HIGHER FOR CfE

MODERN STUDIES

INTERNATIONAL ISSUES

D0928949

Frank Cooney, Gary Hughes,
Pauline Kelly and Steph O'Reilly

HODDER
GIBSON
AN HACHETTE UK COMPANY

The Publishers would like to thank the following for permission to reproduce copyright material:

Photo credits

Chapter opener images: **p.1** © frank11 – Fotolia.com; **p.49** © Gang – Fotolia.com; **p.84** © Anna Omelchenko – Fotolia.com; **p.131** © Aleksandar Todorovic – Fotolia.com; **p.166** © Rawpixel – Fotolia.com

p.2 (left) © Photodisc/Photolibrary Group Ltd; (right) © Florian Franke/Corbis; **p.5** © Sandy Huffaker/Corbis; **p.8** © Ron Chapple/Corbis; **p.9** © Glow Images/photolibrary.com; **p.10** © Ron Chapple/Corbis; **p.11** © Washington Post/Getty Images; **p.12** © Rex Features; **p.18** (top) © Democrat Party (United States); (bottom) © Republican Party (United States); **p.19** © KPA/Zuma/REX; **p.20** © Scott Olson/Getty Images; **p.21** © Gabriella Demczuk/Stringer/Getty Images; **p.22** © Chip Somodevilla/Getty Images; **p.25** © Andres Rodriguez – Fotolia.com; **p.27** (all images) © Whitehouse.gov (Creative Commons Attribution 3.0 License); **p.28** © Monkey Business – Fotolia.com; **p.31** (left) © Christopher Pillitz/Getty Images; (right) © GIPhotoStock Z/Alamy; **p.35** © Image Source/Getty Images; **p.36** © LARRY W. SMITH/epa/Corbis; **p.44** © Alliance Images/Alamy; **p.52** © By: Lintao Zhang/Getty Images; **p.55** © STAFF/Reuters/Corbis; **p.57** © By: XAUME OLLEROS/AFP/Getty Images; **p.61** © SALVATORE DI NOLFI/AP/Press Association Images; **p.62** (left) © Mitsuru Tamura/AP/Press Association Images; (right) © AFP/Getty Images; **p.64** © CATHERINE HENRIETTE/AFP/Getty Images; **p.65** (top) © HuiTuan Wang – Fotolia.com; (bottom) © Mathew Imaging/FilmMagic/Getty Images; **p.66** © Sovfoto/Universal Images Group/Getty Images; **p.68** © SeanPavonePhoto – iStockphoto via Thinkstock; **p.70** (left) © Lou Linwei/Alamy; (right) © Xiaoyang Liu/Corbis; **p.72** © ullsteinbild/Topfoto; **p.74** © Quirky China News/Rex Features; **p.75** © Jonathan Browning/REX; **p.80** © DON EMMERT/AFP/Getty Images; **p.81** © Ju Peng/REX; **p.84** © Goddard_Photography – iStockphoto via Thinkstock; **p.86** © Tetra Images/Alamy; **p.90** © AndreaWillmore – iStockphoto via Thinkstock; **p.92** © Louise Gubb/CORBIS SABA; **p.93** © Facundo Arrizabalaga/Rex Features; **p.96** © Xinhua News Agency/REX; **p.97** © Africa Media Online/Alamy; **p.99** (top) © Robin Laurance/Alamy; (bottom) © Eco Images/Universal Images Group; **p.104** © By: RAJESH JANTILAL/AFP/Getty Images; **p.108** © Gallo Images/Getty Images News; **p.110** © SIPHIWE SIBEKO/Reuters/Corbis; **p.113** © Stock Connection Blue/Alamy; **p.114** (left) © African National Congress; (top right) © Democratic Alliance; (bottom right) © Economic Freedom Fighters; **p.115** (top left) © Inkatha Freedom Party; (bottom left) © National Freedom Party; (top right) © United Democratic Movement; (bottom right) © Congress of the People; **p.116** © ZUMA/REX; **p.117** © Gallo Images/REX; **p.119** © SIPHIWE SIBEKO/Reuters/Corbis; **p.135** (left) © Stockbyte via Thinkstock; (right) © Joe Gough – Fotolia.com; **p.137** © mrallen – Fotolia.com; **p.138** (left) © Syner-Comm/Alamy; (right) © Frans Lanting/Corbis; **p.139** © Education Images/Getty Images; **p.142** © Sam Valtenbergs/Getty Images; **p.144** © GRANT NEUENBERG/Reuters/Corbis; **p.145** © Raul Touzon/National Geographic Creative/Corbis; **p.146** © Sipa Press/REX; **p.147** (left) © Joe Gough – Fotolia.com; (right) © somartin – Fotolia.com; **p.148** (left) © Imagestate Media; (right) © david pearson/Alamy; **p.149** © Michael Kemp/Alamy; **p.153** © African Union/Courtesy of Wikipedia; **p.156** (left) © Unicef; (right) © By: PIUS UTOMI EKPEI/AFP/Getty Images; **p.158** © imagebroker/Alamy; **p.159** © www.marysmeals.org.uk; **p.161** (both) © Oxfam; **p.164** © Joel Goodman/LNP/REX; **p.166** © David Sheerin; **p.169** © David Sheerin

Acknowledgements

Table 1.2 'Powers of national and state government' reproduced with permission Ben's Guide to the U.S. Government, U.S. Government Publishing Office; Extract 'Exercise the right to vote' reproduced with permission The Chronicle, 2015; Case study: Rock the Vote – extracts used with permission www.rockthevote.com; Extract from 'Solving America's Inequality Puzzle' reproduced from www.USAnews.com with permission © U.S. News & World Report LP; Extract from 'FBI: Mass Shooting Incidents Occurring More Frequently' by Evan Perez reproduced from CNN.com with permission Turner Broadcast Systems, Inc.; Extract from report by the Pew Research Centre reproduced from http://www.brookings.edu/blogs/fixgov/posts/2013/12/04-us-international-influence-declining-galston with permission Brookings Institution Press; Extract from 'South Africa reports of police brutality more than tripled in the last decade' by David Smith, reproduced with permission © Guardian News & Media Ltd 2013; Extract from 'South Africa's expanding global influence' reproduced by permission SAnews.gov.za; Extract from 'BRICS Bank – a new lender in global development'© 2014 Reuters.com. All rights reserved, used by permission and protected by the Copyright Laws of the United States. The printing, copying, redistribution, or retransmission of this content without express written permission is prohibited; The table on qualitative and quantitative research is reproduced from www.snapsurveys.com with permission Snap Surveys Ltd, copyright © Snap Surveys Limited 2015

Every effort has been made to trace all copyright holders, but if any have been inadvertently overlooked the Publishers will be pleased to make the necessary arrangements at the first opportunity.

Although every effort has been made to ensure that website addresses are correct at time of going to press, Hodder Gibson cannot be held responsible for the content of any website mentioned in this book. It is sometimes possible to find a relocated web page by typing in the address of the home page for a website in the URL window of your browser.

Hachette UK's policy is to use papers that are natural, renewable and recyclable products and made from wood grown in sustainable forests. The logging and manufacturing processes are expected to conform to the environmental regulations of the country of origin.

Orders: please contact Bookpoint Ltd, 130 Park Drive, Milton Park, Abingdon, Oxon OX14 4SE. Telephone: (44) 01235 827720. Fax: (44) 01235 400454. Lines are open 9.00–5.00, Monday to Saturday, with a 24-hour message answering service. Visit our website at www.hoddereducation.co.uk. Hodder Gibson can be contacted direct on: Tel: 0141 333 4650; Fax: 0141 404 8188; email: hoddergibson@hodder.co.uk.

© Frank Cooney, Gary Hughes, Pauline Kelly and Steph O'Reilly 2015

First published in 2015 by

Hodder Gibson, an imprint of Hodder Education,

An Hachette UK Company

211 St Vincent Street

Glasgow G2 5QY

Impression number	5	4	3
Year	2019	2018	2017

Cover photo OJO Images Ltd/Alamy

Illustrations by Integra Software Services Pvt. Ltd., Pondicherry, India and Jeff Edwards

Typeset in Minion Pro 12/15 by Integra Software Services Pvt. Ltd., Pondicherry, India

Printed in Dubai

A catalogue record for this title is available from the British Library

ISBN: 978 1471 835865

Contents

1 The United States of America

Background

The United States of America is the third largest country in the world, in terms of land mass. It covers an area of 9,826,675 km², making it about half the size of Russia and a little smaller than Canada. It is about twice the size of the European Union. It has land borders with two other countries: Canada and Mexico. It is spread over 3000 miles from east to west between the Atlantic and Pacific Oceans.

In 2014, the United States population reached a new record of 317,297,938 people, according to US Census Bureau estimates. That means the US is currently the third most populous country on the planet, behind only China (1.35 billion) and India (1.23 billion).

American people

Just who can call themselves an American?

The Statue of Liberty was given by the people of France to the people of the USA in 1886 in recognition of their friendship during the American Revolution. Today, the statue symbolises freedom and democracy as well as

Figure 1.1 **The states of the USA**

1 VERMONT
2 NEW HAMPSHIRE
3 MASSACHUSETTS
4 RHODE ISLAND
5 CONNECTICUT
6 NEW JERSEY
7 DELAWARE
8 MARYLAND

Alaska and Hawaii are not to scale

this international friendship, a colossal symbol of freedom to millions around the world. Its inscription reads:

> 'Give me your tired, your poor,
> Your huddled masses yearning to breathe free,
> I lift my lamp beside the golden door!'

These words, written by Emma Lazarus in 1883, have come to portray the statue's universal message of hope and freedom for immigrants coming to America and people seeking freedom around the world.

Figure 1.2 **The Statue of Liberty**

American society has often been described as a melting pot but, in recent years, it has also attracted other definitions such as 'salad bowl'.

For centuries the USA has attracted people in search of a share of 'the American dream' from all corners of the world. In fact, US history is one of immigration. Today there is a raging debate between opponents of illegal immigration who are calling for even tougher laws, and pro-immigrant campaign groups who argue that America's economy needs them and that the country was built by immigrants and will collapse without them (see pages 5–7).

Ethnic composition of America

The 317 million people making up the population of the United States can be categorised into five main ethnic groups (see Figure 1.4). It is estimated that the population rises by 1 per cent each year. If this continues, then by 2050 the US population will have risen to around 440 million people. Non-Hispanic whites are currently the largest ethnic group in the United States. However, the fastest-growing group is Hispanics (see fact file). In 2015, California became the second US state in which the largest ethnic group was Hispanics – New Mexico was the first.

Figure 1.3 **The USA is a melting pot of different cultures**

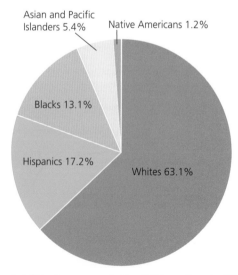

Figure 1.4 **Ethnic groups in the USA, estimated 2014**
Source: US Census Bureau

Fact file

- It is expected that about 20 per cent of Americans, or one in five, will be immigrants by 2050, compared with 12 per cent in 2008.
- The Hispanic population is currently the country's largest ethnic minority group and is expected to triple in size by 2050, accounting for most of the nation's population growth from 2010 to 2050. Hispanics will make up 29 per cent of the USA population in 2050, compared with 15.1 per cent in 2008.
- The white population is expected to increase more slowly than other ethnic groups and will become a minority group by 2050 at 47 per cent.

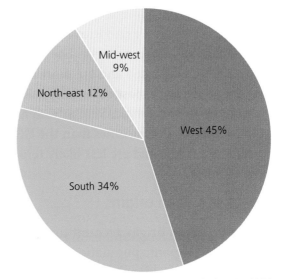

Figure 1.5 **Hispanic percentage of population by USA region of residence, 2013**
Source: US Census Bureau

Hispanics

There are estimated to be about 55 million Hispanics currently living in the USA, making up over 17 per cent of the population. Hispanics are the largest ethnic minority group, having overtaken black Americans in number in 2001. The growth of the Hispanic population since then has been mainly due to births in the USA, not immigration from abroad.

Around two-thirds (64 per cent) of Hispanics in the USA are of Mexican origin. The other third are from the remaining nine Hispanic origin groups of: Puerto Rican, Cuban, Salvadoran, Dominican, Guatemalan, Colombian, Honduran, Ecuadorian and Peruvian. These ten Hispanic groups differ in terms of numbers who are foreign-born, numbers who are US citizens by birth, and their proficiency in English. There are also differences in terms of their education levels, home ownership rates, income and poverty rates.

Hispanics of Mexican origin

Hispanics of Mexican origin account for 64 per cent of the US Hispanic population, over 30 million people.

Mexicans (along with Puerto Ricans) tend to be less well educated than the other Hispanic groups. Only 9 per cent of Mexicans aged 25 and above have obtained a bachelor's degree compared with an average 12.6 per cent in the other groups. As far as income levels and poverty rates are concerned the numbers are similar for most Hispanic groups but lower than those for the US population as a whole. The number of Mexicans living in poverty in 2013 was 21 per cent, which is roughly the same as the other Hispanic groups at 20.5 per cent.

Hispanics of Puerto Rican origin

There are currently 4.2 million Hispanics of Puerto Rican origin living in the USA, which is more than the population of Puerto Rico itself at 3.9 million. Around two-thirds of the Puerto Rican population was born in the USA and one-third was born in Puerto Rico itself. Anyone who is born in Puerto Rico is considered to be an American citizen by birth. They are generally less well educated and are more likely to be unemployed than most other Hispanics or the US population as a whole. Similarly, as a rule, they achieve lower incomes than the US population as a whole and are less likely to own their own homes.

Hispanics of Cuban origin

Hispanics of Cuban origin account for 3.4 per cent of the US Hispanic population. Cubans generally tend to be older than the US population and other Hispanics. Around 70 per cent of Cubans live in Florida. Cubans tend to be better educated than the other Hispanic groups, with 26 per cent of those aged 25 and above having obtained a bachelor's degree compared with 9 per cent of Mexicans. As far as income levels are concerned, the numbers are higher than for all other Hispanic groups but lower than for the US population as a whole. The number of Cubans living in poverty in 2013 was 19 per cent, which is lower than the other Hispanic groups at 26 per cent but slightly higher than the US population as a whole at 16 per cent.

Asian and Pacific Islanders (APIs)

The 12 million Asian and Pacific Islanders account for 5.4 per cent of the US population and are the third largest ethnic minority group in the USA. They are a diverse ethnic group who have come from countries in Asia such as Korea and China or the Pacific Islands. APIs are generally well educated and have the highest educational attainment levels and median annual income of all the ethnic minority groups. As a result they also have one of the lowest poverty rates. Hawaii is the only US state in which Asian Americans or Pacific Islanders are the largest racial/ethnic group.

Black Americans

Black people account for about 13 per cent of the US population and are the second largest ethnic minority group in the USA. The 41 million black Americans are descendants of African slaves brought over to the USA from Africa to work on the plantations of the southern states in the seventeenth and eighteenth centuries. Slightly more than half of this group are concentrated in the states of the south and south-east; the rest are to be found in the industrial cities of the north-east, and in central and Pacific Coast states.

After the Civil War (1861–65), slavery was abolished but black Americans still faced massive political, social and economic inequality, especially in the South. The civil rights movement of the 1960s and subsequent civil rights acts finally gave them full equality. However, the 2014 riots in Ferguson over the death of a black teenager shot by the police were also about a perceived injustice in American society that condemns so many black Americans to a life of poverty (see Social and economic inequality section, page 24–25).

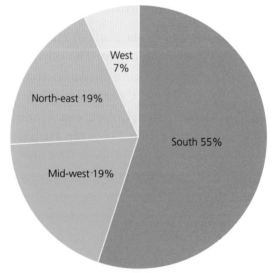

Figure 1.6 **Black percentage of population by USA region of residence, 2012**
Source: US Census Bureau

Native Americans

Native Americans account for 1.2 per cent of the total American population. This ethnic group is known as the 'original' Americans. Nearly 5 million Americans identify as Native American or Alaska Native solely or in combination with one or more races. Of them, more than 2 million identify as purely Native American or Alaska Native. In the most recent census figures, 70 per cent of Native Americans live in urban areas. Alaska has the highest Native American population, followed by New Mexico, South Dakota, Oklahoma and Montana.

Immigration

Immigration is a controversial issue in the USA. President Obama found it difficult to carry out his promise to reform immigration and to persuade Congress to pass new legislation. However, in his second term, which began in January 2013, there were high hopes that a new law could be passed. Both Democrat and Republican Senators agreed to a joint (bi-partisan) approach and passed the Border Security, Economic Opportunity and Immigration Modernisation Acts (2013). Unfortunately, the Republican-controlled House of Representatives failed to pass the bill. In November 2014, the Republicans gained control of the Senate, ending any possibility of immigration reform in the foreseeable future. President Obama made the controversial decision to use an Executive Order to grant amnesty to 5 million immigrants (see pages 6–7).

Just what is the problem?

The problem is that 40 million people in the USA are immigrants, with illegal immigrants accounting for around 12 million of these. In addition, around 1.5 million more immigrants enter the country each year, mainly through the 2000-mile-long Mexican border. For many more, however, entry is blocked.

The Border Security, Economic Opportunity and Immigration Modernisation Acts (2013)

The bill had three main parts:

1 to provide a road to citizenship for several million unauthorised immigrants and overhaul the family immigration system
2 to provide extra funding to create stringent new border enforcement deportation measures
3 a mandate that employers use an electronic employment and eligibility verification system.

Figure 1.7 **The border between the USA and Mexico**

Many immigrants lack any formal education and therefore seek work as unskilled labourers. They often take the sort of jobs that most native-born Americans refuse to do for the wages offered. For example, a lot of California's agricultural sector is dependent on thousands of immigrant labourers.

Why is the issue so tense?

The situation has caused tension between those who are opposed to the increase in immigration and who want increased border controls, and the supportive employers who want cheap migrant workers. Immigrants themselves have also entered the debate, claiming that restrictions only block their 'right to citizenship'.

Politicians are aware of the growing immigrant electorate and so are reluctant to annoy and put off potential voters. The Republican Party faces confrontation from its social conservatives and the business lobby because of the view from some that a harder line is required and illegal immigrants should be criminalised.

Similarly, the Democratic Party is trying to avoid conflict with trade unions who claim that the Guest Worker Programs only drive down wages and cause unemployment for American employees.

Groups opposed to illegal immigration have formed Minutemen groups. These comprise armed residents who patrol the US borders and assist federal guards in arresting illegal immigrants.

What are the key issues?

The key issues are focused around controlling illegal entry. In the aftermath of 11 September 2001, the influx of illegal immigrants may pose a threat to national security. The US business sector claims that immigrants are a necessary workforce for the economy and so supports changes in the law to control entry and to clear up issues surrounding those already in the country illegally. The business sector would like to see illegal immigrants being allowed to remain in the country legally and wants the Guest Worker Program extended.

Others want tougher enforcement of the land borders and existing laws on immigration. For example, some want to extend the fencing that already exists along a part of the US–Mexican border and introduce tougher penalties for businesses caught employing illegal migrants. Despite objections from the Mexican government, this fence has been extended by 700 miles and is now patrolled by several thousand reserve soldiers of the USA National Guard.

Barack Obama enforces US immigration overhaul

President Obama: 'I wasn't going to sit idly by and not do at least what I was authorised to do.'

US President Barack Obama has said he will press for further immigration reform, after Republicans condemned his use of executive powers on the issue. Mr Obama said he had no choice but to act, accusing the Republicans of blocking a bill in Congress, and vowed to make permanent reform a reality. The current move means that more than 4 million illegal immigrants will be allowed to apply for work permits.

Republicans say it will encourage more people to arrive unlawfully. Republicans have been weighing their response to Mr Obama's executive action, but the dilemma they face is how to oppose his immigration reforms without alienating Hispanic voters – whose support they will need in the next election, the BBC's David Willis in Washington reports.

Speaking in Las Vegas, where he first outlined his plans two years ago, President Obama said: 'I will never give up. We're going to keep on working with members of Congress to make permanent reform a reality. But until that day comes, there are actions that I have the legal authority to take that will help make our immigration system more fair and more just, and this morning I began to take some of those actions.

'When members of Congress question my authority to make our immigration system work better, I have a simple answer – pass a bill.' Mr Obama said the moves that he had taken under his executive action meant that 'not everybody will qualify'. 'That's the truth. That's why we're still going to have to pass a bill … This is a first step, it's not the only step.'

Mr Obama added: 'The bottom line is, mass amnesty would be unfair, but mass deportation would be both impossible and contrary to our country's character. That's not who we are. We didn't raise the Statue of Liberty with her back to the world. We did it with her light shining as a beacon to the world.'

Earlier on Friday, Republican Speaker of the House John Boehner said Mr Obama's action had sabotaged any chance of enacting cross-party reforms and damaged the presidency itself. He said the president had acted unilaterally 'like a king or emperor' and not through a democratic process.

There are estimated to be just under 12 million illegal immigrants in the US. More than 4 million of them are expected to benefit from the reform package forced through using executive action, which allowed Mr Obama to bypass Congress.

Only parents who have lived in the US for five years will qualify. Another part of the package will extend a programme that gives temporary legal status to people who arrived in the US as children.

Currently only those under the age of 30 who arrived before 2007 can apply for the programme, which was launched in 2012 and already covers roughly 1.2 million people. Mr Obama has abolished the age limit and extended the cut-off point to 2010, potentially extending the programme to a further 300,000 people. The US leader said his measures would allow illegal immigrants to 'come out of the shadows and get right with the law'.

- The only undocumented immigrant mentioned in the speech was Astrid Silva.
- She was brought to the US aged four, with just her doll, a cross and the dress she wore.
- She is now working on her third College degree.

Source: adapted from BBC News, 21 November 2014

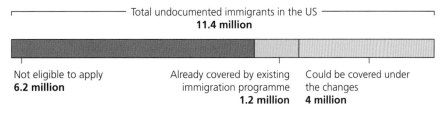

Total undocumented immigrants in the US
11.4 million

Not eligible to apply
6.2 million

Already covered by existing immigration programme
1.2 million

Could be covered under the changes
4 million

Figure 1.8 **Many people are affected by the immigration reforms**
Source: Migration Policy Institute

Show your understanding

1 Describe the five main ethnic groups that make up the population of the USA.
2 Identify the distinct groups into which the Hispanics can be subdivided and compare the income differences between Mexicans, Puerto Ricans and Cubans.
3 Why is immigration such a controversial issue in the USA?
4 Describe the actions taken by President Obama in his Executive Order of November 2014.

Added Value idea

Immigration is obviously a controversial issue. Research the arguments both for and against immigration. Also find out more about Astrid Silva, referred to by President Obama.

The political system

The US Constitution

The US Constitution and system of government was written by the founding fathers, after the 13 colonies gained their independence from Britain in 1783. The then 13 states agreed to devise a new form of government – a federal state. Here power would be divided between the national (federal) government and the respective states. A second compromise was to have a Congress made up of two Houses: the Senate and the House of Representatives. In the Senate there would be equal representation for all states. In contrast, in the House of Representatives there would be representation proportional to the population of each state. Another compromise was to have the president elected indirectly by the people. The citizens would elect the Electoral College and the latter would choose the president. A Bill of Rights would protect the rights of all citizens.

All these compromises and more helped to create the written Constitution of the USA, based on federalism, separation of powers and checks and balances. The Constitution is a set of rules by government establishing how it should be run. The Constitution is the supreme law of the USA, and it defines the relationship and allocation of powers between the Executive, Legislature and Judiciary. This separation of powers or doctrine of shared powers ensures that no one branch of government can dominate and thus protects the fundamental rights of US citizens.

Alastair Cooke, a British journalist, wrote that the American Constitution was founded upon three great principles: compromise, compromise and compromise. Unfortunately, the hostility of Republicans towards President Obama has now created gridlock, gridlock and gridlock.

Bill of Rights

The first ten amendments to the Constitution are referred to as the Bill of Rights, which is a series of constitutionally protected rights of citizens. The first two are:

First Amendment Right to freedom of religion, speech and the press, and the right to assemble peaceably, and to petition the government for a redress of grievances.

Second Amendment Right to bear arms in common defence.

The tenth reads as follows:

Tenth Amendment Powers not listed in the Constitution are retained by the state and the people.

Figure 1.9 **The US Congress sits in the Capitol building in Washington**

The federal government

The federal government deals with matters concerning collective state issues and also foreign affairs. All powers not allocated to the federal government are retained by the respective states. The 50 states have the right to make their own laws on internal matters. At present many states are in conflict with the federal government over President Obama's health reforms.

The federal government has authority over:

- the armed forces
- the post office
- the currency of the USA
- disputes between states
- foreign relations, for example, declaring war.

The separation of powers

The American political scientist, Richard Neustadt, wrote that 'the Constitution had created a government of separated institutions sharing powers', while his UK counterpart, Professor Samuel Finer described the Legislature and Executive as being 'like two halves of a bank note – each useless without the other'. This separation of powers or doctrine of shared powers ensures that no one branch of government can become dominant.

The Legislative branch makes laws

Established by Article 1 of the Constitution, the USA Congress comprises two chambers: the Senate and the House of Representatives. Congress is the legislative (law-making) and oversight (government policy review) body of the national government. For a law to be made, it has to be passed by both chambers by a simple majority and finally signed by the president. Under the Constitution, each state is entitled to be represented by two senators (each serving a six-year term) and at least one representative (serving a two-year term).

The House of Representatives has several powers exclusively assigned to it, such as the impeachment of federal officials.

The Senate has the sole power to ratify treaties and to approve senior posts such as appointments to the Supreme Court.

The Executive branch carries out laws

The chief executive of the USA is the president. The president is responsible for implementing and enforcing the laws written by Congress. The president appoints the heads of federal agencies, including the Cabinet. Each Secretary (Cabinet member) is in charge of a Department of State, which employs thousands of people to do the day-to-day work. The president is elected to a four-year term, and may only be elected to serve two terms.

Figure 1.10 **The White House is the president's official residence**

The Judicial branch interprets these laws

Article 111 of the Constitution establishes the Judicial branch. The Supreme Court is the highest court of the USA and the only one specifically created by the Constitution. Members of the Supreme Court are appointed by the president and confirmed by the Senate. The Supreme Court consists of nine Justices who are appointed for life and are replaced only when they resign, retire or die. In 2009, President Obama appointed the liberal Sonia Sotomayor, with the approval of Congress, to fill a vacancy in the Supreme Court, making her the first Hispanic Justice. Federal courts hold the sole power to interpret the laws. The judges determine whether a law that has been passed is constitutional or not. The Judicial branch determines whether Legislative or Executive acts conform to the Constitution. For example, in 2012 the Supreme Court ruled that Obama's health reforms were not illegal as Congress had the authority to regulate interstate commerce. Below are two other recent Supreme Court decisions:

- **2010 Citizens United v. Federal Election Commission** The Supreme Court ruled 5–4 that the government cannot restrict the spending of corporations on political campaigns, maintaining that it is their First Amendment right to support candidates as they choose.

- **2013 Shelby County v. Holder** The Supreme Court struck down Section 4 of the Voting Rights Act, which established a formula for Congress to use when determining if a state or voting jurisdiction requires prior approval before changing its voting requirements.

Figure 1.11 **The Supreme Court**

Table 1.1 **The three branches of the US Government**

Legislative branch	Executive branch	Judicial branch
Checks over the Executive branch: • May override presidential vetoes with a two-thirds vote • Has the power over the purse strings to actually fund any executive actions • May remove the president through impeachment • Senate approves treaties • Senate approves presidential appointments Checks over the Judicial branch: • Creates lower courts • May remove judges through impeachment • Senate approves appointments of judges	Checks over the Legislative branch: • Has power to veto legislation • Has ability to call special sessions of Congress • Can recommend legislation • Can appeal to the people concerning legislation and more Checks over the Judicial branch: • President appoints Supreme Court and other federal judges	Checks over the Executive branch: • Judges, once appointed for life, are free from controls from the Executive branch • Courts can judge executive actions to be unconstitutional through the power of Judicial Review Checks over the Legislative branch: • Courts can judge legislative acts to be unconstitutional.

What is meant by the 'separation of powers' and 'checks and balances'?

The Constitution outlines the different powers/authority for the three branches of government – Legislative, Executive and Judicial. The Constitution allows each branch to check and balance the others. For instance, the president can veto bills approved by Congress and nominates individuals to the Federal Judiciary; the Supreme Court can declare a law enacted by Congress or an action by the president as unconstitutional; and Congress can impeach and remove the president and Federal Court justices and judges.

The Legislative branch is given the powers to make the laws. The Executive branch is given the power to carry out the laws. The Judicial branch is given the power to interpret the laws. Table 1.1 shows how the branches check and balance each other.

Show your understanding

1 Why is the US Constitution such an important document?
2 Explain how the checks and balances separate and limit the powers of the three branches of government.
3 Describe how power is separated between the three branches of government.

The powers of the president

Article 2 of the Constitution sets out the powers of the president. They are both defined and limited by the Constitution.

The constitutional powers can be divided into three categories:

1 legislative powers
2 head of state powers
3 executive powers.

Chief legislator

As chief legislator, the president is expected to suggest proposals on laws to Congress. The president can refuse to sign a bill that he or she does not feel is in the best interests of the American people. Article 1 of the Constitution lays down the president's veto power:

> 'Every bill … shall, before it becomes a law, be presented to the President of the United States; if he approves he shall sign it, but if not he shall return it, with his objections, to that house from which it shall be originated.'

However, Congress has the power to override the veto with a two-thirds majority in both houses.

The president uses the annual State of the Union address to expand the legislative role of the presidency. At the start of each session in Congress, the president outlines important issues that have affected the country. The president discusses the Executive's actions in the past year and the intended actions of the next 12 months in office. At this stage Congress may pass proposed legislation on behalf of the president. In his second State of the Union address, President Obama reiterated his determination to complete his health reforms in 2010 (see page 12).

Figure 1.12 **President Obama delivering his State of the Union address to Congress in 2010**

The president can also submit an annual budget to Congress with great fanfare – perhaps at a ceremony in the White House. All presidents, even if their party controls Congress, must try to work in a bipartisan way. For example, George W. Bush achieved his education reforms – No Child Left Behind – in 2002 because he worked with leading Democrats such as the late Edward Kennedy to enable the bill to be passed. Barack Obama had hoped to create a bipartisan Immigration Bill in 2013 and this was achieved in the Senate but blocked by the Republican-controlled House of Representatives (see pages 6–7).

Head of state

The president is the chief public representative of the USA, embodying a sense of national pride. The presidential role combines the duties that in the UK would be carried out by a monarch and a prime minister. The president and vice president are the only elected members of the government. A president carries out the following duties:

- meets with leaders of other countries
- makes treaties
- appoints ambassadors.

Passing legislation in the USA: Obama's Affordable Health Bill 2009–13

Presidents can outline their legislative goals in their State of the Union address. However, it can be very difficult, as stated earlier, to get their policies through – even when their party has a majority in Congress. President Clinton only enjoyed two years of a Democratic-controlled Congress. At the first mid-term elections the Republicans gained control and, for the remaining six years of Clinton's presidency, the Republicans controlled Congress. It was therefore no surprise that Clinton's health reforms were never implemented.

In contrast, President Obama seemed to be in a perfect position to push his health reforms through a Congress controlled by the Democrats. By late December 2009, Obama seemed to have achieved success in his health reforms. Both the House of Representatives and the Senate had passed their respective Health Bill versions. All that was required in January 2010 was for the two bills to be combined and a joint version passed by each chamber. The Republicans would not be able to use the filibuster (this enables a senator to block almost any measure just by continuing

to talk), as under Senate rules the assent of three-fifths of senators can prevent a filibuster. In March 2010, the House of Representatives passed the bill by 219 votes to 212. On 23 March 2010, President Obama signed the health-care reform bill into law.

Figure 1.13 President Obama signing the Health Bill

However, the Republicans gained control of the House in the mid-term 2010 elections and tried to change aspects of the bill. Again, some Republican-controlled states challenged its legality. However, the Supreme Court ruled in favour of the president and it finally was implemented on 1 October 2013. This would be the high point of Obama's legislative programme.

Commander in Chief of the Armed Forces

Article II Section 2 of the US Constitution, the Commander-in-Chief clause, states that: '[t]he President shall be Commander in Chief of the Army and Navy of the United States, and of the Militia of the several States, when called into the actual Service of the United States.'

The questions of whether, and to what extent, the president has the authority to use the military in the absence of a Congressional declaration of war have proven to be sources of conflict and debate throughout American history. Some scholars believe the Commander-in-Chief clause confers expansive powers on the president, but others argue that, even if that is the case, the Constitution does not precisely define the extent of those powers. However, this power explains why presidents have far greater international powers than domestic.

The terrorist attacks of September 2001 created new complications for the separation of powers within the war powers sphere. After September 11, the United States Congress passed the Authorization for Use of Military Force against Terrorists (AUMF). While the AUMF did not officially declare war, the legislation provided the president with more authority upon which to exercise his constitutional powers as Commander in Chief. The USA led a coalition which sent troops to Iraq and Afghanistan. President Obama has used these powers by taking action against ISIS in Syria and Iraq, by imposing sanctions on Russia, and by sending troops to West Africa to help contain the spread of Ebola (see pages 45–6).

Chief executive

As chief executive, the president is responsible for the implementation of laws and policy: 'he shall take care that the laws be faithfully executed'.

The president has a duty to uphold the decisions of the Supreme Court.

Executive Order The president can use this in certain emergency circumstances. This has the power of law but does not need Congress to pass it. The decision by President Obama to use his executive powers to introduce immigration reforms was attacked by the Republicans as an abuse of presidential powers (see pages 6–7).

Power of 'patronage' The president controls the civil service, meaning that he or she can fill government offices. Therefore, the president appoints the top four layers of departments:

- Cabinet
- officials of the Executive office
- heads of independent Executive agencies
- independent regulatory commissions.

Control of Congress

In the USA, where the Executive and Legislature are elected separately, there is no guarantee that the president's party will be in majority in either house of Congress. Nor is it guaranteed that the president will have any control over his or her party in the Legislature.

- President Clinton was more of a 'defensive president' as he faced a hostile Congress dominated by Republicans. He failed to get his Health Bill through and used the veto 36 times. The Republican Congress tried to impeach Clinton. The House of Representatives passed two articles of impeachment by simple majority. The Senate conducted the trial and failed to obtain a two-thirds majority that would have removed Clinton from office. (President Nixon resigned rather than face certain impeachment.) Therefore, Congress can remove the president, but the president cannot remove Congress.

- President George W. Bush was more of an 'imperial president'. In his first six years he was allowed to expand the office of presidency, partly due to the fact that his own party controlled both chambers and partly due to the crisis created by 9/11. This all changed when the Democrats regained control of Congress in December 2006. Bush had not used his veto in his first six years; in his last two he used the veto 11 times. Congress overrode four of his regular vetoes, including his veto of the 2008 Food Conservation and Energy Bill.
- President Obama faced a predominately Democratic Congress in his first term and this enabled him to appoint a Latino liberal judge to the Supreme Court and to get through his health-care reforms. However, in the mid-term elections of 2010 the Republicans gained control of the House and then in 2014 gained control of the Senate. Obama is now described as a 'lame duck president' and faces both a hostile House and Senate. This explains why Obama has failed to implement key policy priorities such as new gun control laws and a new immigration bill. Right-wing Republicans with links to the Tea Party are very hostile towards President Obama. In September 2013, House Republicans using the 'power of the purse' refused to continue funding the federal government unless Obama agreed to a one-year delay to the implementation of his health bill. The president refused and this triggered a government shutdown from 1 October. Many non-essential services were suspended and federal workers were not paid.

Congressional Committees

In the USA, no Executive staff are members of Congress and there is no equivalent of 'Question Time' in the House of Commons, in which members of the UK Government are grilled by the opposition parties. As a former president once wrote: 'Congress in session is Congress on public exhibition, whilst Congress in its committee rooms is Congress at work.' Congressional Committees in the USA are far more independent and powerful than their UK counterparts. Overall, there are 199 committees and subcommittees in Congress.

Standing Committees

Congressional Standing Committees are permanent policy specialist institutions which play a strategic role both in legislation and in overseeing the Executive branch. In 2008, members of President Bush's Cabinet made 68 appearances in front of Standing Committees.

They are permanent legislative panels established by the House of Representatives and the Senate rules. Standing Committees consider bills and issues and recommend measures for consideration by their respective chambers.

Select Committees

Congress can also set up Select Committees to investigate Executive action. The House of Representatives set up a committee to investigate the terrorist attack on the American embassy in Iraq in 2012. The final report was highly critical of President Obama's foreign policy.

Conference Committees

These ad hoc (short-term) committees are set up towards the end of the legislative process. Bills tend to have a House version and a Senate version and members from each chamber try to create an agreed form of the bill. If agreement is reached, the full Congress votes to accept or reject – no amendments can be made.

The Republicans eventually backed down in late October, having damaged both the US economy and US democracy. In November 2013, a Gallup Poll had Congress's approval rating at just 9 per cent, an all-time low.

State government

Powers not assigned to the federal government are retained by each of the 50 states. Each state has its Executive, led by a governor, and all have state legislatures. States collect their own local taxes and can decide on issues such as the use of capital powers (see Table 1.2). The death penalty currently applies in 33 states, with Texas having the highest number of executions. Citizens at the state level can also take part in direct democracy by putting forward proposals to change state laws, which are referred to as ballot measures (see page 17).

In addition to their exclusive powers, both the national government and state governments share the power of being able to:

- collect taxes
- build roads
- borrow money
- establish courts
- make and enforce laws
- charter banks and corporations
- spend money for the general welfare
- take private property for public purposes, with just compensation

Table 1.2 **Powers of national and state government**

National government	State government
• Print money • Regulate interstate (between states) and international trade • Make treaties and conduct foreign policy • Declare war • Provide an army and navy • Establish post offices • Make laws necessary and proper to carry out these powers	• Issue licences • Regulate intrastate (within the state) businesses • Conduct elections • Establish local governments • Ratify amendments to the Constitution • Take measures for public health and safety • May exert powers the Constitution does not delegate to the national government or prohibit the states from using them

Source: The US Government Printing Office

Show your understanding

1 Outline the powers of the president.
2 Explain the constraints placed on the president's powers.
3 Compare the presidencies of Clinton, Bush and Obama.
4 Describe the workings of committees in Congress.
5 What powers do the states have?

Rights and responsibilities of US citizens

Rights of US citizens

Most rights fall into one of three general categories:

- security
- equality
- liberty.

Security

Security means protection from unfair and unreasonable actions by the government. The government, for example, cannot arrest, imprison, or punish people or search or seize their property without good reason and without following certain rules. The principle of 'due process of law' protects these rights for all Americans. The due process clause, which is found in the Fifth and Fourteenth Amendments, states that no person shall be deprived of 'life, liberty, or property, without due process of law'. Due process means that the laws must be fair and reasonable, must be in accordance with the Constitution, and must apply to everyone equally.

Equality

The right of equality means that everyone is entitled to the equal protection of all the laws in the USA. That is, all people have a right to be treated the same, regardless of race, religion, or political beliefs.

Liberty

Our fundamental freedoms fall into this category. Most of them are spelled out in the Bill of Rights.

Duties and responsibilities of US citizens

US citizens have an obligation to carry out certain duties and responsibilities. Duties are things citizens are required to do; if citizens fail to perform them, they may be subjected to legal penalties, such as fines or imprisonment. Responsibilities are things people should do. We can fulfil these obligations voluntarily. Fulfilling both duties and responsibilities helps ensure that citizens have good government and continue to enjoy their rights.

Duties include:

1 Obeying the laws
2 Paying taxes
3 Defending the nation
4 Serving in court
5 Attending school

Responsibilities include:

1 Being informed about the government and knowing your rights in order to preserve them
2 Participating in government
3 Respecting the rights of others
4 Respecting diversity

In theory these freedoms and rights cannot be taken away from US citizens. However, since 9/11 national security issues can threaten these rights. Both President George W. Bush and President Obama have ordered the extra-judicial killing of suspected terrorists around the world and some US citizens have been denied the procedural protections of the Bill of Rights. The Executive branch of government has claimed the right to search hostile journalists' email accounts or to listen in to their phone calls.

Political participation

In the USA, people may participate in politics in many ways. They can write to their Representative or Senator or work for a candidate or political party. They can make presentations to their local school board or city council, or call the police to complain about the neighbour's dog. They can join interest groups; for example, one very powerful group is the National Rifle Association (NRA). Partly because of the federalist system, people have many opportunities to participate in US democracy on federal, state and local levels. Turnout at national elections in presidential election years (for example, 2012) is significantly higher than mid-term elections (for example, 2014). Ballot measures are one way that voters can directly be involved in political change (see below).

Ballot measures in the USA

At state level, citizens can make and amend the laws of their respective state by voting on a range of propositions (in the UK the equivalent would be referenda; for example, the September 2014 referendum on Scottish independence). Propositions have included setting budget priorities, setting the minimum wage, marijuana use and gay rights. In the 2012 elections, 188 ballot measures were put forward in 39 states, of which 118 were approved. For example, citizens of California have legalised the use of marijuana.

Supporters of ballot measures argue that they encourage local engagement in decision making and can increase voter turnout. They can hold elected officials to account and can help to overturn unpopular policies. Ballot measures can also recruit, mobilise and energise citizens and make them feel that their votes really count.

However, critics of ballot measures argue that they can undermine democracy by enabling well-funded business interests to manipulate the process; for example, gaming and the gun industry. They can also undermine the ability of elected officials to control state finances; for example, in California, Proposition 13 limited the property tax powers of the state government.

Show your understanding

1 Outline the main rights and responsibilities of US citizens.
2 In what ways can US citizens participate in the political process?
3 Outline the arguments for and against the use of ballot measures in the USA.

Political parties

Political parties in the USA are different from those in the UK. They are more state-based than national. Political parties in the USA are decentralised. They do have a national party organisation, but its role is mostly limited to the choice of presidential candidate at their respective national conventions, held every four years.

The USA is often described as a 'two-party system'. This refers to the fact that the Democrat and Republican parties dominate politics. Most elected officials serving as president, members of Congress and state governors are members of these two main parties.

The Republican Party is the more conservative of the two parties. Yet there are 'moderate Republicans' in the north-east of the country, 'right-wing Republicans' and 'Christian conservatives'. In the 2000 presidential election, George W. Bush popularised the term 'compassionate conservatives'.

The Democratic Party contains both 'liberal Democrats' (such as President John F. Kennedy, who pushed for civil rights for African Americans) and 'conservative Democrats' who are mainly from the south.

However, over the last three decades both parties have become more ideologically based. The large conservative wing of the Democratic Party – mainly from the south – has gradually transferred their support to the more naturally conservative Republican Party. And the liberal wing of the Republican Party – mainly from the north-east – has moved support to the more naturally liberal Democratic Party.

The Democratic Party

Its agenda states that it is 'committed to keeping our nation safe and expanding opportunity for every American'. It ensures that this commitment is reflected by:

- strong economic growth
- affordable health care for *all* Americans
- retirement security
- an open, honest and accountable government
- securing the nation while protecting civil rights and liberties.

Figure 1.14 The donkey, symbol of the Democratic Party

Democratic presidents

- John F. Kennedy
- Bill Clinton
- Barack Obama

Democratic supporters

The Democratic Party tends to gain support from the poorer classes, ethnic minorities, women and people who strongly agree with its liberal views.

The Republican Party

Its agenda states that 'the United States has been blessed with a unique set of individual rights and freedoms available to all'. Republicans share many of the party's main beliefs:

- People can succeed through hard work, family support and self-discipline.
- Helping through voluntary giving and community support is better than taxation or redistribution.
- Government should never become too powerful and infringe on the rights of the people.
- A commitment to lower taxes.
- The armed forces should protect and defend our democracy.

- George H.W. Bush
- George W. Bush

Figure 1.15 The elephant, symbol of the Republican Party

Republican supporters

The Republican Party tends to gain support from men, the middle and wealthier classes, whites and people with more conservative views.

Republican presidents

- Ronald Reagan

Presidential elections

One of the most important events in US government and politics is the election of the president. This event is held every four years and is often compared to a race. It is said that someone is 'running for office' and that the 'presidential race'

is on. Choosing presidential candidates can begin more than two years before the actual election.

A nominee needs a majority of the Electoral College votes to win the presidency. The race is over as soon as one of the nominees gets one vote more than half, or 270, of the total electoral votes. Although the elections are held in November, the new president does not take office until the following January.

Did you know?

The Constitution allows each state to have as many electoral votes as it has representatives in Congress. The size of the state's population is the basis for the number of representatives. No state has fewer than three electoral votes. This is because each state has two senators and at least one representative in the House of Representatives.

When citizens vote for the president of the USA they are actually voting for the electors nominated from their state, who will cast their votes based on which presidential candidate had won the popular vote.

Presidential election 2008

Democratic Party nominee Senator Barack Obama and running mate Senator Joe Biden defeated Republican Party nominee Senator John McCain and running mate Governor Sarah Palin in the 2008 presidential election.

Figure 1.16 **Democratic candidates Barack Obama and Joe Biden in the 2008 presidential race**

McCain secured the Republican nomination by March 2008, but the Democratic nomination was marked by a sharp contest between Obama and initial frontrunner Senator Hillary Clinton, with Obama not securing the nomination until early June. Early campaigning had focused heavily on the Iraq War and the unpopularity of outgoing Republican President George W. Bush, but all candidates focused on domestic concerns as well, which grew more prominent as the economy experienced the onset of the Great Recession and a major financial crisis that peaked in September 2008.

Barack Obama achieved a decisive victory over McCain, winning both the popular vote and the Electoral College, with 365 electoral votes to McCain's 173; he received the largest percentage of the popular vote for a Democrat in nearly half a century. Obama's successes in obtaining a major party's nomination and winning the general election were both firsts for an African American.

Obama won:

- 365 electoral college votes
- 52.5 per cent of the overall popular vote.

McCain won:

- 173 electoral college votes
- 46 per cent of the popular vote.

Voting patterns

Voter turnout in the 2008 presidential election was 62.8 per cent, the highest since the 1960s. There are many factors that influence a person's voting preference, such as gender, age or geographical area. This presidential election saw a significant increase of first-time voters casting their votes. Of these first-time voters, 69 per cent voted in favour of Obama and the Democrats while 30 per cent voted for McCain and the Republicans. The exit polls showed that Obama and the Democrats had overwhelming support from black people; a staggering 95 per cent of the black electorate voted for the first black president.

Table 1.3 **Votes by race and gender in 2008 presidential election**

Democrats	Republicans
White 43%	White 55%
Black 95%	Black 4%
Hispanics 67%	Hispanics 31%
Men 49%	Men 48%
Women 56%	Women 43%

Table 1.4 **Presidential election results, 2004–12**

Results: 2004	Votes	Won
George W. Bush	62,039,572	50.8%
John F. Kerry	59,027,453	48.3%
Others	1,188,537	1.0%
Results: 2008	**Votes**	**Won**
Barack Obama	69,492,376	53.0%
John McCain	59,946,378	45.7%
Others	1,703,390	1.3%
Results: 2012	**Votes**	**Won**
Barack Obama	62,611,250	50.6%
Mitt Romney	59,134,475	47.8%
Others	1,968,682	1.6%

Presidential election 2012

Figure 1.17 **Republican candidate Mitt Romney in the 2012 presidential race**

332 Obama   270 to win   Romney 206

In the US presidential election of 2012, the Democratic nominee, President Barack Obama, and his running mate, Vice President Joe Biden, were re-elected to a second term, defeating the Republican nominee, former Governor of Massachusetts Mitt Romney, and his running mate, Representative Paul Ryan from Wisconsin.

Overview of results

The gender vote was split between the two candidates: Obama won 55 per cent of the female vote and Romney won 52 per cent of the male vote. Obama once again won the ethnic minority vote. Young voters favoured Obama, but less so than in 2008.

Table 1.5 **Voting by age, income, religion and ethnicity in the 2012 presidential election**

Age	18–29	30–49	50–64	65+
Obama	60%	52%	47%	44%
Romney	38%	47%	52%	56%
Income	**Up to $49,999**	**$50,000–$99, 999**	**$100,000–$199,999**	**Over $200,000**
Obama	60%	46%	44%	45%
Romney	38%	52%	54%	53%
Religion	**Protestant**	**Catholic**	**Jewish**	**Mormon**
Obama	43%	50%	69%	21%
Romney	56%	48%	30%	78%
Ethnicity	**White**	**African American**	**Hispanic / Latino**	**Asian**
Obama	39%	93%	71%	73%
Romney	59%	6%	27%	26%

Source: National Election Pool, a consortium of ABC News, Associated Press, CBS News, CNN, FoxNews and NBC News

Comparing 2008 and 2012

Voter turnout dipped from 62.8 per cent of eligible citizens voting in 2008 to 57.5 per cent in 2012. That figure was also below the 60.4 level of the 2004 election but higher than the 54.2 per cent turnout in the 2000 election. Despite an increase of over 8 million citizens in the eligible population, turnout declined from 131 million voters in 2008 to an estimated 126 million voters in 2012 when all ballots were tallied. Some 93 million eligible citizens did not vote.

113th Congress, January 2009 –December 2014

- House of Representatives: 233 Republicans, 205 Democrats and 3 vacant seats.
- Senate: 53 Democrats; 2 Independents, who caucus with the Democrats; and 45 Republicans.

During this time:

- a record 102 women (18.8 per cent of total membership) were in Congress
- there were 44 African American Members (8.1 per cent of the total membership) in Congress: 42 served in the House of Representatives and 2 served in the Senate
- there were 37 Hispanic or Latino Members in Congress, 6.9 per cent of the total membership: 33 served in the House and 4 served in the Senate
- there were 13 Asian, South Asian, or Pacific Islander ancestry Members in Congress (2.4 per cent of the total membership: 12 of them (all Democrats) served in the House, and 1 (a Democrat) served in the Senate
- there were 2 American Indian (Native American) Members of the 113th Congress, both of whom were Republican Members of the House.

Source: The Congressional Research Service, July 2014

The Congressional Black Caucus

Figure 1.18 **The Congressional Black Caucus, January 2015**

'Since its establishment in 1971, Members of the Congressional Black Caucus have joined together to empower America's neglected citizens and to address their legislative concerns. For more than 40 years, the CBC has been committed to utilizing the full Constitutional power, statutory authority, and financial resources of the government of the United States of America to ensure that everyone in the United States has an opportunity to achieve their version of the American Dream.'

Source: The Democratic Caucus

The Congressional Black Caucus (CBC) is an organisation representing the African American members of the United States Congress. The Black Caucus consists of all the black members of the House of Representatives. This group can prove influential when passing a bill through this chamber. There were 42 African American members of the House of Representatives in the 113th Congress and if their votes were cast together they could deliver around 20 per cent of the votes required. The Black Caucus provides a united front and requires that both Democrats and Republicans vote together.

The Congressional Hispanic Caucus

Figure 1.19 **The Congressional Hispanic Caucus**

'The CHC aims to address national and international issues and the impact these policies have on the Hispanic community. The Caucus is dedicated to voicing and advancing, through the legislative process, issues affecting Hispanics in the United States, Puerto Rico, and the Commonwealth of the Northern Mariana Islands.'

Source: The Congressional Hispanic Caucus

The Congressional Hispanic Caucus (CHC) was founded in December 1976 as a legislative service organisation of the United States House of Representatives. The CHC is dedicated to voicing and advancing, through the legislative process, policies affecting Hispanics in the United States, Puerto Rico and the US Territories.

There were 26 CHC Members in the 113th Congress representing congressional districts in California, Texas, Florida, Illinois, Arizona, New Mexico, New Jersey, New York, Puerto Rico and the Northern Mariana Islands.

2014 mid-term elections

In the 2014 mid-term elections, the Republicans increased their majority in the House of Representatives and won control of the Senate,

which they had lost in 2006. The Republicans gained eight seats in the Senate to achieve a comfortable majority and increased their numbers in the House to 243 (the Democrats had 178 seats in the House). The Democrats also did badly at the state level, losing five governors' posts.

Show your understanding

1 Using the information in this chapter, describe a typical Democrat supporter and a typical Republican supporter.
2 Compare the election results from the 2008 and 2012 presidential elections. Include statistics in your answer.
3 Describe the ethnic minority representation in the Congress elected in November 2012.
4 Describe the activities of the Black Caucus and the Hispanic Caucus groups.
5 In what way were the results of the November 2014 congressional elections disappointing for President Obama?

The youth vote

Around 45 per cent of young people aged 18–29 voted in 2012, down from 51 per cent in 2008. The youth vote varied greatly by gender and race. Young black and Hispanic women were the strongest supporters of President Obama. Although 60 per cent of US citizens between the ages of 18 and 29 have enrolled in college, 71 per cent of young voters have attended college, meaning that college-educated young people were over-represented among young people who voted.

Why youth voting matters

● Voting is habit-forming: when young people learn the voting process and vote, they are more likely to do so when they are older. If individuals have been motivated to get to the polls once, they are more likely to return. So, getting young people to vote early could be key to raising a new generation of voters.

- Young people are a major subset of the electorate and their voices matter:
  - 46 million young people aged 18–29 in the USA are eligible to vote, while 39 million seniors are eligible to vote
  - young people (aged 18–29) make up 21 per cent of the eligible voting population in the US.
- Young people's participation can influence election results.
- Involving young people in election-related learning, activities and discussion can have an impact on the young person's household, increasing the likelihood that others in the household will vote. In immigrant communities, young voters may be easier to reach, are more likely to speak English (cutting down translation costs), and may be the most effective messengers within their communities.

There have been numerous campaigns over the years to encourage the youth to vote in the USA, as highlighted in the following quotation:

'Declare yourself. Rock the vote. Choose or lose. Vote or die. Whatever it is you do, do whether you're a Republican or a Democrat. A Libertarian or Green. Whether you're a Poli Sci major or hate politics in all its forms. Whether you actually like Kerry or just can't stand Bush. Whether you're voting on Iraq, voting on abortion or voting on taxes. Just vote.

If there is one thing that we can all learn from the struggle for democracy in Afghanistan and Iraq, it is that we need to be thankful for our right to vote. We need to be thankful that every four years, we, as citizens of the United States, have a hand in electing our leaders.'
(*'Exercise the right to vote'*, The Chronicle, *2015*)

Case study: Rock the Vote

Rock the Vote's mission is to engage and build political power for young people in our country. Rock the Vote is the largest non-profit and non-partisan organization in the United States driving the youth vote to the polls. Fusing pop culture, politics, and technology, Rock the Vote works to mobilize the millennial voting bloc and the youth vote, protect voting rights, and advocate for an electoral process and voting system that works for the 21st-century electorate.

Since 1990, Rock the Vote has revolutionized the use of pop culture, music, art and technology to inspire political activity. Now, for almost 25 years, Rock the Vote has pioneered ways to make voting easier by simplifying and demystifying voter registration and elections for young adults.

Whether it's Madonna wrapping herself in the flag for the first Rock the Vote PSA or Snoop Dogg launching our bus tour in 2004, Rock the Vote represents the historic and groundbreaking intersection of culture and politics.

Rock the Vote's online voter registration tool has been translated into 13 languages. By educating thousands of young people through its 'Democracy Class' initiative and conducting groundbreaking research with its polling arm Young Voter Strategies, Rock the Vote has become the pre-eminent authority on how to mobilize young voters.

By consistently seeking out novel ways to reach new voters, we have run the largest voter registration drives for young people on record during the past six presidential elections. Additionally, in 2008 and again in 2012, our on-the-ground efforts, online organizing, and cutting-edge tools and technologies made us the largest non-partisan voter engagement campaign in the nation.

All of these efforts have resulted in Rock the Vote registering over 6 million new voters, bringing millions more to the polls, and becoming a trusted resource for young people, government agencies, and technological innovators passionate about political discourse and engagement.

Source: www.rockthevote.com

Social and economic inequality

Social factors	Economic factors
Education	Poverty/low income
Health	Unemployment
Housing	
Family structures	
Crime and justice	

The USA is one of the most affluent countries in the world, with a leading system of higher education; it is also the world's most industrialised country but has one of the most uneven distributions of wealth. A recent CNN news article highlighted that Americans face inequalities and the gap between rich and poor is not only widening but also affecting other social and economic factors.

According to data from the Organization for Economic Cooperation and Development (OECD), the USA ranked tenth out of 31 OECD countries in income inequality based on 'market incomes' – that is, before taking into account the redistributive effects of tax policies and income-transfer programmes such as social security and unemployment insurance.

'It's not just income inequality. It's lifespan inequality, education inequality and declining economic growth.' *(CNN Money)*

'The 400 richest people in the USA have more wealth than the bottom 150 million put together,' said Berkeley professor and former Labor Secretary Robert Reich on a 2014 CNN Money panel on inequality. Meanwhile, the median wage earner in America took home 9 per cent less last year than in 1999. But the rising income gap is manifesting itself in American society in other ways too. Social scientists have long said income inequality is bad for society. Figure 1.20 clearly shows a contrast between American citizens achieving academically in relation to their income status. More worryingly, Figure 1.21 highlights the life expectancy gap between the poor and the rich in the USA.

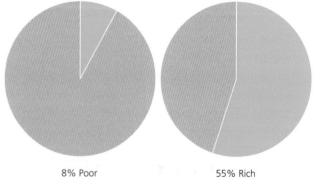

8% Poor   55% Rich

Figure 1.20 **Percentage of rich and poor American citizens who attained a four-year degree**
Source: Department of Health and Human Services

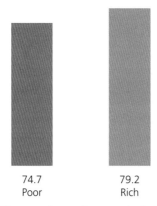

74.7
Poor

79.2
Rich

Figure 1.21 **Life expectancy (in years) of rich and poor American citizens**
Source: Department of Health and Human Services

For Americans born in the early 1960s, 5 per cent of poor people went to college and 35 per cent of rich people did, according to the Russell Sage Foundation. They defined rich and poor as the top and bottom 25 per cent for income. Only one generation later, Americans born around 1980, the number of rich people who went to college jumped by 20 per cent. For poor people, it rose by only 3 per cent. That further emphasises the cycle of income inequality, as an increasing number of middle-class jobs favour the more educated.

Education

Educational attainment, which represents the level of education completed (i.e. a high school diploma or equivalency certificate, a bachelor's degree, or a master's degree), is an important indicator in determining employment levels and income. Too many of America's most disadvantaged children grow up without the skills needed to thrive in the twenty-first century. Inequality persists, whether in educational attainment between income groups or racial/ethnic groups or across geographic locations. Low levels of performance among the most disadvantaged create long-term problems, particularly in an economy in which higher skill levels are more and more valued and the wages available to less-skilled workers are diminishing.

In a Brookings Institution/Hamilton Project study from June 2013, the observation was made that 'children from well-off families are disproportionately likely to stay well off, and children of poor families are very likely to remain poor'. It is widely understood that the single best predictor of future financial success is educational achievement, yet educational opportunities seem to be sorely lacking for all but the families at the top of the income ladder. A 2010 study of the most selective higher education institutions by Georgetown University researchers Anthony Carnevale and Jeff Strohl concluded that 'the wealthiest students out-populate the poor students by a margin of 14 to 1'.

College tuition costs

College tuition in the USA is increasing by about 8 per cent per year. If this continues, college costs could double every nine years or so and this is likely to make a college education beyond the reach of most average Americans. Attainment of a college degree correlates with income, wealth creation and therefore economic growth, so will have an impact on the future of the USA.

Figure 1.22 **College graduation in the USA**

Fact file

College graduates have average earnings 70 per cent higher than those of high school graduates.

The National Centre for Education statistics stated that, in 2013, some 34 per cent of 25–29-year-olds had earned a bachelor's or higher degree. Between 1990 and 2013, the size of the white–black gap at this education level widened from 13 per cent to 20 per cent, and the white–Hispanic gap widened from 18 per cent to 25 per cent.

Between 1990 and 2013, the percentage of 25–29-year-olds who had received at least a high school diploma or its equivalent increased for:
- whites – from 90 to 94 per cent
- blacks – from 82 to 90 per cent
- Hispanics – from 58 to 76 per cent
- Asian/Pacific Islanders – from 92 to 95 per cent.

The size of the white–black attainment gap at this education level narrowed from 8 to 4 per cent, and the white–Hispanic gap narrowed from 32 to 18 per cent.

Between 1990 and 2013, the percentage of 25–29-year-olds who had attained a bachelor's or higher degree increased for:
- whites – from 26 to 40 per cent
- blacks – from 13 to 20 per cent
- Hispanics – from 8 to 16 per cent
- Asian/Pacific Islanders – from 43 to 58 per cent.

Between 1990 and 2013, the gap in the attainment rate at this education level between white people and black people widened from 13 to 20 per cent, and the gap between white people and Hispanics widened from 18 to 25 per cent.

Government response

When he became president in 2008, Obama stated, 'I'll invest in early childhood education.' This promise was achieved through the investment of billions of dollars in Head Start and Early Head Start federal programmes that promoted pre-school education for low-income families. Part of the Head Start programme provided nutrition to poorer pupils. The Obama Government also invested heavily in high school education through the federal programme Race to the Top, which created over 300,000 new teachers with performance-related pay. The American Recovery and Reinvestment Act also invested $30 billion towards college scholarships for poorer families.

Making college affordable

'We will provide the support necessary for you to complete college and meet a new goal: by 2020, America will once again have the highest proportion of college graduates in the world.'
(President Obama, 2009)

The US Government have admitted that there are inequalities in educational attainment and have highlighted poverty/income as a factor that requires attention.

'Over the past three decades, the average tuition at a public four-year college has more than a tripled, while a typical family's income has barely budged. As a result, more students than ever before are relying on student loans to pay for their college education. Today, 71 per cent of students earning a bachelor's degree graduate with debt, which averages $29,400. While most students are able to repay their loans, many feel burdened by debt, especially as they seek to start a family, buy a home, launch a business, or save for retirement.'
(www.whitehouse.gov)

On 9 June 2014, President Obama signed a new Presidential Memorandum directing the Secretary of Education to propose regulations that would allow an additional almost 5 million federal direct student loan borrowers the opportunity to cap their student loan payments at 10 per cent of their income. The memorandum also outlines a series of new executive actions aimed to support federal student loan borrowers, especially vulnerable borrowers who may be at greater risk of defaulting on their loans.

Fact file

Making college affordable

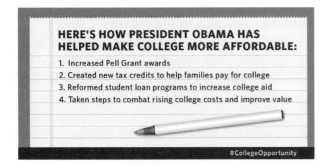

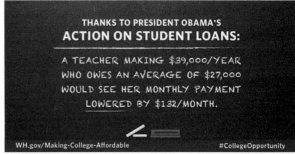

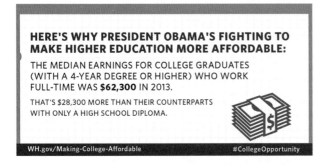

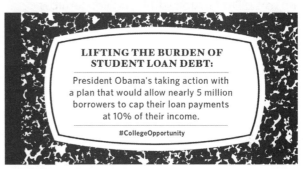

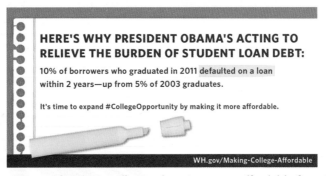

Figure 1.23 President Obama's ways of making college education more affordable for millions of American citizens

Increasing Pell Grant awards

Low-income students can apply for a Pell Grant to help fund their college education. The grants do not need to be repaid (unlike a loan).

The President has raised the maximum Pell Grant award to $5,730 for the 2014–15 award year – almost a $1,000 increase since 2008. Under the ⇨

Fact file (continued)

President's leadership, the number of Pell Grant recipients has expanded by 50 per cent over that time, providing college access to millions of additional low-income and middle-class students across the USA. The Obama Administration's landmark investment in the Pell Grant was enacted in the Health Care and Education Reconciliation Act of 2010, which ended student loan subsidies for private financial institutions and banks and shifted over $60 billion in savings back to students.

New tax credits to help families pay for college

President Obama established the American Opportunity Tax Credit in 2009 to assist families with the costs of college, providing up to $10,000 for four years of college tuition for families earning up to $180,000. Around 11.5 million families are expected to now benefit from the American Opportunity Tax Credit.

Reforming student loan programmes to increase college aid

The education-related initiatives funded by the Health Care and Education Reconciliation Act are fully paid for by ending the government subsidies currently given to financial institutions that make guaranteed federal student loans. Starting 1 July, all new federal student loans will be direct loans, delivered and collected by private companies under performance-based contracts with the Department of Education. According to the non-partisan Congressional Budget Office, ending these wasteful subsidies will free up nearly $68 billion for college affordability and deficit reduction over the next 11 years.

Source: www.whitehouse.gov/Making-College-Affordable

Show your understanding

1 Describe the income inequality which exists in America and its impact in terms of education and health.
2 Why is entry to college/university education difficult for those experiencing social inequality?
3 To what extent have all ethnic groups in the USA achieved success in education?
4 Outline the actions taken by President Obama to improve education, including making college education more affordable.

Health

Unlike the UK, the USA does not have a National Health Service (NHS) that is free to use. American citizens currently pay for their medical bills through private medical insurance: they have to pay for their health care. Medical insurance finances a person's health-care expenses. The majority of American citizens have private medical insurance coverage, primarily through an employer; many others obtain health

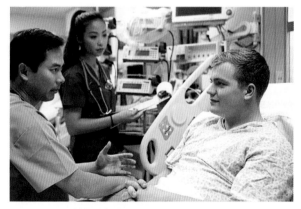

Figure 1.24 **US citizens must pay for their health care**

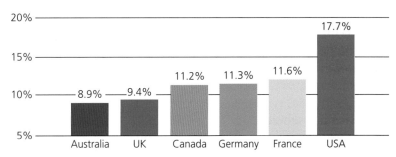

Figure 1.25 **Health spending as a percentage of the economy**
Source: OECD

insurance through programmes offered by the Government. In 2013, the percentage of Americans with health insurance (for all or part of their health needs) was 86.6 per cent.

Other individuals do not have health insurance at all; there were approximately 42 million (13.4 per cent) Americans who were uninsured in 2013.

The USA, which has a mostly private health-care system, spends more on its public health-care system than countries where the health-care system is almost entirely public. The US Government spends more, as a percentage of the economy, on public health care than Canada, the United Kingdom, Japan or Australia. And then it spends even more than that on private health care (see Figure 1.25).

Medicaid and Medicare are two government programmes that provide medical and health-related services to specific groups of people in the USA. Although the two programmes are very different, they are both managed by the Centers for Medicare and Medicaid Services, a division of the US Department of Health and Human Services.

- Medicaid is a means-tested health and medical services programme for certain individuals and families with low incomes and few resources. In 2013, 17.3 per cent of citizens were covered by Medicaid.

- Medicare is a federal health insurance programme that pays for hospital and medical care for elderly and certain disabled Americans. In 2013, 15.6 per cent of citizens were covered by Medicare.

Medicare now accounts for 15 per cent of the total federal budget and 21 per cent of total national health care spending.

Who experiences inequalities?

The main people who will experience inequalities in health are the uninsured American citizens:

Young people (2013)

- The percentage of children under age 19 who were uninsured was 7.6 per cent.
- The uninsured rate for children under age 19 in poverty, 9.8 per cent, was higher than the uninsured rate for children not in poverty, 7.0 per cent.

Ethnic groups (2013)

- 9.8 per cent of whites were uninsured
- 14.5 per cent of APIs were uninsured
- 15.9 of blacks were uninsured
- 24.3 per cent of Hispanics were uninsured.

Low-income groups (2013)

The US Census Bureau states that household income correlates with health insurance coverage and health insurance type. Among people with health insurance coverage, those with lower household income were likely to have coverage through government health insurance programmes while people with higher household income tend to have private coverage.

- 26.7 per cent of people with household income below $25,000 had private coverage, compared with 89.8 per cent of people with household income at or above $150,000.
- 62.5 per cent of people with household income below $25,000 had government health

insurance, compared with 14.1 per cent of people in the highest income category.

Government response

The Affordable Care Act (ACA), known as 'Obamacare', was passed by Congress and signed into law by President Obama on 23 March 2010. It became law on 1 October 2013. The Act promises 'comprehensive reforms that improve access to affordable health coverage for everyone and protect consumers from abusive insurance company practices'.

Fact file

The Affordable Care Act

The law helps you by bringing down health-care costs and making sure your health-care dollars are spent wisely. Insurance companies will now be accountable to their customers for how they are spending premium dollars, and how much they are raising rates. Plus, the new law will help lower costs through new tax credits and new marketplaces where insurers will have to compete for your business.

Value for your premium dollar

Thanks to the Affordable Care Act's 80/20 rule, if insurance companies don't spend at least 80 per cent of your premium dollar on medical care and quality improvements rather than advertising, overheads and bonuses for executives, they will have to provide you with a rebate. In 2012, 8.5 million people received half a billion dollars in refunds.

Stopping unreasonable rate increases

In every state, and for the first time ever, insurance companies are required to publicly justify their actions if they want to raise rates by 10 per cent or more.

Small business tax credits

Small businesses have long paid a premium price for health insurance – often 18 per cent more than larger employers. The tax credit will benefit an estimated 2 million workers who get their insurance from an estimated 360,000 small employers who will receive the credit in 2011 alone.

The health-care law builds on what works in our health-care system. And it fixes what's broken by providing you with more health insurance choices and better access to care.

Free prevention benefits

Insurers are now required to cover a number of recommended preventive services, such as cancer, diabetes and blood pressure screenings, without additional cost sharing such as deductibles. Already, 54 million Americans with private health coverage have received better preventive services coverage as a result.

Coverage for young adults

Under the law, most young adults who can't get coverage through their jobs can stay on their parents' plans until age 26 – a change that has already allowed 3.1 million young adults to get health coverage and given their families peace of mind.

Coverage for Americans with pre-existing conditions

Before the law, many Americans with pre-existing conditions were locked or priced out of the health insurance market. More than 50,000 Americans with pre-existing conditions have gained coverage through the new Pre-Existing Condition Insurance Plan. This temporary programme makes health coverage available and more affordable for individuals who are uninsured and have been denied health insurance because of a pre-existing condition. In 2014, insurance discriminating against anyone with a pre-existing condition will be illegal.

Affordable Insurance Exchanges

Affordable Insurance Exchanges are one-stop marketplaces where consumers can choose a private health insurance plan that fits their health needs. Starting in 2014, they will offer to the public the same kinds of insurance choices members of Congress will have. Exchanges will select health plans qualified to offer coverage; facilitate consumer assistance, shopping and enrolment; and co-ordinate eligibility for the Exchange and potential premium assistance. Already, 33 states and the District of Columbia are on their way to building Exchanges, having received a total of nearly $670 million in Exchange Establishment Grants.

Source: www.whitehouse.gov

Housing

Figure 1.26 **The difference between poor and rich housing areas in the USA**

Home ownership

In the USA, buying a home is the key to achieving the American Dream. Around 42 per cent of the net worth of all households consists of equity in their homes – this means that, for most Americans, their homes are their single largest asset. Home ownership provides families with the means to invest in education, business opportunities, retirement and resources for the next generation.

However, the banking crisis of 2008 and the collapse of the housing market created misery for millions of people. In the economic boom prior to 2008 many low-paid workers were able to buy their own homes. But with the collapse of house prices and the economic recession of 2008 onwards, many householders realised that their homes were worth much less than their mortgages and many suffered unemployment. As a result, since 2008 almost 11 million homes have been repossessed, 3.5 million more home owners are behind in their payments, and another 1.5 million homes are in the foreclosure process.

The percentage of Americans who own their homes has fallen from 69 per cent in 2004 to about 65 per cent today.

According to the US Census Bureau, figures for the home ownership rate for the second quarter of 2014 are as follows:

- White home owners were highest at 72.9 per cent.
- API and Native American home owners were second at 54.7 per cent.
- Hispanic home owners were third at 45.8 per cent.
- Black home owners were lowest at 43.5 per cent.

Inner-city areas

These are older central parts of a city which are run down and in which low-income groups predominate.

- People living in inner-city areas make up 21 per cent of the US population living in poverty. That's 8 million people.
- People living in these areas make up 15 per cent of the US unemployed. That's 2 million people.
- In inner-city areas 3 in 10 people live in poverty.
- In the suburbs 1 in 10 people live in poverty.

Government response

The Department of Housing and Urban Development (HUD) plays a crucial role in providing affordable homes and shelter and

support to the homeless and to those in need, such as the elderly and the sick. Its mission statement is 'to create strong, sustainable, inclusive communities and quality affordable homes for all'. In 2011, Congress allocated $46 billion dollars to the agency. The collapse in the housing market and HUD's involvement in providing financial assistance for low-income families has created significant challenges for the agency. Below are some of the wide-ranging federal programmes it provides for individuals and communities in partnership with states, local government and housing associations.

HUD programmes

- **The HOME Investment Partnership Programme** This the largest federal block grant to states and local government to be allocated to provide affordable homes for low-income households. Annually about $2 billion is allocated by HUD.
- **Self-help Homeownership Opportunity Programme (SHOP)** This provides funds to organisations to build their own homes.
- **Community Development Block Grants (CDBG)** This provides financial support to states and local government 'to address a wide range of unique community development needs'.
- **Low Income Tenants' Rental Assistance Programme** This provides financial assistance to help low-income tenants to pay their rents.

Other important programmes cater for the elderly, the disabled and those in ill health, for example, HIV/AIDS sufferers.

Criticism of HUD

An Inspector General's Report to Congress in 2010 highlighted grave weaknesses in the running of the HUD agency. Through mismanagement, duplication and fraud the Report identified almost $1 billion of public funds 'that could have been spent providing housing aid to those in need'. It discovered that HUD rental assistance payments were being given to 652 deceased people and that HUD had spent $12.2 billion acquiring foreclosed houses but had only recovered $6 billion in resales. HUD's affordable housing block grant programme had spent $400 million on over 600 projects that had been abandoned. Millions had also been wasted on paying slum landlords who failed to modernise their properties and simply banked the money. President Obama has reformed HUD's largest mortgage programme, the Federal Housing Administration (FHA), which lost millions of dollars through its investment in high risk loans. New rules will ensure that the individual can afford mortgage payments loans. In future, loans will not be provided to rich individuals to buy luxury flats in, for example, Manhattan in New York. In one case a developer had received $5.5 million in HUD funds since 2006 to build houses in Anaheim, California, but no construction had occurred.

Family structure

There has been a significant change in family structure in the USA over the past few decades and a breakdown of the traditional family unit. In the 1960s there were similar statistics of married couples within each of the ethnic groups, but the decline in marriage since then has been particularly severe for black families. Black children are significantly less likely than other children to be living with two married parents. For example, in 2013, 34 per cent of black children were living with two parents, compared with 83 per cent of Asian children, 74 per cent of white children, and 58 per cent of Hispanic children.

Single-parent families tend to have much lower incomes than two-parent families do, while cohabiting families fall in between. The US Census Bureau stated that family households and married couple households had the highest median income in 2013 ($76,509), followed by households maintained by men with no wife present

($50,625). Those maintained by women with no husband present had the lowest income ($35,154).

Most children who live with just one parent, regardless of ethnic group, live with their mothers. This is the case for more than half of all black children, and more than one-quarter of all Hispanic children; among white and Asian children, smaller proportions (about one in seven, and one in ten, respectively) live with their mothers only.

- Among the race groups, Asian households had the highest median income in 2013 ($67,065).
- White households' median income was $58,270.
- Hispanic households' median income was $40,963.
- Black households' median income was $34,598.

Government response

> 'Fighting for working families; strengthening our economy.'
>
> 'I want all our children to go to schools worthy of their potential – schools that challenge them, inspire them, and instil in them a sense of wonder about the world around them. I want them to have the chance to go to college – even if their parents aren't rich. And I want them to get good jobs: jobs that pay well and give them benefits like health care, jobs that let them spend time with their own kids and retire with dignity.' *(Barack Obama, 2008)*

The US Government continues to highlight that a strong nation is made up of strong families. 'Every family deserves the chance that so many of our parents and grandparents had – to make a better future for themselves and their children. Strong families will always be front and centre of President Obama's agenda.'

Fact file

Strengthening families

President Obama was raised by a single parent and knows the difficulties that young people face when their fathers are absent. He is committed to responsible fatherhood, by supporting fathers who stand by their families and by encouraging young men to work towards good jobs in promising career pathways. The president has also proposed an historic investment in providing home visits to low income, first-time parents by trained professionals. The president and First Lady are also committed to ensuring that children have nutritious meals to eat at home and at school, so that they grow up healthy and strong.

Supporting working families

President Obama is committed to creating jobs and economic opportunities for families across America. And he is restoring fairness to the tax code and increasing child care so that working families have the support they need. Ten days after taking office, the president established a White House Task Force on Middle-Class Working Families, led by Vice President Biden. The Task Force is focused on raising the living standards of middle-class, working families across America.

The President's American Recovery and Reinvestment Act provided needed support to families enduring difficult times.

- The Act protects health coverage for 7 million Americans who have lost their jobs, by giving a 65 per cent COBRA (Consolidated Omnibus Budget Reconciliation Act) subsidy to make coverage affordable.

- The Act also boosts family incomes by expanding the Child Tax Credit to cover an additional 10 million children in working families and creating a new Make Work Pay tax credit.
- To help working mothers and fathers obtain quality child care, the Act includes an additional $2 billion for the Child Care and Development Block Grant, $1 billion for Head Start and $1.1 billion for Early Head Start.
- To fight hunger, the Act includes a $20 billion increase for the Supplemental Nutrition Assistance Program (SNAP), formerly known as Food Stamps, as well as funding for food banks and the Special Supplemental Nutrition Program for Women, Infants, and Children (WIC).
- The Act increases the Weatherization Assistance Program by $5 billion to help low-income families save on their energy bills by making their homes more energy efficient.
- The Act increases job training funds for those who need them most, with $3.95 billion in additional funding for the Workforce Investment system, which will support green job training, summer jobs for young people, and other opportunities.
- The Act provides increased income support, including an increase of $25 per week for Unemployment Insurance recipients and incentives for states to expand unemployment insurance eligibility, as well as an extra $250 payment to Social Security and Supplemental Security Income beneficiaries and new resources for the Temporary Assistance for Needy Families (TANF) programme.

Source: www.whitehouse.gov

Show your understanding

1 Describe the inequalities that exist in health between different ethnic groups.
2 In what way does the Affordable Care Act improve the health of those who experience social inequality?
3 Why is housing an area of social concern in the USA?
4 To what extent has HUD met the housing needs of American citizens?
5 Compare the family structures of different ethnic groups in the USA.
6 What actions has the US Government taken to support families?

Crime and law

The FBI estimated that, in 2012, the number of violent crimes in the USA increased by 0.7 per cent. However, property crimes decreased by 0.9 per cent. Statistics show that the estimated rate of violent crime was 386.9 offences per 100,000 inhabitants, and the property crime rate was

Figure 1.27 **A prisoner inside a US federal prison**

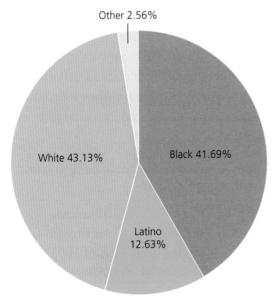

Figure 1.28 **Current US death row population by race, July 2014**

2,859.2 offences per 100,000 inhabitants. While the violent crime rate remained virtually unchanged when compared to the 2011 rate, the property crime rate declined by 1.6 per cent.

Most crimes that are committed in the USA take place in inner-city areas. Many different factors can contribute to making certain cities dangerous to live or work in within the USA. There can be issues with armed robberies, lack of police funding, gang-related violence and much more that contributes to the lack of safety within city limits.

Is justice colour-blind?

The February 2012 killing of 17-year-old black American Trayvon Martin by neighbourhood watch volunteer George Zimmerman in Sanford, Florida, became a national issue, sparking protests, debate and a personal statement from President Obama. The case has raised questions about race, guns and justice, and led to numerous federal, state and local investigations.

George Zimmerman shot Trayvon Martin while he was walking back from a convenience store in Sanford, Florida, where he had bought a bag of sweets and a drink. Zimmerman claimed he killed the teen in self-defence after a scuffle. Initially the police did not charge Zimmerman. However, in March 2012 President Obama commented on the case, saying he thought the shooting should be investigated, telling reporters: 'If I had a son, he'd look like Trayvon.' As a result Zimmerman was charged with second-degree murder in the shooting. However, at the trial in July 2013 Zimmerman was found not guilty.

The Ferguson riots

The acquittal of a white police officer charged with the murder of an unarmed black teenager, Michael Brown, in Ferguson, a run-down suburb of St Louis, in November 2014 highlights the issue of race in American justice and the continuation of racial segregation. In 1990 the population of Ferguson was about 75 per cent white, today it is 67 per cent black. Yet 80 per cent of its six-member local council are white and only three of the 53 police officers are black. The police are accused of systematically targeting black people for minor or non-existent traffic offences and imposing heavy fines which, if they cannot pay, give them a criminal record for life.

The not guilty verdict led to further riots in Ferguson but also significantly led to 170 peaceful protests across the USA by people of all races displaying solidarity for the non-white and poor community of Ferguson.

Figure 1.29 Protestors facing a line of riot police in Ferguson following the death of Michael Brown

It is estimated that 500 people were killed by the police in the USA during 2013 but, in most cases the police were defending themselves against people carrying guns. However, according to ProPublica, a website for investigative journalism, between 2010 and 2012 young black males were 22 times more likely to be fatally shot by police than young white males.

Below is a list of 2014 deaths of unarmed black citizens at the hands of the police:

- 20 November 2014: Akai Gurley, a young black father, was shot dead by a white police officer as he climbed the stairs to his flat. He was unarmed and the police officer panicked in the dim lighting.
- 22 November 2014: A police officer in Cleveland, Ohio, shot dead Tamir Rice, a 12-year-old black boy who was holding an air gun.
- 4 December 2014: A grand jury acquitted a police officer of killing an unarmed black man, Eric Garner, in New York. In July 2014, Garner, who had been selling illegal cigarettes, was placed in a chokehold (a chokehold is banned under NYPD policy). The incident was filmed by passers-by and in the video Garner clearly stated, 'I can't breathe'.
- 4 April 2015: a police office in North Charleston shot dead Walter Scott, an unarmed black man whose brake light was malfunctioning. Police officer Michael Slager claimed he felt threatened and was forced to shoot. However, video evidence clearly shows Scott running away and being shot 8 times in the back. Slager was arrested and charged with murder.

Table 1.6 **Firearm ownership and homicide by firearm figures by country/territory, 2010**

Country/ territory	Average firearms (per 100 people)	Homicide by firearm (per 100,000 population)
USA	88.8	2.97
Switzerland	45.7	0.77
Finland	45.3	0.45
Serbia	37.8	0.46
Cyprus	36.4	0.46

FBI: Mass shooting incidents occurring more frequently

Mass shootings have been occurring more frequently in recent years, an FBI study shows, with nearly one incident a month from 2000 to 2013.

The study reported 160 incidents during that time, with 486 people killed and 557 wounded. Those figures don't include the deaths or injuries of the shooters.

The bureau called such shootings 'active shooter incidents', which the report described as 'individuals actively engaged in killing or attempting to kill people in populated areas (excluding shootings related to gang or drug violence)'.

In 40 per cent of the cases studied, the shooters killed themselves.

Most of the shootings were carried out by males. Only six of the 'active shooters' in incidents during that time period were female. Seventy per cent of the incidents 'occurred in either a commerce/business or educational environment', the FBI said.

Source: CNN (Washington)

Case study: Mass shootings in the USA

Among the incidents studied by the FBI for the report was the Sandy Hook Elementary School shooting in Newtown, Connecticut, on 14 December 2012. Gunman Adam Lanza, 20, killed 20 children, ages 6 and 7, and six adults at the school before killing himself. Police later found the body of Lanza's mother at her home.

'In at least nine incidents, the shooter first shot and killed a family member(s) in a residence before moving to a more public location to continue shooting,' the FBI report said.

Another case studied for the report was the mass shooting at an Aurora, Colorado, movie theatre in 2012. Twelve people were killed and 58 wounded. Accused gunman James Holmes pleaded not guilty by reason of insanity to the killings; his trial is due to begin in 2015.

In April 2007, Virginia Tech student Seung-Hui Cho shot and killed 32 people and wounded dozens more in a classroom building and a dormitory on campus before killing himself.

Major Nidal Malik Hasan killed 13 people and wounded 32 more at Fort Hood, Texas, during a shooting rampage on 5 November 2009. He was convicted in 2013 and sentenced to death.

Government response

On 16 January 2013, President Obama put forward a specific plan to protect children and communities by reducing gun violence. The plan combines executive actions and calls for legislative action that would help keep guns out of the wrong hands, ban assault and high-capacity magazines, make schools safer, and increase access to mental health services.

The proposed plan:

- requires background checks for all gun sales and strengthens the background check system;
- provides states with monetary incentives – $20 million in 2013 and a proposed $50 million in 2014 – to share information so that records on criminal history and people prohibited from gun ownership due to mental health reasons are more readily available;

- bans military-style assault weapons and limits magazines to a capacity of ten rounds;
- urges Congress to pass the administration's $4 billion proposal to keep 15,000 state and local police officers on the street to help deter gun crime;
- provides training for 'active shooter' situations to 14,000 law enforcement, first responders and school officials;
- helps schools invest in safety. The president's plan calls for more school resource officers and counsellors in all schools through the Community Oriented Policing Services hiring programme. The plan also calls for the federal government to assist schools in developing emergency management plans;
- improves mental health awareness through enhanced teacher training and referrals for treatment. It calls for the training of 5000 additional mental health professionals nationwide. The plan also calls for coverage of mental health treatment under the Patient Protection and Affordable Care Act and the Mental Health Parity and Addiction Equity Act of 2008.

However, the Republican-controlled House of Representatives refused to support this modest gun reform and no action was taken. This highlights the limitations of presidential powers.

Income and poverty

'We are true to our creed when a little girl born into the bleakest poverty knows that she has the same chance to succeed as anybody else, because she is an American; she is free, and she is equal, not just in the eyes of God but also in our own.'
(Barack Obama, Inaugural Address, 21 January 2013)

In 2013, the official poverty rate was 14.5 per cent; this amounts to 45.3 million people living in poverty in the USA.

This figure was a decrease from 15.0 per cent in 2012 (see Figure 1.30).

How the poorest are faring

The recession also pushed many more people into poverty. In 2010, the poverty rate peaked at 15.1 per cent, and has barely fallen since then. This is the first time the poverty rate has remained at or above 15 per cent for three years running since 1965.

Those making $23,492 a year for a family of four, or $11,720 for an individual, were considered to be living in poverty.

While the ranks of the poor are still elevated from the recession, overall poverty remains far below the 22.4 per cent it was in 1959 when the Census first began tracking the data. Over the last 25 years, the poverty rate has averaged at just over 13 per cent.

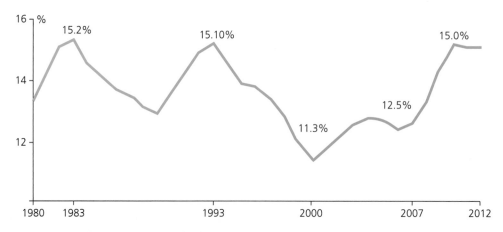

Figure 1.30 **US poverty rate, 1980–2012**
Source: US Census Bureau

Race and ethnicity

The incidence of poverty among African Americans and Hispanics exceeds that of whites by a factor of 2–3 times. In 2013, the following were considered to be living in poverty:

- 27.2 per cent of blacks (11.0 million)
- 23.5 per cent of Hispanics (12.7 million)
- 9.6 per cent of whites (18.8 million)
- 10.5 per cent of Asian and Pacific Islanders (1.8 million).

Although black people represent only 13.0 per cent of the total population, they make up 24.4 per cent of the poor population; Hispanics, who represent 17.3 per cent of the population, account for 28.1 per cent of the poor. Poverty rates for Hispanics fell from 25.6 per cent in 2012 to 23.5 per cent in 2013, as did the number of poor Hispanics, from 13.6 million in 2012 to 12.7 million in 2013. Poverty rates and the numbers estimated as poor were statistically unchanged from 2012 to 2013 for white non-Hispanics, black people and Asian and Pacific Islanders (APIs).

Government response

President Obama has been a lifelong advocate for the poor. As a young college graduate, he rejected the high salaries of corporate America and moved to the South Side of Chicago to work as a community organizer. As an organizer, President Obama worked with Chicago residents, churches, and local government to set up job training programs for the unemployed and after-school programs for kids. As President, his life experiences inform his efforts to create a path of opportunity for all hard-working Americans to enter the middle class. President Obama will lead a new federal approach to revitalize communities stricken by the economic crisis as well as communities that were hurting before it began.

Expand opportunity

President Obama is committed to creating the opportunity for all Americans to grab the first rung on the ladder to the middle class. That includes investing in strategies to make work pay, expanding access to affordable housing, and helping low-income Americans build the job skills to succeed in the workforce.

Stem the tide

The economic crisis has hit low-income American families particularly hard. President Obama will help vulnerable Americans through this crisis by making sure they have the resources they need to put food on the table and keep a roof over their heads, while also extending tax credits to low-wage workers.

The American Recovery and Reinvestment Act (see page 34) included broad investments to alleviate the poverty made worse by the economic crisis.

- To fight hunger, the Act includes a $20 billion increase for the Supplemental Nutrition Assistance Program (SNAP), formerly known as Food Stamps, as well as funding for food banks and the Special Supplemental Nutrition Program for Women, Infants, and Children (WIC).
- The Act also provides for $2 billion in new Neighbourhood Stabilization Funds to help maintain ailing neighbourhoods and $1.5 billion in Homelessness Prevention Funds to keep people in their homes or rapidly rehouse them.
- The Act increases funding for the Community Services Block Grant, which helps to alleviate the causes and conditions of poverty in communities, by $1 billion.

Tax relief for middle-class families

President Obama has cut taxes for middle-class families every year since he has been in office, ⇨

and federal taxes for middle-class families are currently at nearly their lowest levels in decades.

A typical middle-class family has benefited from a tax cut of $3,600 over the last four years – more if they were putting a child through college.

- President Obama's Making Work Pay credit provided 95 per cent of working families with a tax cut of $400 per person or $800 per couple in 2009 and 2010.
- The President's payroll tax cut provided 160 million workers with a 2 per cent reduction in payroll taxes, cutting taxes for a typical family earning $50,000 a year by $1,000 – or $40 per paycheck – in 2011 and 2012.

- Families putting a child through college can receive as much as $10,000 of help over four years from the President's American Opportunity Tax Credit, the equivalent of a 30 per cent discount on tuition at a typical state university. For many families, the American Opportunity Tax Credit provides thousands of dollars more help with college expenses than they could have received from pre-existing tax credits.
- Federal income taxes on middle-income families are now at nearly their lowest level (as a share of income) since the Eisenhower Administration, and total federal taxes on middle-class families also remain at nearly the lowest levels in decades.

Source: www.whitehouse.gov

Labour force and ethnicity

Labour-market differences within racial and ethnic groups are associated with many factors, not all of which are measurable. These factors include variations across the groups in educational attainment; the occupations and industries in which the groups work; the geographic areas of the country in which the groups are concentrated, including whether they tend to reside in urban or rural settings; and the degree of discrimination encountered in the workplace.

White people made up the majority of the labour force (63.5 per cent) in 2013. Around 16 per cent of the labour force were people of Hispanic or Latino ethnicity. Black people and Asian and Pacific Islanders made up an additional 12 per cent and 6 per cent, respectively. Native Americans and Alaska Natives made up 1 per cent of the labour force.

Despite the decreasing unemployment figures, rates were highest for black people (13.1 per cent), Native Americans (12.8 per cent) and Hispanics (9.1 per cent) and lowest for APIs (5.2 per cent) and for white people (6.5 per cent).

Earnings

Among the major race and ethnicity groups, Hispanics and black people continue to have considerably lower earnings than white people and APIs in 2013.

The median usual weekly earnings of full-time wage and salary workers were $578 for Hispanics and $629 for black people, compared with $802 for white people and $942 for APIs. Among men, the earnings of white people ($884), black people ($664) and Hispanics ($594) were 83 per cent, 63 per cent and 56 per cent, respectively, of the earnings of APIs ($1,059).

The median earnings of white women ($722), black women ($606) and Hispanic women ($541) were 88 per cent, 74 per cent and 66 per cent, respectively, of the earnings of Asian and Pacific Islander women ($819).

Government response

Long-term unemployment is falling, but still work to do

'The recent labour market data have been encouraging. Businesses have now added nearly 10 million jobs over 53 straight months of job growth, the longest streak on record. Total job gains have exceeded 200,000 in each of the last six months, the first time that has happened since 1997. And the unemployment rate has fallen rapidly since mid-2013 to reach 6.2 per cent in July, 1.1 per cent less than a year ago.

'The Administration has also taken steps to help more of the long-term unemployed get back to work. Earlier this year, the President unveiled a set of "best practices" being taken by leading employers – including over 80 members of the Fortune 500 and over 20 members of the Fortune 50 – around recruiting and hiring the long-term unemployed, to remove some of the barriers that make it harder for them to navigate the hiring process.'

Source: www.whitehouse.gov

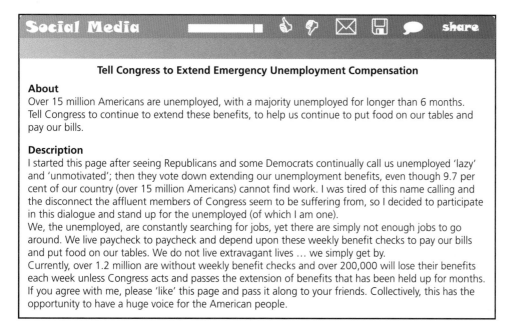

Social Media

Tell Congress to Extend Emergency Unemployment Compensation

About

Over 15 million Americans are unemployed, with a majority unemployed for longer than 6 months. Tell Congress to continue to extend these benefits, to help us continue to put food on our tables and pay our bills.

Description

I started this page after seeing Republicans and some Democrats continually call us unemployed 'lazy' and 'unmotivated'; then they vote down extending our unemployment benefits, even though 9.7 per cent of our country (over 15 million Americans) cannot find work. I was tired of this name calling and the disconnect the affluent members of Congress seem to be suffering from, so I decided to participate in this dialogue and stand up for the unemployed (of which I am one).

We, the unemployed, are constantly searching for jobs, yet there are simply not enough jobs to go around. We live paycheck to paycheck and depend upon these weekly benefit checks to pay our bills and put food on our tables. We do not live extravagant lives … we simply get by.

Currently, over 1.2 million are without weekly benefit checks and over 200,000 will lose their benefits each week unless Congress acts and passes the extension of benefits that has been held up for months. If you agree with me, please 'like' this page and pass it along to your friends. Collectively, this has the opportunity to have a huge voice for the American people.

Figure 1.31 **Content adapted from a real Facebook page**

Show your understanding

1 What evidence suggests that the USA is a violent society?
2 Describe incidents of mass shootings in the USA.
3 Why do most ethnic minorities feel that they are discriminated against in terms of law and order issues?
4 Compare the income, poverty and unemployment experiences of different ethnic groups.

Show your understanding

Group task

Create groups of three or four pupils.

Each group should choose one social or economic factor.

Your task is to create a handout of your chosen factor – this will be given to everyone in the class to use as a study aid.

Research your chosen factor and make detailed notes on:

- inequalities and those who experience inequalities
- what the government is doing to help
- whether any progress has been made.

12-mark question

Analyse the policies introduced by a world power you have studied to solve socio-economic issues.

20-mark question

To what extent do individuals or groups in a world power you have studied experience social inequality?

International relations

Background

After the Second World War in 1945, two nations competed for global influence: the capitalist USA and the communist Soviet Union. Both were referred to as 'superpowers' and their rivalry was known as the 'Cold War'. Both set up military alliances to challenge each other's dominance. NATO (North Atlantic Treaty Organisation), which still exists today, included the USA, Canada and the countries of Western Europe, and the Warsaw Pact consisted of the Soviet Union and countries of Eastern Europe.

However, by 1991 Communism had collapsed in Eastern Europe and the Soviet Union had disintegrated. Democratic governments were set up in the countries of Eastern Europe and many, such as Poland, have since joined NATO (see Figure 1.32). New countries such as Georgia and the Ukraine were formed after the collapse of the Soviet Union and what was left of the Soviet Union became the new state of Russia.

In this section we will examine American involvement and influence in international organisation and the challenge it faces from Russia, China and extremist groups. President Obama's recent address to the Security Council of the United Nations highlights the challenges faced by the international community to maintain peace and security and the need for collective action to eradicate world poverty and disease (see pages 45–46).

Key

■ NATO member countries

Figure 1.32 **The NATO member countries**

Table 1.7 **Top six countries by military spending, 2011**

Country	Spending ($bn)	World share (per cent)
United States*	739.3	45.7
China*	89.8	5.5
Britain*	62.7	3.9
France*	58.8	3.6
Japan	58.4	3.6
Russia*	52.7	3.3

*Nuclear power
Source: International Institute for Strategic Studies, 2012

USA world dominance

For almost 25 years the USA has been the dominant economic and military power across all continents of the world. From the United Nations to NATO to the G8 group, the US influences global events and has used its military might to take action against states and organisations that threaten the security of the West. Table 1.7 highlights the massive military might and spending of the USA, which includes nuclear weapons. However, there is a perception today that America's dominance is on the decline. Both the banking crisis of 2008 and the subsequent economic recession have weakened the US economy and have led to many Americans questioning US involvement abroad (see Pew Research findings on the next page). The failure to destroy al-Qaeda and the Taliban, and the rise of ISIS in Syria and Iraq, explain why public approval of President Obama's foreign policy is at an all-time low. The USA also faces the emergence of an aggressive Russia willing to use military force in Eastern Europe and a confident China no longer willing to accept US dominance in Asia.

A report by the Pew Research Centre underscores the extent to which development at home and abroad have altered Americans' attitudes towards international engagement.

Among the report's key findings:

- For the first time in surveys dating back decades, a majority of Americans (53 per cent) see the USA as playing a less important and less powerful role in the world than it did a decade ago.
- Also for the first time, 52 per cent of Americans agree that 'the USA should mind its own business internationally and let other countries get along the best they can on their own'.
- Around 70 per cent (up from 56 per cent in 2009) believe that the USA is less respected by other countries than in the past.
- By a margin of 80 to 16 per cent, Americans endorse the idea that 'We should not think so much in international terms but concentrate more on our national problems and building up our own strengths and prosperity here at home.'

The public's long-range foreign policy goals reveal the intensification of a long-standing inward focus. The goals receiving more than 60 per cent support as top priorities include:

- protecting the USA from terrorist attacks
- protecting American jobs
- preventing the spread of weapons of mass destruction
- reducing dependence on imported energy.

The goals receiving less than 40 per cent support as top priorities include:

- strengthening the United Nations
- dealing with global climate change
- promoting and defending human rights in other countries
- helping to improve living standards in developing nations
- promoting democracy in other nations.

Source: Pew Research Centre, July 2012

Figure 1.33 **US aircraft carrier, the USS Abraham Lincoln**

USA and the United Nations

The USA played a leading role in setting up the United Nations after the Second World War and this is reflected in its headquarters being in New York. The USA has one of the five permanent seats on the UN Security Council along with Russia, China, France and the UK. The Security Council can impose economic sanctions on a country and can also take military action, such as sending 30,000 UN soldiers to the Darfur region of Sudan. However, all of the permanent members must agree to any action and can use a veto. This can lead to no action being taken by the UN. For example, the USA, the UK and France wished to condemn and take action against the Assad regime in Syria. However, both China and Russia vetoed such a move. This highlights the limits of US influence in the Security Council as it cannot impose its foreign policy objectives.

However, the USA has been far more influential in the humanitarian work of the specialised agencies of the UN such as WHO (World Health Organization). The UN declared the Ebola outbreak in West Africa an international public health emergency and the USA, alongside the UN, has acted swiftly to provide doctors, scientists and military support to tackle the crisis in the countries affected. To date, more than 8000 people have died from the Ebola virus in seven countries.

Below is an extract from President Obama's address to the UN Security Council in September 2014:

'As we gather here, an outbreak of Ebola overwhelms public health systems in West Africa and threatens to move rapidly across borders. Russian aggression in Europe recalls the days when large nations trampled small ones in pursuit of territorial ambition. The brutality of terrorists in Syria and Iraq forces us to look into the heart of darkness.

'We believe that right makes might – that bigger nations should not be able to bully smaller ones, and that people should be able to choose their own future.

'And these are simple truths, but they must be defended. America and our allies will support the people of Ukraine as they develop their democracy and economy. We will reinforce our NATO Allies and uphold our commitment to collective self-defense. We will impose a cost on Russia for aggression, and we will counter falsehoods with the truth. And we call upon others to join us on the right side of history.

'Moreover, a different path is available – the path of diplomacy and peace, and the ideals this institution is designed to uphold. The recent cease-fire agreement in Ukraine offers an opening to achieve those objectives. If Russia takes that path – a path that for stretches of the post-Cold War period resulted in prosperity for the Russian people – then we will lift our sanctions and welcome Russia's role in addressing common challenges. After all, that's what the United States and Russia have been able to do in past years – from reducing our nuclear stockpiles to meeting our obligations under the Nuclear Nonproliferation Treaty, to co-operating to remove and destroy Syria's declared chemical weapons. And that's the kind of co-operation we are prepared to pursue again – if Russia changes course.

As we speak, America is deploying our doctors and scientists – supported by our military – to help contain the outbreak of Ebola and pursue new treatments. But we need a broader effort to stop a disease that could kill hundreds of thousands, inflict horrific suffering, destabilize economies, and move rapidly across borders. It's easy to see this as a distant problem – until it is not. ⇨

America is pursuing a diplomatic resolution to the Iranian nuclear issue, as part of our commitment to stop the spread of nuclear weapons and pursue the peace and security of a world without them. And this can only take place if Iran seizes this historic opportunity. My message to Iran's leaders and people has been simple and consistent: Do not let this opportunity pass. We can reach a solution that meets your energy needs while assuring the world that your program is peaceful.

America is and will continue to be a Pacific power, promoting peace, stability, and the free flow of commerce among nations. But we will insist that all nations abide by the rules of the road, and resolve their territorial disputes peacefully, consistent with international law.

America is committed to a development agenda that eradicates extreme poverty by 2030. We will do our part to help people feed themselves, power their economies, and care for their sick. If the world acts together, we can make sure that all of our children enjoy lives of opportunity and dignity.

America is pursuing ambitious reductions in our carbon emissions, and we've increased our investments in clean energy. We will do our part, and help developing nations do theirs.

I have made it clear that America will not base our entire foreign policy on reacting to terrorism.

Instead, we've waged a focused campaign against al Qaeda and its associated forces – taking out their leaders, denying them the safe havens they rely on. As an international community, we must meet this challenge with a focus on four areas. First, the terrorist group known as ISIL must be degraded and ultimately destroyed. This group has terrorized all who they come across in Iraq and Syria.

In this effort, we do not act alone – nor do we intend to send US troops to occupy foreign lands. Instead, we will support Iraqis and Syrians fighting to reclaim their communities. We will use our military might in a campaign of airstrikes to roll back ISIL. We will train and equip forces fighting against these terrorists on the ground. We will work to cut off their financing, and to stop the flow of fighters into and out of the region. And already, over 40 nations have offered to join this coalition.

Together with our partners, America is training and equipping the Syrian opposition to be a counterweight to the terrorists of ISIS and the brutality of the Assad regime.

We recognize as well that leadership will be necessary to address the conflict between Palestinians and Israelis.

Source: adapted from President Obama's address to the United Nations General Assembly, 24 September 2014

USA and China

In 2013, the new leader of China, Xi Jinping stated that 'the vast Pacific Ocean has enough space for the two large countries of China and the United States'. China's new confidence is now challenging US dominance of south-east Asia. Tension has always existed between the two countries over the island of Taiwan; when the Chinese Communists gained control of mainland China, the defeated Chinese Government fled to Taiwan and set up their own independent China. The US protects Taiwan and provides it with up-to-date military equipment to deter a mainland attack. There is also tension over Hong Kong, a former British colony, now ruled by China. Recent student demonstrations there in support of free elections could lead to military intervention by China. Neighbouring countries such as Japan and the Philippines look to America for protection. China has territorial demands against these countries, and there is a danger of this leading to military conflict. China has, for example, fuelled anti-Japanese riots in its cities and has challenged Japan's control over uninhabited islets. The US fleet still dominates the Pacific but China will soon have in service its first aircraft carrier (the US has 11 worldwide). The USA has military bases in South Korea and Japan and China wishes to challenge US dominance in the region.

Both countries depend on each other for trade. The Asia-Pacific Economic Co-operation (APEC) summit of November 2014 was held in Beijing, reflecting the new economic might of China (it is estimated that by 2015–16 China will overtake America to become the world's largest economy).

USA and NATO

The USA has been the dominant member of NATO (North Atlantic Treaty Organisation) since its inception in 1949. NATO was set up as a political and military alliance to defend the freedom and security of its members. NATO now has 28 members including countries from the former Russian-controlled Eastern Europe (see below). NATO will defend its members from aggression and an attack on one member is regarded as an attack upon them all. This explains why Georgia and the Ukraine are anxious to join as they have both been threatened by Russian aggression. Over the last 20 years, the US and its NATO allies have played an important role in crisis management and peacekeeping in areas such as the former Yugoslavia and Afghanistan.

The expansion of NATO

The new members of NATO are:

- Albania
- Bulgaria
- Croatia
- Czech Republic
- Estonia
- Latvia
- Lithuania
- Poland
- Romania
- Slovakia
- Slovenia.

Russian aggression

Under President Putin, Russia is now determined to challenge US and NATO's dominance in Eastern Europe. In 2008, Georgia sent troops into South Ossetia (part of Georgia) to crush rebel groups. Putin sent in Russian forces to eject the Georgian forces from South Ossetia and Abkhazia. In early 2015, the area still had not been returned to Georgia and pro-Russian rebels remained in control. The USA, NATO and the European Union (EU) condemned this invasion and provided Georgia with $6 billion in humanitarian aid. Aware of the lack of action by the West, Putin raised the stakes and set out to effectively partition the Ukraine and destabilise the country. Obama in his address to the Security Council described the situation as follows:

'After the people of Ukraine mobilized popular protests and calls for reform, their corrupt president fled. Against the will of the government in Kyiv, Crimea was annexed. Russia poured arms into eastern Ukraine, fueling violent separatists and a conflict that has killed thousands. When a civilian airliner was shot down from areas that these proxies controlled, they refused to allow access to the crash for days. When Ukraine started to reassert control over its territory, Russia gave up the pretense of merely supporting the separatists, and moved troops across the border.'

The USA and the EU have imposed economic sanctions on Russia, which has weakened her economy. NATO troops have stepped up military exercises in Eastern Europe and the USA has reassured Poland of NATO's support if Russia violates its territory. Putin's objective has been achieved: Crimea has been taken from Ukraine, and Russian troops control part of eastern Ukraine. Meanwhile, the USA and NATO are helpless. Their leaders and citizens do not wish to engage in military conflict in a far-off country, and Putin is aware of this.

USA and international terrorism

America's response to 9/11 in 2001 was to mobilise the international community and launch a 'war on terrorism'. Iraq was invaded by coalition forces and its leader, Saddam Hussein, executed. Afghanistan was also invaded to root out Al-Qaeda and to remove the Taliban Government. All this was quickly achieved but both these countries did not enjoy peace. Democracy failed to take roots in both countries and civil war took place. When Obama became president in January 2009, he stated, 'we will kill Bin Laden. We will crush al-Qaeda'. The former was achieved in May 2011 when American special forces killed Bin Laden and numerous drone attacks wiped out 30 top leaders of the group. Obama also carried out his promise to take all troops out of Iraq and to begin a gradual reduction from Afghanistan; however, by the time US troops withdrew from Iraq over 4000 of their comrades had been killed.

However, fast-forward to 2015 and US foreign policy objectives of bringing peace and stability to the region are in ruins. Obama failed to act in Libya in 2011, leaving it to its European partners to use air power to enable the rebels to depose the dictator Gaddafi. Extremist groups used the chaos in Libya to seize huge stockpiles of weapons to start conflict in Syria. This new fundamentalist group ISIS (Islamic State of Iraq and Syria) has launched a 'holy war' to set up their Islamic state in Syria and northern Iraq. Obama has responded by co-ordinating US-led coalition airstrikes to push back ISIS.

Show your understanding

1. What evidence supports the view that the USA is the world's superpower?
2. Why is there a perception today that US domination is on the decline?
3. What evidence suggests that the US public wants the USA to reduce its international role?
4. Describe US involvement in international organisations such as the UN and NATO.
5. What action has the US taken against international terrorism?
6. To what extent is China a threat to US dominance in south-east Asia?
7. Read Obama's address to the UN Security Council and list the problems faced by the international community and the actions taken by the USA.

20-mark question

To what extent has a world power you have studied had influence in international relations?

2 The People's Republic of China

Background

The People's Republic of China has the largest population in the world (1.35 billion), with one in five people in the world living in China. Geographically, it is a very large country, the fourth largest in the world behind Russia, Canada and the USA, with an area of 9,596,961 km². China's population is split between urban and rural areas and it has a very diverse population in terms of wealth, language and culture. The country is bordered by 14 other countries: Afghanistan, Bhutan, India, Kazakhstan, Kyrgyzstan, Laos, Mongolia, Myanmar (Burma), Nepal, North Korea, Pakistan, Russia, Tajikistan and Vietnam. The way in which the country has developed is a direct result of its geography. Most of its major cities lie along the eastern seaboard, ideal for shipping China's produce around the world. Its major geographical features include the world's tallest mountain (Everest) and two major rivers (the Yangtze and the Yellow River). China's main ethnic group is the Han Chinese who make up 91.6 per cent of the population. The other 8.4 per cent is made up of over 55 other minority groups (see Table 2.1).

China has experienced remarkable economic growth over the last 30 years and in 2011 China's economy became the second largest in the world. It is now challenging American dominance in south-east Asia. The Chinese Communist Party (CCP) came to power in 1949 under Chairman Mao and it has ruled China ever since.

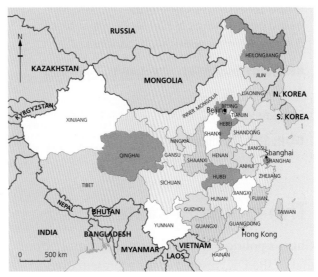

Figure 2.1 **China**

Table 2.1 **China's main ethnic groups**

Ethnic group	Number of people
Han	1200 million
Zhuang	16 million
Manchu	10 million
Hui	9 million
Miao	8 million
Uighur	7 million
Yi	7 million
Mongol	5 million
Tibetan	5 million

China

Capital: Beijing

Population: 1.354 billion people

Main language: Mandarin

Major government ideology: Communism based on teachings of Karl Marx, a nineteenth-century German political philosopher

Religions: Buddhism, Christianity, Islam and Taoism

Currency: Yuan

GDP: $8.227 trillion

The political system

China's political system differs enormously from that of the UK. Instead of the representative democracy which we have, China has a very authoritarian, communist government which permeates every aspect of people's lives. China is ruled by the Chinese Communist Party (CCP), which has ultimate political control over its citizens and allows for no real form of political opposition. Although the CCP tolerates the existence of other political parties, they must be ideologically similar to the CCP and there is little representation of other political ideas. The CCP has been in control of China since 1949, and its strict communist regime is founded on the principle of strong state intervention, based on the communist teachings of the political philosophy of Karl Marx, whereby the CCP dominates every aspect of people's lives – what they watch on television, what they can access on the internet and which religion they can practise freely.

The Communist Party of China (CCP)

Political parties in China work very differently from those in the UK. Despite the fact that the CCP is the largest political party in the world with 85 million members, it is a very exclusive organisation which only allows admission after several years of a lengthy application process. Potential members of the CCP must complete substantial written applications, interviews, pass exams that test their political ideology and suitability, have to be sponsored by a current member of the Party and serve a full year's probationary period. Gaining party membership often comes down to who you know, as this elite group usually admits people to the CCP who have family connections. Indeed, the current leader of the CCP, Xi Jinping, has been nicknamed as a 'Princeling', as he has managed to ascend to a position of power within the CCP because of his own family connections to the Party: Xi Jinping's father was Xi Zhongxun – one of the Communist Party's founding fathers. As a direct result of this type of admission, the Party is largely unrepresentative of China as a whole; only a quarter of the CCP are under 35 and even fewer are women. Selection to the CCP from within means it is very difficult for ordinary citizens to infiltrate the Party.

Many people still wish to join the Communist Party, as it is seen by many as a ticket to success in communist China. In 2013, many university students applied to join the Party (indeed 40 per cent of the new intake to the CCP that year were students); a far cry from 30 years ago when students protested against Communist-Party rule in Tiananmen Square.

Joining the Communist Party in China is attractive as members are usually guaranteed better government jobs, which are crucial to being economically successful in China. The vast influence which the Party has in society ensures that members have access to the best schools for their children and better health care. The privileges of Party members are taken much further than occupational benefits, however; corruption is rife within the Communist Party, where officials accepting bribes is common practice. When Xi Jinping came to power in 2012, he stated that tackling corruption was his main priority as he believed it could lead to 'the collapse of the Party and the downfall of the state' (see page 56).

The influence of the CCP in China extends much further than that of the political parties within the UK. The CCP controls exactly what is taught in schools, which includes a vast history of the CCP and China's political greatness and history. It also censors the internet to a large extent, blocking major sites like Facebook and ensuring that Chinese people have no anonymity on micro-blogs like Twitter. The different levels at which the Party functions ensures there are always local village representatives, meaning the CCP is always aware of what is happening in every area of society.

The CCP is very insular and all major political decisions are made by CCP Party officials without the influence of the public. The General Secretary of the Party is Xi Jinping, who is also the president of China and the Chairman of the Military Commission. It is the Party's job to appoint and promote all its government officials, the majority of whom come from the CCP itself. Underneath Xi Jinping in terms of influence is the seven-member Politburo Standing Committee or PBSC (reduced from nine members in the 18th Communist Party Conference November 2012), which acts like the president of the USA's

Cabinet. The head of the PBSC is China's Premier, Li Keqiang. Most of the PBSC's work is carried out in private, and this is where the majority of the major political decisions for China are made. This group effectively runs China. Underneath them in terms of power is the 25-member Politburo (which includes the seven members of the PBSC), which is the CCP's decision-making body.

Figure 2.2 **The structure of the CCP**

National Party Congress

Roughly once every five years, the CCP holds a National Party Congress (not to be confused with the National People's Congress – China's parliament) where major political decisions made by the CCP are announced and where the policies for China for the next five years are announced – the Five-Year Plan. The 18th Party Congress took place in November 2012, where there was major party overhaul. Xi Jinping took over as the General Secretary of the CCP/president from Hu Jintao after his ten-year rule. It is at this meeting that the members of the Politburo and PBSC are chosen.

The CCP has several major institutions:

- The Politburo Standing Committee (PBSC)
- The Central Committee of Politburo
- The Central Military Affairs Commission.

The Central Military Affairs Commission

In an authoritarian communist country, the army plays a vital role in national security and policing the nation. Xi Jinping recently said that commitment to the CCP is the 'the soul and lifeblood' of the People's Liberation Army (PLA). The army has maintained order recently during protests in Tibet (over its freedom from Chinese rule) and it is an integral part of the Chinese political system. China is a country with nuclear weapon capabilities and where the CCP is permitted, by the Central Military Affairs Commission (CMAC), to control China's armed forces (the PLA) and nuclear weapons. The CMAC has 11 members and it is their job to make decisions regarding army deployment, appointing high-ranking military personnel and arms spending. The CCP holds ultimate power over the CMAC, as Xi Jinping is also the Chairman of the CMAC. Many have observed that the Government and the army in China are one and the same thing, as all army personnel are members of the CCP and pledge allegiance to serve the Party.

Xi Jinping's 'Chinese Dream'

In his first speech as leader of China, Xi Jinping pledged he wanted to crack down on corruption within the CCP and fight for the 'Chinese Dream'.

Figure 2.3 Xi Jinping, China's new strong leader

Xi Jinping claimed the 'Chinese Dream' was his new vision for China. The CCP would continue to raise the living standards of its people and to assert China's right to be treated by America as an equal. Many have observed that Xi Jinping wants to strengthen China's military forces and world influence, something many surrounding countries are anxious about (see page 81). Others have stated that it is a similar concept to the 'American Dream' – that Chinese citizens should enjoy freedoms to make money and improve their living standards, albeit within strict government supervision and CCP guidance. This has inspired many students at the country's universities who feel that the 'Chinese Dream' will inspire them to give back to China by working hard in the education sector and paying back to society through their work contributions.

Others are more sceptical, and feel that Xi Jinping's notion of a 'Chinese Dream' is just a media ploy to inspire another generation of Chinese citizens to follow the CCP's beliefs and values. Many people's version of the 'Chinese Dream' would be to have fairer human rights and the observation of the 'rule of law'. China often has flare-ups of civil unrest because of a lack of political freedoms, which we will look at in greater detail later in this chapter.

Show your understanding

1 Create a brief fact file on China.
2 Explain how China's political system differs from our own.
3 Describe the process Chinese citizens must undertake to join the CCP.
4 Briefly explain the structure of the CCP and explain who holds the real power.
5 Outline what is meant by Xi Jinping's 'Chinese Dream'.

Structure of the national government

As we have already mentioned, the Chinese political system is a communist system dominated by the CCP. It has a system of 'collective leadership' whereby the president (currently Xi Jinping) and the seven members of the Political Bureau Standing Committee have different ranks and roles within the Government, and power is shared to a small extent. Power is shared more now in China than it was in Chairman Mao's time, when the Government was much more of a 'one-man-band'. Although there is a State Constitution, which outlines how the government of China should share powers and observe people's rights, party members and government officials are encouraged instead to abide by the Party's Constitution as their supreme code of conduct, which means people's rights are often overlooked. The Constitution of China can be overruled in practice by the CCP on any decision and there are many protests for the Constitution (as it is on paper) to be upheld. The national government consists of the State Council, the president and the National People's Congress.

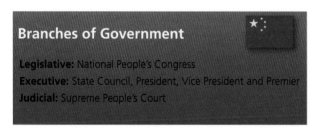

Branches of Government

Legislative: National People's Congress
Executive: State Council, President, Vice President and Premier
Judicial: Supreme People's Court

Figure 2.4 **The three branches of central Government in China**

The National People's Congress (NPC)

The Congress meets for ten consecutive days every year in March. Around 3000 delegates attend, who are elected for a five-year period, and their main job is to approve laws and the appointments of senior party officials. According to Articles 57 and 58 of the Chinese Constitution the NPC is 'the highest organ of state power' which can 'exercise the legislative power of the state' (make laws). However, in practice this is not the case. The NPC merely approves or 'rubber-stamps' laws that have been made by the PBSC and the Politburo. The NPC has its own Standing Committee of 161 officials who meet once every two months. This group is made up of retired government officials and representatives from the eight 'democratic parties' (see page 56) and they appoint the new state president and vice president.

The State Council

The State Council is led by China's premier, Li Keqiang (also a member of the PBSC), and it meets monthly. It is in charge of carrying out party policy at all levels. It often prepares draft laws which are sent to the NPC. The State Council also has members from each of the Government departments for internal politics, national defence, finance and the economy. It is in charge of managing China's Five-Year Plan and the budget.

Supreme People's Court

China's Supreme Court is unlike a Western Supreme Court. In theory, the Supreme Court is the highest judicial administration in the land with the power to protect the rights of citizens. In practice, however, this is not the case, and the court mainly works to represent CCP interests by outlining controls on the people.

Local politics in China

The political system of China is very complex. Having looked at the national government, it is also important to look at the other administrative levels within the country. Because of China's sheer size and massive population, the CCP also has officials on regional and local levels to ensure it always has ultimate control and that its policies are implemented. There are four levels of government administration: national, provincial, protectorate and county. All major decisions are made at national level and 'trickle down' through these lower levels of government. There are local village elections in which Chinese people can choose their local representatives. The lowest level is the Village Committees.

Village Committees

In the 1980s, official Village Committees (VCs) were introduced at a grass-roots level. They are elected every three years and consist of a handful of members made up of a Chairperson, Vice Chairperson and Representatives. This allows Chinese people to vote on a local level and also to stand as a candidate for election. Women are also playing a larger role within these committees and they are supposed to be guaranteed equal representation, although this is still not the case in practice. However, this makes China no different from countries like the USA and the UK, where women are still vastly under-represented. Voters are now supposed to be granted a secret ballot, aimed at reducing bribes, corruption and election-related violence. According to Article 2 of the Villagers' Committees Law, however, 'the Villagers' Committee is the primary mass organisation of self-government, in which the villagers manage their own affairs, educate themselves and serve their own needs and in which election is conducted, decision adopted, administration maintained and supervision exercised by democratic means'. Figures show that, in 2011, 98 per cent of Village Committees in China were elected by direct elections.

However, the village Party secretary is the most important person within the village and is always a member of the CCP overseeing the work done by the VCs. Village Committees therefore have little real power, although they are often involved in the running of village schools and enforcing family-planning regulations. This is the only level at which people can vote directly in Chinese politics. Even at village level, there are often 'irregularities' within the votes cast and some people are suspicious of the way in which the votes are counted. Also, CCP officials can step in at any time to oversee elections as they have the ultimate power within the political process.

Many Western observers are sceptical about the CCP's motivations for allowing local village elections. Many have noted that this move has been to merely justify and legitimise the CCP's leadership; allowing people to vote for the CCP makes people feel that they have been involved in the political process and it is perceived therefore to be fairer.

Checks and balances on government

By Western standards, it may seem that the Chinese political system does not meet with our concept of what a democracy should be. Limited human rights, discussed later in the chapter, along with a lack of choice over which political party to vote for and being unable to choose your national representatives, means that the Chinese Government can rule with very few checks and balances and limited scrutiny from the people. Although China does have a written Constitution, which outlines the rights of all people, the Government is not held accountable by the people, who are heavily restricted in their right to protest. Indeed, it is not a government for the people or by the people, but instead a government the people must obey.

However, it would be naive not to recognise the changes to China's political system which have made it more democratic in recent years at the

Successful protests, Wukan Village, Guangdong

In 2011, hundreds of protestors gathered in Wukan Village, Guangdong, to show their anger at local officials who had seized their land without fair compensation. There has been a rise in local government officials seizing land on behalf of the Government and compensating villagers very poorly. This land is often then sold on for larger profits which are used for personal gain of the local officials or the Government. Although this is an example of corruption, and a lack of democracy in China, these high profile protests are becoming increasingly common and many are effectively challenging the political process. As a result of these protests, two local officials were sacked from their jobs and the village was given the right to take part in local elections to hire new officials. As these protests become more common in China, many Western observers believe that China is listening to the people more.

Figure 2.5 Villagers watch candidates in Wukan's Village Committee election give speeches

local level. Local village elections add an element of democracy that has allowed villagers to choose their village leaders and co-operate with them in many local victories. Land disputes, for example, have been settled with the villagers winning compensation and also the right to stay in their homes thanks to this type of grass-roots leadership. Many areas have seen a rise in participation in politics; in Wukan Village in 2011, for example, locals took to ousting their local government and won the right to hold new elections there (see fact file above). There also seems to be a restriction on the amount of time each president in China can serve: two five-year terms, which can put limits to lengthy leadership as seen in Chairman Mao's era. However, recent events in Hong Kong suggest that, while the Chinese leadership will accept some criticism of its actions and Party officials, it will not tolerate any attempt to challenge the totalitarian rule of the Communist Party.

Challenges facing the CCP

In recent years, the two biggest challenges facing the CCP have been corruption and international pressure to implement the 'rule of law'. In terms of the latter, the CCP sees the laws and the Constitution to be flexible guidelines that can be stretched/overruled by the CCP/Government. It believes that the law is in place to give the power to the Government and not necessarily to protect the rights of citizens. However, the international community and many Chinese protestors have called upon the CCP to abide by the rule of law, meaning that citizens' rights are protected above those of the Government. The Supreme Court of China can only scrutinise members of the CCP for misconduct if they have first gained permission from the CCP, meaning it is not a fully democratic court – it does not work independently from the Government.

China's political parties

Although the CCP has ultimate political power in China, there are actually eight other minor political parties. The Chinese Government describes China as a 'multi-party state' but in practice it merely tolerates the other political parties which have no real political power or influence. All political decisions are made by the CCP, which can get rid of any of the other political parties at any time. The other political parties must swear to work under the CCP, share its values and, as a result, cannot be described as opposition parties. The CCP puts limits on the size of membership of these parties and their combined membership is less than 1 million people, far less than the CCP's 85 million members. The eight parties may be called 'democratic parties', and the CCP would argue that they allow China to be a democracy, but this is a far cry from the democratic political systems that we are accustomed to. Therefore, in the Western world of multi-party politics, where elections often result in different parties winning in different years or even coalition governments, we still consider China to be a 'one-party state'.

There have been numerous attempts by brave individuals to bring real democracy to China as outlined below:

- **Liu Xiaobo, 2010 Nobel Peace Prize Laureate, Leader of Charter 08**
  In December 2009, Liu received 11 years' imprisonment for 'inciting sedition'. His crime was to circulate Charter 08 demanding political reform. The Charter demanded the elections of all political representatives, freedom of expression, association and religion. In November 2011, the world acknowledged his courage by awarding him the Nobel Peace Prize.
- **Ms Wang Zheng, leader of the Zhi Xian Party**
  In November 2013, Ms Wang Zheng, a university professor, set up her own political party – the 'China Zhi Xian Party' (which translates as 'the Supremacy of the Constitution'). She set up the party in homage to the disgraced Chinese leader Bo Xilai who was found guilty of corruption and given a life sentence in September 2013 (see below). The party insisted that it was not an opposition party, but simply wished the Chinese Government to abide by China's written Constitution and stand by the rights that it is supposed to guarantee its citizens.

In a country like China where the constitution of the land is not upheld, and your family connections or *guanxi* can guarantee you power, corruption is rife. Xi Jinping vowed to reduce corruption within the Chinese political system and as a result over 37,000 people were tried for corruption in 2013.

In October 2014, the CCP published a document that would use the Constitution to establish the rule of law. The document declared that 4 November would henceforth be National Constitution Day and that all Party officials would swear an oath of allegiance to the Constitution. The document stated that 'they must regard the Constitution as the fundamental guidelines of

their activities'. As stated earlier, the Constitution does not offer the rights that we take for granted in the West but exists only to promote the socialist values of the people and the CCP. Mr Xi wishes to strengthen the enforcement of the Constitution to root out corrupt Party officials. However, some argue that his campaign against corruption was also used to remove any possible opposition to his rule. Supporters of the now disgraced regional party chief, Bo Xilai, claim that is what happened to their leader. Bo had been the popular party leader of Chongqing province before being arrested by Xi and found guilty of corruption.

Evidence of improving political rights

In the aftermath of the Beijing Olympic Games in 2008, there has been much speculation from the West as to whether or not China has become more democratic or politically open. The year 2014 represented an important anniversary for China, marking 25 years since the Tiananmen Square student protests, and since then there have been some signs that China's political system has allowed for more citizen participation and political rights. In recent years, there have been a number of high-profile protests over land seizures, internet freedom and the environmental impact of

Chinese's rapid economic growth, many of which have been permitted by the CCP. Recent cases have seen a rise in compensation being awarded to citizens from the CCP for judicial mistreatment.

The Chinese Government permits freedom of expression, such as mass demonstrations, when it suits their goals. All over China, citizens have marched in protest against Japan's actions in disputed islands. However, China finds it difficult to control spontaneous workers' protests against poor working conditions and communities protesting against the seizure of their land and property.

Limits of political expression

In 1984, Britain signed the Sino-British Joint Declaration on the Question of Hong Kong which set out arrangements for the transfer of sovereignty over Hong Kong, a British colony, to China from Britain under the 'one country, two systems' principle. This agreement enshrined democratic rights for the citizens of Hong Kong and was expected to last for at least 50 years after the 1997 handover. However, China has refused to fulfil the terms of the Declaration that the people would be able to elect representatives of their choosing, and has stated that all candidates must be approved by the CCP before the people can vote.

Figure 2.6 Protesters in Hong Kong, 2014

In September 2014, Hong Kong's students took to the streets to demand free democratic elections just

as the students had done in Tiananmen Square in 1989 – before they were massacred by the Chinese Army. However, with Hong Kong being the wealthiest city in China and with the eyes of the world watching, the Chinese Government was reluctant to send in the army and hoped that the protest would run its course. The UK protested (see page 82) but was told not to meddle in Chinese affairs. Through strict censorship, the Chinese leaders ensured that the protests were not reported in mainland China.

The protesters were demanding that they should be able to vote for any candidate of their choosing in the 2017 elections for the post of chief executive. At one stage over 100,000 protesters armed with umbrellas (which have become the symbol of protest) marched on government buildings. The central business centre was also the centre of action, dubbed 'Occupy Central'. The present leader of Hong Kong has met with the student leaders but has simply stated that 'they have the universal suffrage that was promised'. (In mainland China no universal suffrage is permitted above the local level.) Mr Xi, the leader of China, was determined to tighten, not weaken, Party control. Media censorship was intensified, dissenters were arrested and brutal measures were taken in Tibet and Xinjiang against nationalist supporters (see page 61). In December 2014, riot police armed with pepper spray, batons and shields charged the remaining student protesters, ending the occupation.

Show your understanding

1 Briefly outline the roles of the National People's Congress, State Council and the Supreme Court.
2 Explain how Village Committees are elected and what their main role is.
3 Explain why the power of Village Committees is limited by the Village Secretary.
4 Who has the main power within the Chinese Government? Explain your answer.
5 What are the two main problems facing the CCP at the moment?
6 What happens to people who start up opposition parties in China? Give examples.
7 What evidence is there of improving democracy/political rights in China?
8 Describe and explain the actions of protesters in Hong Kong.

20-mark question

To what extent does the Chinese political system provide an effective check on its government?

Human rights

As stated from a Western perspective, China appears to have very limited human rights and the strict control of the CCP dominates every aspect of people's lives. However, in recent years there has been some relaxing of the strict control the CCP has and Chinese people have been able to enjoy more social and economic freedoms. People are now allowed greater property rights, economic freedoms to start their own businesses and, on the surface, control over the internet has been reduced to allow foreign businesses to operate more effectively. Since the Beijing Olympic Games in 2008, foreign journalists have had more freedom to report stories from within the country.

The Constitution does provide a range of political and social rights but they can only be exercised in the interests of the socialist policies of the CCP (see page 59). While the new Chinese leaders promise a fairer legal system, the reality is completely different (see the fate of Xu Zhiyong, a Chinese lawyer, right). Many organisations like Amnesty International have highlighted the religious, social and political freedoms that people within China still do not have. According to Amnesty International, there are currently 500,000 people being held in detention camps without charge or trial and the country's legal system is geared towards protecting the Government not the people.

Xu Zhiyong, founder of the New Citizens Movement

Mr Xu is a lawyer and a founder of the New Citizens Movement, a group seeking to work within China's system to improve the rule of law. The group had demanded the disclosure of the senior communist officials' personal wealth (several foreign journalists have been expelled from China for disclosing the wealth of top Party members). Among other demands were compensation for people harmed in food safety scandals. In January 2014, Xu and four of his associates were found guilty of 'assembling a crowd to disrupt order in a public place' and sent to prison for four years.

Fact file

Political rights

According to Article 35 of the Chinese Constitution, citizens have the right to 'freedom of speech, of the press, of assembly, of association, of procession and of demonstration'. On top of this people can:

- vote in the Local Peoples' Congress and village elections. Candidates must be approved by the CCP.
- submit petitions to the Chinese Government. In 2013, China launched a new online website that accepts e-petitions. People can submit petitions, but they must also provide their full name, address and passport number and many people are worried that anyone submitting petitions will then be monitored by the Government.
- hold protests/demonstrations with the permission of the Government.
- join the CCP. They have to apply and be recommended by members of the CCP. There are now around 85 million members of the CCP (5 per cent of the population) and 14 per cent of those who applied to join were accepted in 2011.

Internet freedom

China has the world's largest population of internet users, 618 million in 2014, who are based mainly in urban areas. Many academics have noted that the rapid growth of the internet in China has led to groups of like-minded people forming blogs, online forums and social networking groups to share political opinions, facts and complaints about the Government and CCP officials. People can now freely post political viewpoints and protests about the CCP, sometimes anonymously, and the Government in China is extremely concerned about the increase of 'cyber-democracy' and calls for more political opposition in China. As a result, the CCP has introduced extreme methods of censorship to prevent loss of government control. Although anyone in China can use the internet, with the idea being that the internet can stimulate economic growth and strengthen communication for businesses, individual citizens are subject to scrutiny and website restrictions. The 'Great Firewall of China' is used to block Chinese citizens from accessing Western news websites like the BBC, human rights organisations like Amnesty International and even information on sexually transmitted infections (STIs) and HIV/AIDS. The Government employs a large number of workers to monitor the internet and remove 'sensitive' political content; it also encourages self-censorship by issuing rules for internet users and even employs bloggers to blog favourably about the CCP on high-profile websites.

Internet censorship is a very complex issue. Although there are some signs of decreasing government control, with websites such as Facebook and Twitter being unblocked in the Free Trade Zone in Shanghai, overall the internet is still heavily monitored and vetted. In 2014, the new Chinese Internet Security and Information group headed by Xi Jinping was formed as a matter of 'national security' looking at 'cleansing' the internet. Even the television Chinese people watch online is monitored and restricted by the CCP; in 2014, four American TV shows including *The Big Bang Theory* were removed from television streaming web services in China because of their 'inappropriate content'. In 2012, 5000 people in Beijing alone were arrested for internet crimes and 260 internet cafés were forced to close down, showing the sheer strength of government monitoring over the internet and free speech.

Hong Kong – the invisible protest

For more than four months their fellow citizens in Hong Kong have been demanding free elections and democratic reforms, yet the vast majority of the people in China are unaware of the protests and sit-ins (see page 57). And those who are aware and try to inform others are arrested. The army of Chinese internet censors has been scrutinising Weibo (a Chinese micro-blogging website) to delete any reference to Hong Kong. The Chinese leadership is aware that this is the first large-scale student protest for democracy to erupt in a Chinese city since 1989.

Freedom of religion

According to Amnesty International, many religious groups face huge discrimination in China, if not persecution. Although Article 36 of China's Constitution says that Chinese citizens should have freedom to practise whatever religion they choose, this is not the case.

Falun Gong

Practitioners of spiritual movements like Falun Gong are often persecuted for their beliefs and for assembling in large groups, something the CCP does not allow. Initially Falun Gong was encouraged by the Government as it was seen to be good exercise with its Tai Chi-like movements and mental health benefits. However, after membership exceeded 100 million members, the group was heavily scrutinised by the Government and shut down over fears of protests against the Government and 'illegal activities'. Falun Gong describes itself as a peaceful, spiritual movement whereas the CCP has labelled it a dangerous cult. As a result of its increasing popularity and membership the movement was banned in 1999, and since then it is estimated that over 3000 Falun Gong practitioners have been killed and tens of thousands have suffered from violence and persecution in Chinese Laogai (reform) camps.

Christians

Religions like Christianity are permitted by the Government, but they are confined by very strict monitoring and regulations. In Chairman Mao's era, religion was totally banned by the state, but since the 1980s it has once again been allowed. However, the official religious stance of the CCP is atheism and many people who practise different religions are often persecuted by the state. CCP government officials are concerned about the rapid growth of Christianity within China and have shut down many churches as they are 'illegal buildings'. New places of worship must be registered with the Government, and people may not practise their religion in the streets in any form of demonstration. In April 2014, 'mega-churches' in Wenzhou were demolished because they were illegal buildings, contravening CCP rules which state that religious groups break government regulations by holding meetings outside the church. CCP officials have said that Christianity is spreading through the country too rapidly and must be controlled by the state (see Table 2.2). The American Pew Research Centre estimates there were 58 million Protestants and 9 million Catholics in China in 2012. Church Aid, an American church group, estimates that in 2013 more than 7400 Christians suffered persecution in China.

Table 2.2 Christians in China

Year	Christians (millions)
1950	3
1980	4
1995	15
2012	67
2020 (estimated)	100

Tibet

Tibet is an autonomous region of China, although many believe it should be an independent state. The Chinese Government clearly sees Tibet as part of China and says that it is ruled by Beijing. However, many Tibetans believe that it should be a separate nation and seek independence for Tibet. This has led to several bloody uprisings between Tibetans and the Chinese authorities, most recently during the 2008 Beijing Olympics and their aftermath. Western news channels frequently reported on Free Tibet protestors' objections to holding the Olympics in China, given the treatment of Tibetans by the Chinese Government. It is thought that, since 2009, 120 Tibetans have set themselves on fire (self-immolation) in the ultimate protest against Chinese rule. While the Dalai Lama, Tibet's exiled leader, does not encourage these acts, he has openly praised the courage of those involved for making the ultimate sacrifice for their cause. However, Xi Jinping in a speech of 2014 stated that these protestors were 'terrorists'.

Security in Tibet's capital is intense – security personnel are everywhere and surveillance cameras monitor its citizens' every movement.

Figure 2.7 **Buddhist monks protesting against Chinese rule of Tibet**

The Tibetan people are denied their cultural identity and the Chinese occupiers control all stations of influence – the political leaders are all Chinese and Tibetans are not even allowed to display pictures of their religious leader, the Dalai Lama. Foreign journalists are not allowed to visit Tibet to report on the plight of the Tibetan people.

Xinjiang

Xinjiang is another province where there is strong opposition to Chinese rule. The Uighurs, who are Muslim and live in Xinjiang, feel that their culture is being slowly destroyed by the Chinese Government. Mass immigration of millions of Chinese citizens to the province has taken place and the Han Chinese now account for over 40 per cent of the population and dominate urban communities. Xinjiang has been under Chinese control since 1949 as an autonomous region in China (similar to Tibet).

In 2009, fierce fighting erupted in the main city of Urumqi when a group of Uighurs attacked Chinese citizens. This was followed by Uighurs fighting with Chinese troops. Over 200 people were killed before the Chinese military regained control. The ringleaders were executed but China's goal of ending unrest has not been achieved. Since 2012, China has been subjected to a number of high-profile and violent terrorist attacks by Uighur separatists. In October 2013, five Uighur suspects were arrested for an attack in Tiananmen Square which led to the deaths of five people when a 4×4 car was driven into the square. This was closely followed by another attack when nine knifemen attacked people in a railway station in Kunming, killing at least 29 people and injuring around 130.

Show your understanding

1 Briefly explain the political rights that people in China have.
2 Explain how internet use in China is restricted and how it is monitored and influenced by the Chinese Government.
3 Are people in China free to practise their religion? Explain with examples.
4 Why have there been violent uprisings in Tibet?
5 Why does the Chinese Government refer to Uighur separatists as terrorists?

Figure 2.8 **Xinjiang terror attack**

Torture and lack of legal rights – the Laogai system

China's Laogai system was set up in the 1950s in order to 're-educate' or reform criminals 'through labour'. Prisoners held within Laogai camps are often forced into slave labour to produce goods cheaply for mass export; prisoners are not paid and work up to 14 hours a day. According to the Laogai Research Foundation, this generates millions of dollars in profit for the CCP every year. The system has two elements: the Laogai labour camps where prisoners work in slave-like conditions, and the Laojiao camps which function as re-education camps where authorities can hold people for up to four years without trial. Within the re-education programme, there is also psychiatric treatment for those who show opposition to the Government and these people are often tortured or 'treated' using electric

Case study: Tang Hui

Tang Hui was imprisoned in a Laogai camp in 2013 after seeking justice for her daughter. Tang's daughter, aged 11, was kidnapped and forced into a life of prostitution and abuse in 2006. Tang searched for her daughter and, after eventually finding her three months later and rescuing her with the help of her brothers, she begged the Government for harsher punishment for her daughter's captors. As a result of her protests, Tang was sentenced to 18

Figure 2.9 Tang Hui

months in a Laogai camp for 'disturbing order' and 'exerting a negative impact on society'. This led to a media uproar around the world, and on micro-blogging websites in China, and Tang was eventually released from the Laogai camp after a nine-day ordeal. In 2013, Tang successfully won compensation of £317 from the Government, although there was no official written apology for her treatment. She said she was 'pleased' with the small victory but that she was still 'worried about the future, about upcoming problems and further compensation and justice for my daughter'.

Tang's case shows the sheer lengths that the CCP has gone to in order to maintain public order and protect the Communist Party from criticism. However, it also shows a rare victory in the appeals process in China. In 2014, 109 lawyers and former Party members signed a petition to abolish and reform the Laogai system.

shock. The UN has heavily criticised China for its treatment of prisoners, stating that this directly breaks Article 2 of the UN Convention Against Torture and Other Cruel, Inhuman or Degrading Treatment or Punishment (which China ratified in 1988). Although China put in place laws in 1994 to reform the prison system, including the intention to stop using cruel or inhumane punishment, these are regularly breeched through the Laogai system of prisons. It is thought that over 1000 Laogai camps still exist in China, with between 3 and 5 million people detained in the camps. In December 2013, the Chinese Government announced plans to abolish Laogai camps, but it is too early to tell whether this will happen.

Death penalty

The Supreme People's Court decides on death penalty cases in China. However, it is very difficult to know how widespread executions are in China, as no official figures are ever published by the Government. Many prisoners are often sentenced to death with little or no legal representation and there is a minute chance of appeal. Amnesty International has estimated that China executes more people than the rest of the death penalty states combined and the figure has been put at around 5000 people a year. A total of 55 crimes are punishable by the death penalty in China, including robbery, fraud and selling state secrets.

There have, however, been small improvements to China's death penalty usage. Since 2007, all death penalty sentences have been reviewed by the Supreme People's Court and 10 per cent of these have been overturned in favour of life sentences. Also, the number of crimes that carry the death penalty was reduced from 68 to 55, with most economic crimes being removed from the list. Pregnant women, those under the age of 18 and those over the age of 75 at the start of their trial are also not meant face the death penalty.

Human rights defenders

Throughout China those who try to stand up to the Government, even in the smallest of ways, are often persecuted, tortured, imprisoned without trial or sent to Laojiao camps for 're-education'. In recent years, there have been a number of high-profile cases of human rights defenders in China who have come to the attention of international human rights organisations and the media (see page 64).

China's one-child policy

During the 1970s, the Government was concerned about China's massive population growth rate and as a result introduced the one-child policy in 1979. This policy aimed to curb population growth which was causing a strain on feeding and educating the country. In many areas of China, the policy limited married couples to having only one child although there were some exceptions: for example, families in rural China were allowed to have a second child if their firstborn was a female. This policy is thought to have prevented the birth of around 400 million extra children since its implementation. However, there are many who are strongly opposed to the strict control that the CCP has over family planning.

In China, couples have to apply for a birth permit before they are allowed by the state to have a child, and if they have a second child or have a child without permission they often face a large fine, sterilisation or a forced abortion. The way in which the policy has been implemented in many areas has caused significant human

Case study: Human rights defenders

Shi Tao

The Tiananmen Square pro-democracy protests of 1989 were one of the bloodiest protests in modern history. Several hundred pro-democracy protestors were shot or beaten to death by Chinese military forces after mass peaceful protests were stopped violently by the Government. Shi Tao, a Chinese journalist, was arrested in 2004 after emailing a US-based news station about the Chinese Government's plans to prevent any uprisings on the fifteenth anniversary of the Tiananmen Square protests. He was charged with 'illegally providing state secrets to foreign entities'

Figure 2.10 Hundreds of thousands of Chinese protestors gathered in Tiananmen Square in June 1989

and imprisoned for ten years. His family were put under surveillance by the state and frequently questioned. He was eventually released in 2013 after serving eight years in prison. Amnesty International dubbed Shi Tao as a 'prisoner of conscience' whose only crime was to stand up for his right to free expression; something which the Chinese Constitution says every Chinese person has the right to do.

Pu Zhiqiang

Pu was a participant of the Tiananmen Square protests 25 years ago and he has attended low-key events to commemorate the anniversary every year since the protests happened. A high-profile human rights lawyer in China, Pu has often represented dissidents who have stood up for their human rights, and he is a well-known figure to the Chinese media. In 2014, Pu attended a seminar entitled 'Beijing 4 June 2014 Commemoration Seminar' and as a result Pu, along with up to 16 others, was accused of 'causing a disturbance' against the Government which may see him imprisoned for up to five years. He is currently being detained at the Beijing Detention Centre.

rights violations. According to human rights organisations worldwide, it is thought that the one-child policy has led to over 9000 forced sterilisations in Puning City over a two-month period in 2010. In addition, many thousands of couples were detained in custody if they refused to have the sterilisation procedure carried out.

The policy has also had a negative impact upon Chinese society in many ways. Families who complied with the policy had access to better

health care, benefits and education systems for their children, which has led to huge inequalities for families who did not abide by the rule. It has also had an extremely negative impact on gender equality within the country, with around 90 per cent of abortions carried out in China being on female foetuses and many female babies being put up for adoption. The policy has also led to a gender imbalance within the population; for every 100 baby girls in some areas, there are up to 130 baby boys. Many Chinese people also feel the policy has led to children being spoiled and that it is healthier for children to have siblings so that they learn to share and communicate.

Recently, however, the Chinese authorities have relaxed the one-child policy on account of the increasing elderly population and falling birth rate. People in China are now allowed to have more than one child if either the mother or father is an only child.

Figure 2.11 **A single-child Chinese family**

Case study: One-child policy fines

In 2014, world-famous director Zhang Yimou, responsible for films such as *Hero* and *House of the Flying Daggers*, was fined 7.5 million yuan (£700,000) for violating the one-child policy. Fines for violating this rule in China are based on an individual family's wealth and Zhang Yimou's family were charged so much because of their large income. A total of 20 billion yuan (£1.97 billion) was collected in one-child policy fines in 2013. However, there has been little documentation on how each province has spent the money raised in fines, which is supposed to help each province deal with the burden put upon social services in the area. Many local people talk of money that is unaccounted for, suggesting corruption at a local level is a problem.

Figure 2.12 Zhang Yimou

Show your understanding

1 Explain what the Laogai camps are and how they violate human rights.
2 What is likely to happen to someone who defends their human rights in China? Explain with examples.
3 Briefly outline what the one-child policy is. In what ways has this been relaxed in recent years?

China's economy

China's economic past

Economically, from 1949 to 1976, China was identified as a traditional communist country, where farmers worked under a commune system overseen by China's ruler, Chairman Mao. Under this system, farmers were told what they could grow and how much, and they were not allowed to sell any of the surplus food they grew to make profits. This system severely limited food production and both individual wealth and economic growth. This system was overhauled in the 1980s when Chinese leader Deng Xiaoping introduced agricultural reforms that allowed farmers greater economic freedom. Deng stated that 'to get rich is glorious', which was an unfamiliar concept in a traditionally communist Chinese economy. People became wealthier, businesses were privatised and food production increased. Deng Xiaoping opened up China to trading with the West through the Open Door Policy, and an economically backward China began to take advantage of the world market. It also joined the World Trade Organization in 2001.

China's economy today

Today, China is one of the richest countries in the world with the second largest economy (behind the USA). In 2014, China overtook the USA to become the world's largest trading nation. Economically, China describes itself as a capitalist system with Chinese characteristics, with a modern market economy rather than its traditional state-planned economy. There has been a huge rise in the number of multi-millionaires in China and many Chinese people have amassed huge wealth and purchase many luxury goods because of their high disposable incomes. China has become wealthy in recent years because of its massive economic growth.

Figure 2.13 **Deng Xiaoping**

Fact file

China's wealth

- According to the World Bank, China's annual economic growth rate is 7.8 per cent (2012). To put this into perspective, the UK's annual economic growth rate was only 0.1 per cent for 2012. However, there are signs that China's annual growth rate is slowing slightly; it had its lowest annual growth rate since 1999 in 2013.
- The IMF (International Monetary Fund) has said that, by 2016, China will have the largest economy in the world.
- Economic expansion and technological innovation in China are very fast – between 2008 and 2011, China built 10,000 km of high-speed rail track. In comparison, the UK's new HS2 rail line (announced in February 2013) is going to be 531 km long and it will not be ready until 2033.

Figure 2.14 clearly indicates the significant rise in individual wealth.

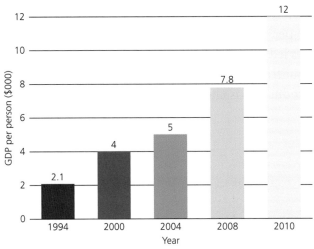

Figure 2.14 **GDP per person ($000) at purchasing power parity**

Foreign direct investment

Foreign direct investment can be simply defined as a company investing money or setting up premises in a different country from where the company is based. In recent years, many British and US firms have set up in China's Special Economic Zones. Foreign direct investment in China increased by 5.3 per cent in 2013, which equated to $117.59 billion.

China's Special Economic Zones (SEZs)

A Special Economic Zone is an area in which foreign direct investment is encouraged. Companies from all around the world were initially encouraged to set up businesses in SEZs

Fact file

China's economic reforms and key events timeline

- 1949: Chairman Mao Zedong founds the People's Republic of China.
- 1958: The 'Great Leap Forward' is introduced – traditional Communism. It was a five-year economic plan that focused on both agriculture and industry. People worked under the commune system where their tools were owned by the Government and they did not work for themselves; everything was run by the state. The outcome was that production of food was reduced and many millions of people starved. People could not make their own profits.
- 1976: Mao Zedong dies.
- 1977: Deng Xiaoping replaces Mao Zedong.
- 1986–1990s: The 'Open Door Policy'. China started to trade more with other countries, and companies from around the world were allowed to set up in China.

- 1992: Three Gorges Dam plans approved. Construction started in 1993.
- 1997: Deng Xiaoping dies.
- 2001: China becomes a member of the World Trade Organization, allowing it to agree further trade agreements with other countries around the world.
- 2003: Hu Jintao becomes the president of China.
- 2008: Beijing hosts the Olympic Games.
- 2011: China celebrates 90 years since the founding of the Communist Party.
- 2011: China becomes the second largest economy in the world (taking the title from Japan).
- 2012: Xi Jinping becomes China's president.
- 2013: China's urban population outnumbers its rural population for the first time.
- 2014: China sets up its first Free Trade Zone in Shanghai.

because of their close proximity to the economically valuable Hong Kong, and because companies were offered low tax rates, cheap labour and reduced building costs. The first SEZs in China were set up in Shenzhen, Shantou and Zhuhai (Guangdong Province) and the city of Xiamen in 1979. Since their introduction in China, they have been seen as pockets of capitalism within an otherwise communist-socialist state. Trading regulations and government control within these areas have been relaxed to allow Westernised companies to function in a capitalist manner. Economic growth within these areas has been revolutionary; Shenzhen, a fishing village of 30,000 people 30 years ago, now has a population of 15 million people, is the largest manufacturing base in the world and home of China's international stock market. Shenzhen attracts hundreds of thousands of migrant workers every year and house prices within the area increased by 20 per cent during 2012–13.

In recent years, however, many economists have noted that China may not keep the 'factory of the world' title for long; there is a demand for increased wages in China (wages have gone up by 13 per cent in Shenzhen in the last year) and this has led to many businesses setting up in other countries, such as Brazil and Vietnam, where production is cheaper.

Figure 2.16 **The location of Guangdong Province in China**

Figure 2.15 **Shenzhen: China's first SEZ**

Production: China as the 'factory of the world'

Guangdong Province has a population of 104 million people. In this province alone, there are an estimated 60,000 factories which every day produce some $300 million worth of goods including one-third of the world's shoes and toys.

Fact file

China's technology and innovation

- Much of China's wealth comes from its natural resources and mining. In 2013, China was the largest producer of steel (50 per cent of the world's steel) and it also has massive reserves of coal and iron.
- China produces 23 per cent of the world's cars; China's car production increased by 12 per cent in 2013 due to an internal increase in demand.
- IHS Global Insight research has shown that in 2010 China made 20 per cent of the world's products and became the largest manufacturer in the world. The USA had previously held that position for around 110 years.
- China's main new industries are in telecommunications, coal, steel and ICT. It is fast becoming the technology centre of the world.

Agriculture

China is responsible for 21 per cent of the world's food production despite the fact it only has 7 per cent of the world's farmland. China's agricultural system faces many challenges; it has to feed the largest population in the world (1.35 billion people). Agricultural trade has increased since China joined the World Trade Organization in 2001. It now produces 38 per cent of the world's fruit and vegetables and 27 per cent of the world's rice.

Industry

In the past, businesses in China would have been predominantly state-owned enterprises (SOEs), but now most are privately run. Today, 40 per cent of China's industries are SOEs; the rest are privately owned. China's agricultural workforce makes up 36 per cent of the population, while the urban workforce is increasingly growing. In 2014, the urban population of China reached a figure of 680 million people, meaning that for the first time there are now more people living in China's cities than in rural areas.

Income

As a result of joining the World Trade Organization, and through foreign direct investment, much of China's urban population has been able to gain well-paid jobs and average income in China has risen by 500 per cent since 2001 (Forbes.com). China is not only producing technological and luxury goods for export; there is now an increasing internal market for these products and many Chinese people are purchasing top-of-the-range cars, appliances and designer clothing. The rise of capitalism in a previously communist country now means that many Chinese people within urban areas have large disposable incomes and there is a growing trend for Western fashion, food and television. This has benefited the UK; China bought one-fifth of the UK's Bentley cars in 2013 as the demand for luxury items, and middle-class affluence, in China increased.

Challenges facing China's economy

China's rapid economic growth and huge manufacturing output has had a massive effect on both China's people and its environment. Subsequently, there are a number of economic challenges that China is now facing.

Environmental damage

China has found that an unfortunate side-effect of rapid economic expansion is significant environmental damage. This impact is felt in cities where the smog and fumes from factories is often so bad that people wear face masks, and the Chinese Government has taken to broadcasting the sunrise and sunset on large television screens in areas like Tiananmen Square because the air quality is so poor the sun cannot be seen through polluted skies. In rural areas, the opening of new factories, as cities expand, has led to chemicals and toxic by-products being released into rivers, killing wildlife and poisoning farms and crops. This has resulted in over 50,000 protests about environmental issues in China, demonstrating how concerned Chinese people are becoming about environmental damage. China is now responsible for 30 per cent of the world's greenhouse gas emissions; an increase of 20 per cent since the 1990s.

Figure 2.17 **Smog is a problem in many Chinese cities**

Migration

Over the last 30 years, 260 million Chinese people have moved from rural areas of China to the cities in the south-east of the country. Unequal economic development has driven these people from rural areas, which tend to be associated with poverty, fewer job opportunities and lower-quality education, to cities where many job opportunities exist. Chinese people are now keen to get their share of wealth, and the capitalist economy has encouraged many to move to the cities in the hope of a better life. Many parents from rural areas have moved to cities, many thousands of miles away, to earn a decent wage to send back to their children at home, who often live with their grandparents. This 'floating' workforce contributes hugely to the success of China's economy, but this mass migration is not without its issues. Many families are separated, with children only seeing their parents a few times a year. In addition, this large-scale migration to certain areas has caused pockets of unemployment where there are often more people in a city than jobs available and also a lack of affordable housing.

Inadequate power supplies

Because of China's massive population and rapid economic growth, there are often energy supply problems. In order to tackle this, the Chinese Government has undertaken a number of controversial projects to ensure adequate power supplies for the country, such as the Three Gorges Dam. The project, built on the Yangtze River, which finished officially in 2012 and is the world's largest hydroelectric system, has caused massive problems for the people of China. Controversially, the project cost $24 billion, caused the displacement of 1.2 million people and resulted in massive environmental damage, not to mention the reported human rights abuses suffered by builders and villagers. The Government, however, maintained that the dam was necessary to provide China with 'flood prevention, river transportation and power generation for the future'.

Figure 2.18 **The Three Gorges Dam**

Show your understanding

1 Briefly explain China's movement from Communism to 'capitalism with Chinese characteristics'.
2 What evidence is there to show that China's economy is growing rapidly? Why is China becoming so wealthy?
3 What is a Special Economic Zone? Outline its main features.
4 What has happened to make China's urban population richer?
5 Briefly outline the main challenges facing China's economy.

Social and economic inequality

Although China's average economic growth rate has been no less than 7 per cent per annum in the last 20 years, wealth distribution is extremely unequal, and economic and social progress throughout the country is varied. Indeed, the poorest 25 per cent of the population own just 4 per cent of the country's wealth. In urban areas, there is a large emerging middle class of consumers who aspire to buy the latest technological goods, luxury items and status symbols. Their rapid accumulation of wealth has led to a huge rise in the number of billionaires in China; according to the Forbes rich list, there are now 168 billionaires in China and the number is ever-increasing in areas of the economy like petrochemicals, telecommunications and steel.

This rapid rise of affluence, however, has been very much an urban phenomenon; people in the countryside have a relatively low average income, which is only around a third of the average urban income. This is reportedly the largest gap in urban–rural incomes since 1978, meaning that, although China's economy is growing rapidly, this is not benefiting China's citizens equally. Many believe that the Chinese Government must do more to tackle rising inequalities in China, and Li Keqiang (currently China's Premier) stated in 2014 that 'China will wage a war against poverty with a stronger resolve' in the future.

Employment and income

The average income in China is now £4600 a year. However, according to Chinese Government figures there are now over 100 million rural poor in China who earn on average 2,300 yuan (£225 a year), although the actual number is thought to be more. Many academics argue that this is due to the Government's over-development of China's east coast in places like Beijing and Shanghai, while largely neglecting to build and develop inner, rural China. The rural–urban difference is also due to different types of employment in the two areas of China: rural areas are associated with poorer paid jobs like farming and mining, while urban jobs are often well paid by comparison and in technologically advanced petrochemical or service industries such as finance, insurance and banking. Although the overall unemployment rate (according to the Chinese Government) is a very low 4 per cent, this is not the case in all areas. According to the *Economist*, urban unemployment in areas like Beijing is thought to be as low as 1.4 per cent, yet it can be as high as 40–60 per cent in some mining towns. The CCP has been accused of covering up the true unemployment figures in rural areas, which are seen as tarnishing China's economic growth.

Rural to urban migration

Lack of job opportunities and the low pay that residents in rural China now face have pushed many people to migrate to urban areas, especially to Special Economic Zones (SEZs). Villagers can see that urban life offers them many luxuries compared with rural life and they now want to achieve the 'Chinese Dream'. Many of these people are seen as China's 'floating population' because they have migrated illegally without permission from the Government, ignoring the Hukou system (household registration required by law, identifying people as resident in a particular area) which is in place. The number of people migrating from rural to urban areas in search of work exceeded 160 million people in 2012 and these floating workers are causing competition for social services and housing, which is leading to overcrowding in areas such as Shanghai and Shenzhen. This problem is expected to worsen over the next three decades, where it is estimated that another 300 million people will move to urban areas to live and work. In the past, many migrant workers would live in the cities, leaving their children behind to live with grandparents in the countryside and sending home money to better their lives. However, according to Li Ben, the Head of the National Population and Family Planning Commission, 60 per cent of those moving to the cities to work are now moving their children with them, exacerbating the lack of housing and schools in some urban areas.

China's middle class

China's rapid growth in GDP from just 1.1 trillion in 2001 to 8.2 trillion in 2013 has led to a marked increase in China's middle-class population. Relaxed government ties over business ownership and state intervention, and taxation incentives, have allowed many Chinese people to start their own businesses, many of which have flourished in China's increasingly capitalist economy. The Chinese middle classes are characterised as having a high level of disposable income, professional careers and a university-level education, and are mass

consumers. It is now thought that 64 per cent of urban residents in Shanghai are classified as middle class and their drive to have the latest products has led to a rapidly expanding internal market for luxury goods. China's initial economic growth resulted from large levels of production of relatively cheap goods and technological goods for export. However, there is now a huge market within China itself for the latest goods: internal consumer spending now makes up around 35 per cent of China's economy.

Figure 2.19 **Enjoying the good life**

Case study: Identifying China's middle class

The average middle-class family in China has around $3000 disposable income a year. The middle class can be identified as people who send their children to private schools, own their own homes (often fashionable apartments in the city), own cars and take up to two holidays a year. These people often have a very different lifestyle from their parents, who would have had very little income, basic food and shelter and no luxuries. Nowadays, China's middle classes can afford tablet computers, top-of-the-range mobile phones and designer clothes, and they are influenced by Western fashion trends and fast food. In China today, 2600 cars are sold every hour and there is a Starbucks coffeehouse opening on average every day in China.

Show your understanding

1 What are the main reasons given for differences in China's wealth between urban and rural areas?
2 Explain why many people from rural areas move to the cities.
3 What has happened in China to allow many people to own their own businesses?
4 Explain in your own words the main characteristics of China's middle class.

Health care

Organising the health-care system for a country with a population of 1.35 billion people brings many challenges. Health care in China is not universal the way it is in the UK; it works through a combined insurance scheme of both individual and employer-based contributions. Structurally, the health-care system is run by the National Health and Family Planning Commission, which has a Bureau of Health in each province. Where health care has to be paid through insurance, there are inherent inequalities, with those who are well off receiving better care than those living in poverty. Currently, 62 per cent of hospitals in China are state-run, with 38 per cent being privately run. Those who can afford to pay for private care often experience shorter waiting lists and better-quality treatment, leading to a two-tier system in terms of the quality of care received.

Economic prosperity and growth, however, have led Chinese people to expect and demand better health care. As a result, the Chinese Government pledged in its 12th Five-Year Plan to begin looking at ways to implement universal health care in China by 2020 and it has set a number of strict health targets and improvements that it wishes to make. The Government has aimed to improve the basic health insurance system and improve access to health-care services in rural areas, spending around $371 billion in its efforts. The impact of these reforms is already being seen; the Social Insurance Law 2011 improved people's access to health insurance and a White Paper on China's health-care reforms highlighted that China has some of the best health in the developed world. Health insurance coverage has increased from 30 per cent of the population in 2003 to 95 per cent in 2012. There has been a massive reduction in infant mortality rates in China (from 29 per cent to 12 per cent between 2002 and 2012) and life expectancy has risen to 75 years.

The system, however, still has its flaws. Patients in China still have to pay directly for around a third of their health care and this can lead to great inequalities between those who can afford to pay and those who cannot. Once a patient is admitted to hospital, their public insurance will pay for around half of all treatment they receive, but this is a far cry from a universal health-care system. As some doctors receive payments from drug companies, they sometimes over-prescribe medicines that patients do not need in order to increase their incomes.

China's health problems

Health concerns in China are now beginning to mirror problems in the West; as lifestyles change so do the types of health problems that a country faces. China's improving access to health care since the 1980s has led to reduced infant and maternal mortality rates, and the country suffers less from curable diseases and conditions such as diarrhoea and pneumonia. However, China's increasingly Westernised lifestyles have created other health problems such as obesity, high smoking rates and alcohol addiction. Because families still have to pay large medical bills for treatment, despite having some of the costs covered by insurance, many mental health issues also go untreated and are often largely ignored.

Fact file

China's health problems

Smoking

Smoking is a huge health issue in China, and it is very gender specific. According to the World Health Organization, only 4 per cent of women in China smoke compared to a staggering 61 per cent of men. This huge difference is thought to be because of the culture within the country that it is socially unacceptable for women to smoke and also due to women's often lower socio-economic status. China is home to around 30 per cent of the world's smoking population. There are now more smokers in China than there are people in the USA. To tackle this the National People's Congress, meeting in March 2014, started to look towards banning smoking in public places in order to reduce the number of smokers in the country and reduce the effects of passive smoking.

Obesity

The rise in disposable incomes for many Chinese people, combined with less exercise, has led to a huge increase in obesity levels which have doubled in the last 30 years. This is a staggering contrast in a country where, 50 years ago, 45 million people died of hunger in the Maoist famines. This rapid change in China reflects developments already seen in countries like the UK and the USA. More and more people are now buying cars when the previously favoured mode of transport was bicycles, and there are now thousands of Western and American fast-food chains in China. Increasingly fatty diets have led to a huge rise in health problems such as type 2 diabetes (affecting 92 million people), heart disease and high blood pressure.

Figure 2.20 China has seen increasing levels of obesity in recent years

Government health reforms

As part of China's health reforms, the Ministry of Health published the 'Healthy China 2020' strategy which set out ten health targets that China was to achieve by 2020. These include raising life expectancy, reducing infant mortality rates and providing basic universal health care to all. It is thought that, by 2020, health spending will account for 7 per cent of the country's GDP – amounting to a total spending of $1 trillion. According to the World Health Organization, China's health-care system is currently ranked 144th in the world and an increase in wealth and standards of living is now pushing the Government to do more about improving health care provision.

Show your understanding

1 Briefly describe how health care is paid for in China.
2 Explain some of China's main health problems and why they are occurring.
3 Briefly explain China's health care reforms.
4 Evaluate how successful health-care reforms in China have been so far.

Education

Figure 2.21 **Students in Shanghai Gezhi High School,** **Shanghai**

China's education system is often renowned as being the best in the world, with the Programme for International Student Assessment (PISA) ranking China as first in the world for maths and science teaching. China has the largest network of universities in the world and educational expectations are extremely high. However, it is a deeply unequal system that is based on location, wealth and postcode-lottery style funding. In China, children are required to undergo nine years of mandatory education, but this does not always happen and children from rural areas often receive sub-standard education. For example, although 84 per cent of teenagers in Shanghai city go on to university, only 5 per cent of children from rural areas do. This large disparity is caused by poorer funding in rural schools, fewer resources and poor standards of teaching. Also, China has highly competitive entrance exams for high school, and children from poorer rural areas tend to do less well in these tests, because of proven links between poverty and poor educational attainment. Many children from rural areas drop out of school to support their families financially or to work the

land. In 2011, 80 per cent of children in urban areas graduated high school compared with only 20 per cent in rural areas.

Challenges facing Chinese education

Although China's education system is ranked by the OECD as one of the best in the world, it is not without flaws. Many people are critical of the system because of the pressure it puts on pupils; admission to the best schools and universities means passing extremely difficult entrance exams or *Gaokao*. These *Gaokao* exams have been reported to last up to nine hours for some institutions and there have been a number of high profile suicides in China in recent years due to the pressure of these exams.

Also, schools receive funding based on their performance, and teachers in rural schools are often paid half of what teachers in top performing urban schools receive. Educational experiences for students across China vary enormously and, although literacy rates for the country have dramatically improved, huge disparities in educational opportunity, quality of schools and teachers still remain.

Migrant children in China often struggle to access education because of the traditional Hukou system of residence registration. If families have migrated to urban areas from rural areas without seeking permission through the Hukou system, they may find it more difficult to access social services and, in particular, schools although laws on this have been relaxed by the Government. According to the OECD, 17 per cent of migrant children are no longer in schools by the time they are 13, leading to a major lack of opportunities for children of these families. Research carried out by REAP (Rural Education

Action Program) in China has found that, although urban schools are mostly rated 'good' and rural schools are rated 'improving', schools that are designed for migrant children in urban areas are rated as 'poor' in terms of teachers, curriculum and resources.

Concern has been raised about the growing wealth division of students in China's elite universities. In the 1970s, 50 per cent of first year students at Tsinghua University, alma mater of President Xi, were from poorer rural areas, according to Mr Dongping of Beijing Institute of Technology. In 2010, that figure was down to 17 per cent.

Government educational reform

China's educational system is undergoing rapid reform. As the economy rapidly advances, China needs a workforce with technological, economic and scientific expertise and the Government recognises this, stating it now needs a country that is 'rich in human resources'. As part of the educational reform 2020 programme, the Chinese Ministry of Education wants China to improve citizens' access to pre-school education and make the overall system more equal. China currently spends 4 per cent of its GDP on education, and this is set to rise by 2020. They also want to increase school enrolment from 82 to 88 per cent.

Housing

Standards of housing all over China vary enormously, with those living in rural areas often suffering from poorer housing and reduced access to water, electricity and sanitation. In contrast, those living in the city often live in nice apartments with many amenities and modern appliances. However, with China's rapid urbanisation the boundaries between urban and rural areas have begun to blur and led to the creation of many urban villages; these are areas that would have been considered to be countryside 20 years ago, but have now been engulfed by urban development from all sides, making them slums within the cities themselves. This has led to a reduction of farmland for farmers whose land has now been filled with skyscrapers and apartment blocks. Inhabitants of these slum areas often live in appalling conditions, with roadways so narrow they cause major fire hazards.

The types of housing that people in China live in have also changed. In the Maoist socialist era, most people lived in work units provided by the Government. However, nowadays in capitalist China there is a scramble over luxury, privately owned housing in cities like Beijing and Shanghai for the wealthiest and dilapidated shared housing for the less fortunate.

Show your understanding

1 Create a table with two columns showing the current positives and negatives of China's education system.
2 Describe the differences between the quality of education that students receive in rural and urban areas.
3 Explain the problem migrant children face when it comes to education.
4 Explain how the Chinese Government wants to improve the education system.

Case study: Urban villages – China's poor

Many people in China now live in what are defined as 'urban villages'; areas that used to be rural until cities were built around them and the rural village itself became a slum part of an otherwise modern city. People living in these areas often suffer from some of the worst housing in China, although it has slowly improved in recent years. Many academics have noted that the urban villages have become areas for local gangs and criminals to work from and that they are now becoming home to mass numbers of China's floating population, as housing can be acquired cheaply. People living in these areas tend to have very low incomes or none at all, and they often rely solely on renting spare rooms of their properties to migrant workers. According to Shenzhen Commercial News, 70 per cent of all crime in the area of Shenzhen occurs within urban villages.

Case study: China's wealthy

In comparison to those living in urban villages, China's wealthy live in unlimited opulence. Many luxurious apartments and penthouses have sprung up rapidly in desirable areas such as Shanghai to house the city's 'super-rich': 166,000 millionaires. Many of these apartments take up whole floors of skyscrapers, have fantastic views of the city and come with a multi-million pound price tag, not to mention the butlers, cleaners and chefs hired to cater for the needs of their owners. This capitalist phenomenon is a far cry from life in Mao's time in the 1950s, when Communism meant that normal Chinese people could not accumulate this level of wealth for themselves.

Housing problems

China's urban revolution and mass migration has caused several problems in its housing market. First of all, there is a clear lack of housing, let alone affordable housing, for the huge numbers of people migrating from rural to urban areas. House prices in Shanghai rose by 24 per cent between 2012 and 2013 and they are set to continue to rise, making affordable housing a real problem for Chinese people. House prices increased 250 per cent in China from 2000 to 2010, making it very hard for young urban couples to get on the property ladder and buy their own homes. Lack of housing is a problem that is predicted to grow enormously in the foreseeable future: with an estimated 300–400 million more people moving to China's main cities in the next 20 to 30 years, demand for housing in urban areas will remain extremely high.

Government housing reforms

The 12th Five-Year Plan (2011–2015) outlines the Government's need to tackle the existing housing crisis by providing 36 million more affordable homes in urban areas where most property is now privately owned. Projects have also been trialled in areas of Beijing where more affordable housing is being introduced by capping the sale price of certain properties and ensuring there are more affordable rental properties for migrant workers. The Government is also looking at relaxing the Hukou system further, allowing migrant workers more rights to access social services such as housing.

Crime

The strict discipline of the CCP seems to have had a trickle-down effect on crime rates in China, with most citizens obeying the laws of the country. The fact that over 50 crimes still carry the death penalty and criminals often face very harsh punishment and lengthy detention seems to have deterred many Chinese citizens from committing crime. China is viewed as being a very safe place to live, with a low crime rate. Violent crime rates, for example, are very low; the UN puts China's murder rate at 1.1 per 100,000 of the population compared with the UK's rate of 1.2 and the USA's rate of 5. However, studying crime rates in China must be treated with an element of caution; the official crime figures put forward by the Government are often seen as unrealistic and there is no uniform way of reporting and recording crimes in different provinces. For example, it has been reported by Chinese academics that deaths resulting from robbery or rape are not classified as murders, resulting in misleading figures. The CCP has not prioritised reducing crime or reforming the criminal justice system in their recent 12th Five-Year Plan, instead focusing on issues it sees as more pressing such as the economy, health-care services and the environment.

Cybercrime

One of China's most recent socio-economic issues is cybercrime. Vast gangs of computer hackers operate on what has become known as the mobile underground by hacking into people's mobile phones, a problem that is only set to grow as 81 per cent of mobile phone users in China have access to the internet on their devices. In recent years, these hackers have used a huge variety of scams, such as signing up mobile phone users to text services and charging them premium rates without their permission, and sending spam emails asking people to log on to false websites to change their banking details. This has led to large profits being made by cyber gangs, something that the Government has been trying to crack down on. In 2012, it was estimated that around 11,000 cybercrime suspects and 620 gangs were unearthed by CCP internet security forces and many websites were heavily fined for selling people's personal data.

Case study: Crime in Shanghai

The large police presence within China and the significant conviction rate for crimes (thought to be as high as 98 per cent in some areas) seems to act as a deterrent to those who would otherwise seek to commit crimes. Certain types of crime in urban areas like Shanghai, however, still present some issues. Crimes committed are mostly petty crimes, for example, theft and pickpocketing, and many have argued this is a result of the huge social and economic disparities that people in China are facing. A number of tourists in recent years have come forward about robberies and sexual assaults they have faced when venturing into unregistered taxis, and tourists are often targeted by Chinese criminals because of their supposed affluence.

Government responses to crime

The Chinese Government has faced a number of difficult internal criminal problems in recent years such as corruption, terrorism, cybercrime and violent riots. In an attempt to reduce terrorism and ethnic riots, Xi Jinping travelled to the Xinjiang region to meet with police officials and the Uighur people. In a speech there he said 'the battle to combat violence and terrorism will not allow even a moment of slackness, and decisive actions must be taken to suppress the terrorists' rampant momentum'. Xi has been accused of promoting the interests of the Han Chinese people in the area, encouraging them to move there through a new system of high-speed rail networks, so that the Uighur people are no longer the majority of the population.

In terms of tackling corruption, Xi Jinping has introduced a large crackdown on this activity, resulting in several thousands of arrests across China. And as cybercrime in China is largely monitored by the Chinese authorities, cyber gangs have been targeted and shut down to reduce economic crime. However, the Government may be condemning actions that it openly pursues itself, as the USA has accused China of cyber attacks on its government and companies. For example, attacks on senior US security officials were apparently traced to the People's Liberation Army facility near Shanghai.

12-mark question

Analyse the policies introduced by a world power you have studied to solve socio-economic issues.

20-mark question

To what extent do individuals or groups in a world power you have studied experience social inequality?

International relations

Is China the new 'superpower'?

China has a huge influence in the international community both economically and politically. It has the largest population in the world at 1.35 billion people and the second largest economy. Many observers have even dubbed China the 'new superpower', set to overtake America economically in some aspects during 2015 and being the biggest exporter of goods in the world. With an economic growth rate of no less than 7 per cent annually over the last three decades, the Chinese economy could be set to double in around ten years, dominating the USA's growth rate of a mere 3 per cent. However, superpower status is not based on economics alone; other factors such as military strength and decision-making influence on an international scale must also be taken into account. In terms of the military, China spent only 1.3 per cent of its GDP on military assets compared with the USA's 4.9 per cent (see Table 2.3).

Table 2.3 **Selected military assets, China and USA**

	China	**USA**
Defence budget 2011 ($ billion)	89.8	739.3
Active personnel (million)	2.3	1.6
Intercontinental missiles	66	450
Bombers	132	155
Nuclear-powered submarines	5	57
Main battle tanks	2,800	6,302
Cruise destroyers	13	18
Frigates	65	28
Aircraft carriers	1*	11

*Aircraft carrier is being built
Source: adapted from various US military sources

In recent years, however, the spotlight has been on China because of major world events like the Beijing Olympics 2008 and how China has dealt with internal problems such as corruption, dissent and terrorism. Chinese relations with neighbouring countries have also been heavily monitored for fear of conflict in east Asia. On the international stage, China is a member of many major organisations like the World Trade Organization, the UN (in which it has a permanent seat on the Security Council) and the G20. It is not a member of NATO or the OECD, although it has strong trade links with the EU.

China and the UN

Founded after the Second World War, the United Nations (UN) plays a vital role in international co-operation, peace and security. The People's Republic of China, as it stands now, has been a member of the UN since 1971 (although parts were previously a member under the Republic of China since 1945). China holds one of the five permanent seats on the UN Security Council, along with the UK, Russia, USA and France, and plays a key role in international relations.

Figure 2.22 **China has a seat on the UN Security Council**

Recently, China has taken a large role in improving international relations around the world. In 2014, Chinese Premier Li Keqiang pledged that China would work with the United Nations Environment Programme (UNEP) on a global scale to reduce emissions, combat climate change and support sustainable development. China also provided the UN with 6.5 per cent of its overall peacekeeping budget, and has offered international assistance to countries all over the world to counter terrorism and violence. In recent years China has been the biggest contributor of peacekeeping troops among the five permanent members of the Security Council. In April 2014, China offered assistance to Nigeria when the terrorist group Boko Haram abducted 250 schoolgirls. China condemned the terrorist acts of Boko Haram and offered to use satellite data and intelligence services to help find the girls, and the terrorists responsible, in a joint mission with the USA. China also sent its first peacekeeping troops to Mali in 2014 to safeguard the presidential elections there and in recent years it has begun to take a more leading role in ensuring international security and peacekeeping.

However, many political observers have criticised China for being too interested in pursuing its own interests in the international community. A number of controversial UN Security Council decisions in recent years have put China at odds with other permanent members of the Council, such as the USA and the UK. In 2012, China used its veto power within the Council to reject proposals to condemn the use of heavy weapons by government forces in Syria and to end war, violence and human rights violations in Syria. The veto power means that any of the five permanent members of the Security Council can prevent actions from being taken in a particular country and, as a result of China using its veto on three occasions regarding the Syrian crisis, the Council has been unable to offer any significant assistance and is still debating actions to help in 2015.

China's challenge to the US in south-east Asia

In 2013, the new leader of China, Xi Jinping, stated that 'the vast Pacific Ocean has enough space for the two large countries of China and the United States'. China's new confidence is now challenging US dominance of south-east Asia. Tension has always existed between the two countries over the island of Taiwan. When the Chinese Communists gained control of mainland China, the defeated Chinese Government fled to Taiwan and set up their own 'independent' China. The US protects Taiwan and provides it with up-to-date military equipment to deter a mainland attack. However, China's long-term aim is to restore Taiwan to Chinese rule, and its military strategy is to build up its navy to deter American military involvement if it ever decided to invade Taiwan. The US fleet still dominates the Pacific but China will soon have in service its first aircraft carrier (the USA has 11 worldwide). The USA has military bases in South Korea and Japan, and China wishes to challenge US dominance in the region. However, China believes that America has been weakened by the global financial crisis and debilitating wars in Afghanistan and Iraq, and that the future dominant power in south-east Asia will be China. Xi's Chinese dream is that of a mighty nation reclaiming its rightful place in the world and ending centuries of humiliation from foreign powers.

China has also been seen to be flexing its military power recently over territorial disputes in areas of the South China Sea. China positioned an oil rig in an area of the South China Sea that Vietnam claimed was its territory. This led to a stand-off between Chinese and Vietnamese ships that became very hostile when China used water cannons to disperse the Vietnamese ships. This has led to knock-on tensions in Vietnam, and a number of bloody anti-Chinese protests within the country. China says the waters belong to them historically. China also has territorial claims against Japan and the Philippines.

China and the G20

Figure 2.23 **Xi Jinping at the 2013 G20 Summit in St Petersburg**

China is a key member of the Group of Twenty countries or 'G20'. This group includes representatives from some of the most important economies in the world – 19 different countries and a representative from the EU. This international organisation accounts for 85 per cent of the world's economic output and focuses on improving world economies (especially in the light of the global economic crisis), trade and employment. In 2014, the G20 Leaders' Summit was held in Brisbane, Australia, and the key focus of the summit was increasing economic growth and co-operation. The previous summit, in St Petersburg, Russia, was the first attended by Xi Jinping, China's leader. During the meeting, Xi Jinping outlined in his speech how successful Chinese economic development had been in recent years, largely avoiding the global financial crisis, and emphasised how China is now a key player in ensuring economic stability for the rest of the world. He also insisted that other G20 countries be more open to wider trading opportunities and that the group should avoid trade protectionism, ensuring that every country within the group can trade more freely.

China's relationships with other countries

China and the European Union

China is obviously not part of the European Union (EU), but relations between the EU and China play a huge role in international diplomacy, foreign affairs and global economic prosperity. The EU is China's largest trading ally and trade between the two in 2013 was estimated to be around €428 billion. However, China does not invest heavily in the EU in terms of foreign direct investment; approximately just 2.6 per cent of the EU's total FDI is from China.

There are signs of friction as well as co-operation between the two powers. The Chinese Government has been coming under fire from developed nations around the world for not doing enough to prevent the production of counterfeit goods; around 65 per cent of the counterfeit goods confiscated by authorities across the EU are thought to have been made in China. Every year since 1997 a China–EU summit has been held and the summit in 2013 looked towards reducing trade tariffs between both groups to allow for freer economic co-operation.

China and the UK

China and the UK are used to working together through international organisations like the UN and the G20. In December 2013, this was strengthened when UK Prime Minister David Cameron visited China. The main aims of the visit were to increase trade between the two countries and look towards building stronger cultural co-operation. As a result of this visit, £5.6 billion of business deals were made between the two countries and 1500 UK jobs were created, with China volunteering to help the UK build its high-speed rail network. There were also calls to negotiate further free-trade deals between the EU and China, the biggest trading partners in the world. This agreement could save the UK up to $1 billion a year in trade tariffs and help push economic growth.

However, in November 2014 relations between China and the UK became tense because of events in Hong Kong. In 1984, Britain signed the Sino-British Joint Declaration on the Question of Hong Kong, which set out arrangements for the transfer of sovereignty over Hong Kong from Britain to China in 1997 under the 'one country, two systems' principle. However, China has refused to implement the agreement that the people of Hong Kong would be able to elect their chosen representatives. Instead the Chinese Government stated that elections would be held but only candidates endorsed by the Chinese Communist Party could stand. The UK Parliament's Foreign Affairs Select Committee had wished to send some of its members to Hong Kong but had been refused entry. Chairman of the Committee, Sir Richard Ottaway MP, said:

'We are not going to be pressured by the Chinese government into abandoning our inquiry, nor are we going to cancel plans to hear from people in Hong Kong. The approach taken by China has been very revealing. The Chinese Deputy Ambassador to the UK stated "Hong Kong came back to China 17 years ago, it is a Chinese territory and we oppose any interference in its internal affairs."'

Show your understanding

1 In what ways can China be described as a 'superpower'?
2 In what ways is China not yet considered to be a 'superpower'?
3 Briefly explain the role that China plays within the UN.
4 What evidence suggests that China wishes to challenge America's dominance in south-east Asia?
5 Why is Taiwan an international problem?
6 Briefly explain the role that China plays within the G20.

20-mark question

To what extent does a world power you have studied have influence in international relations?

The Republic of South Africa

Background

The 'rainbow nation'

South Africa is a nation reborn. In 1994, the country elected its first democratic government after the end of white rule under a system known as apartheid. Nelson Mandela, the leader of the ANC (African National Congress), became the first democratically elected president. Before Mandela, white people had used apartheid to deny non-white people political, social and economic rights: this has left a legacy of vast inequalities between the races which will be discussed later in this chapter. The new 'rainbow nation' has made great progress in the creation of a more prosperous country for all, and in 2010 the football World Cup finals were held in South Africa. It was fitting that South Africa was the first African country to hold such a prestigious event. However, the election of 2014, following the death of Nelson Mandela in December 2013, raised questions about the future path of the country. Will it remain a model of democracy for its neighbours or will the corrupt leadership of President Jacob Zuma and his fellow ANC leaders steer the country towards a one-party dictatorship and a declining economy?

The legacy of the 2010 Football World Cup

South Africa's ten stadiums that were built for the 2010 World Cup symbolise the achievement of a nation reborn. Nobel Peace Prize Laureate and anti-apartheid hero Archbishop Desmond Tutu summed up the majority view by saying 'With all the negative things that are taking place in Africa, this is a superb moment for us. If we are going to have white elephants, so be it.'

Economists also say World Cup construction cushioned South Africa from the global recession and contributed close to R56 billion ($7.3 billion) to the economy. 'It has been a huge blessing for South Africa in view of the recession' said Gillian Saunders of business consultants Grant Thornton.

Nevertheless, the stadiums' spectacular style can perhaps be seen as going way beyond football – the affirmation of the capabilities of a young, democratic country in the face of doubts and cynicism both at home and abroad. 'For the many little boys kicking a ball in the streets of the world's townships and squatter camps, football is the stuff of dreams,' said commentator Tinyiko Sam Maluleke.

Figure 3.1 The Green Point Stadium in Cape Town was built for the 2010 football World Cup

One of South Africa's greatest benefits was the upgrading of its infrastructure – improved national roads and airports and investment in public transport. The Finals put South Africa and Africa on the map and this is reflected in the decision to invite South Africa to join the BRIC Group (see page 127).

The author can testify to the majestic appearance of the Green Point World Cup stadium in Cape Town. Sailing into Cape Town, the dominant landscape is the iconic Table Mountain but nestled below it on the waterfront is the impressive modern stadium.

The land and the people

South Africa is five times the size of the United Kingdom with a population of over 50 million. Owing to its size, it has different climates and landscapes in different parts of the country. Much of the west of the country is desert, while the south, around Cape Town, has a Mediterranean climate. South Africa is divided into nine provinces (see pages 88–89).

Its diverse population is made up of numerous ethnic groups and this is reflected in the recognition of 11 official languages. Black South Africans make up almost 80 per cent of the population (see Table 3.1 on page 86). The most recent Census statistics reveal that 63 per cent of the population now live in urban areas.

Boers, British and Africans

In 1752, a settlement was established by the Dutch East India Company to supply fresh provisions for their trading ships.

By 1806, the British Government had decided to control Cape Colony and consequently took it over. The resultant increase in immigration from Britain established two distinct white communities: the Afrikaners (Boers) and the English-speaking whites (Anglos). With the discovery of diamonds and gold, Britain proceeded to annexe the Afrikaner republics of Transvaal and the Orange Free State. This eventually led to the Boer War (1899–1902), in which the Boers were defeated.

British dominance ended in 1948 when the Afrikaner National Party won the election and began its policy of apartheid and total white control of all aspects of life.

South Africa's economy

South Africa is a middle-income emerging economy with an abundant stock of natural resources. It is served by a modern infrastructure ensuring an efficient distribution of goods to major urban areas. The country has well-developed financial and legal sectors with a stock exchange that ranks among the top ten largest in the world.

Unemployment is a problem. Official figures show 25 per cent unemployed, but the real figure is close to 40 per cent, with about 50 per cent of the population living below the poverty line. Half of all South Africans aged 18–24 are not in education, training or employment. About 70 per cent have no qualifications or work skills. Yet there are many job vacancies, with employers desperate to employ young people with appropriate qualifications and skills.

Massive economic inequalities still exist between the white population and the new black middle class and the majority of black South Africans. South Africa is one of the most unequal societies in the world alongside the USA, China and Brazil, in terms of wealth distribution among its citizens (see Figure 3.23 on page 128).

South Africa is one of the wealthiest countries in sub-Saharan Africa in terms of natural resources and its manufacturing industry. However, the world financial crisis of 2007–08 and the subsequent economic recession has had a far greater impact on South Africa than its neighbours. In April 2014, under revised GDP (Gross Domestic Product) estimates, Nigeria overtook South Africa to become the biggest economy in sub-Saharan Africa (see pages 126–7).

South Africa is the world's largest producer of gold. Large-scale commercial farming ensures an abundant supply of food. In the less fertile areas pastoral farming dominates, with sheep rearing and cattle ranching particularly strong. South Africa is the region's economic superpower. It accounts for 85 per cent of southern Africa's energy consumption and 90 per cent of its GDP.

Ethnic groupings

South Africa's official classifications of race list the four main ethnic groups as follows:

1 The predominant black indigenous population, who are subdivided by tribal group. The two main tribal groups are Xhosa (former presidents Nelson Mandela and Thabo Mbeki) and Zulu (current president Jacob Zuma).

2 Whites are divided into English-speaking and Afrikaans-speaking.
3 The coloured population are of mixed race.
4 Asians, or Indians, are descended from workers who were brought from India to work, especially in Natal, in the nineteenth century.

Figure 3.2 **South Africa's population of 53 million is made up of numerous ethnic groups**

Table 3.1 shows that South Africa's population has now reached 53 million. In 2009, the coloured population overtook the white population – an estimated 800,000 white people have left South Africa since 1994. With a higher birth rate than the other races, the African population has increased by almost 8 million since 1996 and will soon make up 80 per cent of the total population.

Table 3.1 **South Africa's population**

	1996 population (millions)	Percentage	2013 population (millions)	Percentage
Black	31.3	76.8	42.28	79.6
White	4.7	11.4	4.60	8.9
Coloured	3.3	9.0	4.77	9.0
Asian	1.2	2.8	1.33	2.5
Total	**40.5**	**100**	**52.98**	**100**

Source: Statistics South Africa, Mid-Year Population Estimates, 2014

While there are significant inequalities in South Africa based on race, there are also significant inequalities between urban and rural areas. The 2013 General Household Survey, published in June 2014, highlights the fact that regional inequalities are still a feature of South Africa.

Illegal immigrants

Official figures detailing South Africa's population fail to include the millions of Africans who have flocked to the country to escape poverty and persecution in their home nations. It has been estimated by the South African Institute of Race Relations that around 5 million immigrants are living illegally in South Africa. It is ironic that while highly skilled and educated white people leave the country for better jobs abroad (around 800,000 are thought to have left since 1994) and educated black South Africans flock to London to take up jobs in health and education, South Africa is being left with an unskilled and uneducated workforce, which the country, with its unemployment rate of 40 per cent, does not need.

Most refugees originate from the Democratic Republic of Congo, Rwanda, Somalia and Zimbabwe. Around 2 million Zimbabweans are thought to be currently living in South Africa, although many may return home if peace and stability return to Zimbabwe. Illegal immigrants can face great hostility from South Africans. Over the last five years numerous vicious attacks against foreign immigrants have taken place in townships around Johannesburg, Cape Town and in the province of Mpumalanga. In February 2014, in the informal settlement of Refilwe, east of Pretoria, more than a dozen foreign-owned shops were looted. However, many immigrants, especially from Zimbabwe, are well educated and contribute to the economy.

During a stay in Cape Town, the author was surprised by the number of foreigners working in the tourist sector and also learned that many South Africans who live in RDP homes (government low-cost homes) rent their rooms out to foreigners and sleep in their gardens.

Profile of the provinces of South Africa

Province/Capital	**GAUTENG/Johannesburg**
Population	12.7 million
Area km²	18,810 (1.6 per cent of total)
GDP per person ($)	58,000
Agriculture and industry	Gauteng is South Africa's engine room, where about 40 per cent of the country's GDP is generated. Gauteng means 'place of gold' and this is a highly urbanised and industrialised area. It is a magnet area for a large inflow of migrant labourers.
Comment	Pretoria, the administrative capital of South Africa, is situated in the province.

Province/Capital	**NORTHERN CAPE/Kimberley**
Population	1.1 million (1.9 per cent of total)
Area km²	361,800 (29.7 per cent of total)
GDP per person ($)	38,000
Agriculture and industry	Extremely rich in mineral wealth – including copper, manganese and marble.
Comment	It covers the largest area in South Africa and has the smallest population. It is a semi-arid region with low summer rainfall and is the home of the San (bushmen) people.

Figure 3.3 **South Africa's nine provinces**

Province/Capital	**WESTERN CAPE/Cape Town**
Principal language	Afrikaans (55 per cent), English (20 per cent), isiXhosa (23 per cent)
Population	6.0 million (10.9 per cent of total)
Area km²	129,379 (14.4 per cent of total)
GDP per person ($)	50,000
Agriculture and industry	Food basket of South Africa with a harvest of top-grade fruits, vegetables and meats. The head offices of many South African businesses are in Cape Town. Some 96 per cent of its population is urbanised.
Comment	Cape Town is the legislative capital of the country.

Province/Capital	**FREE STATE/Bloemfontein**
Population	2.8 million
Area km²	129,480 (10.6 per cent of total)
GDP per person ($)	38,000
Agriculture and industry	'The granary of the country' with 31 per cent of the potentially arable land of South Africa. Its main economic base is mining.
Comment	It lies in the heart of South Africa and is the third-largest province (size).

Province/Capital	**NORTH WEST/Minabatha**
Population	3.6 million
Area km²	116,190 (9.5 per cent of total)
GDP per person ($)	22,000

| Agriculture and industry | Its main economic base is mining with its major agricultural products being maize and sunflowers. High unemployment levels in the province contribute to the poverty experienced by many of its citizens. |
| Comment | It is developing its tourist industry through national parks. |

Province/Capital — **EASTERN CAPE/Bisho**

Population	6.6 million
Area km²	169,600 (13.9 per cent of total)
GDP per person ($)	21,000
Agriculture and industry	Includes rich agricultural and forestry land. The urban areas of Port Elizabeth and East London are based primarily on manufacturing.
Comment	Includes the former homelands of Transkei and Ciskei.

Province/Capital — **LIMPOPO/Pietersburg**

Population	5.5 million
Area km²	123,280 (10 per cent of total)
GDP per person ($)	20,500
Agriculture and industry	Extremely rich in minerals including coal, copper and platinum. Unemployment is high. The per capita income is by far the lowest in the country.
Comment	The province is the country's gateway to the rest of Africa as it shares borders with Botswana, Zimbabwe and Mozambique.

Province/Capital — **MPUMALANGA/Nelspruit**

Population	4.1 million
Area km²	78,370 (7.3 per cent of total)
GDP per person ($)	25,000
Agriculture and industry	Produces sub-tropical fruits and its tree plantations supply half of the country's total timber needs. It is rich in coal reserves and the country's three biggest power stations are based in the area.
Comment	Mpumalanga (formerly Eastern Transvaal) means 'place where the sun rises'. The province attracts migrant labour from neighbouring states. Suffers from extreme levels of poverty and low levels of literacy.

Province/Capital — **KWAZULU-NATAL/Pietermaritzburg/Ulundi**

Principal language	isiZulu (79 per cent), Afrikaans (2 per cent), English (16 per cent)
Population	10.4 million (21.2 per cent of total)
Area km²	92,180 (7.6 per cent of total)
GDP per person ($)	24,000
Agriculture and industry	Durban is one of the fastest growing urban areas in the world. Huge gap between the urban and rural per-capita income.
Comment	The only province with a monarchy specifically provided for in the 1993 Constitution. Ulundi is the traditional capital of the Zulu monarchy.

Source: SA Government Yearbook, 2013

Western Cape – goodbye to the ANC?

In January 2014, I visited South Africa and had the opportunity to take the social and political pulse of the citizens of the Western Cape four months prior to the 2014 elections. I have been writing about South Africa since 1985 and my visit was an opportunity to experience the new rainbow nation and to assess recent social and economic progress.

The Western Cape's political and population profile is unique to South Africa. It is the only province not controlled by the ANC and also the only province that does not have a black majority – the coloured population is the largest population group.

We stayed in a modern hotel overlooking the sea, with the iconic Table Mountain as a stunning background. Most of the staff were black and the majority of the guests were tourists. The hotel was based in a residential complex occupied by all shades of the rainbow nation and protected by CCTV and patrolling guards. Only the wealthy South Africans experience this racial togetherness in their neighbourhood, workplace and in the beautiful and opulent shopping malls in the centre of Cape Town. In our tours across the Western Cape, we passed the sprawling Khayelitsha township, which consists of planned new RDP homes (recognised by their red roofs) and the informal settlements with sub-standard dwellings that are plagued by violent crime.

Our driver, Robert, enjoyed our wide-ranging discussions. Robert is coloured and had originally supported the ANC, but in the 2009 election had voted Democratic Alliance (DA) and would do so again in 2014. The ANC was no longer the party of liberation and hope but had become the party of maladministration, greed and corruption. He was

Figure 3.4 Cape Town

confident that the DA would retain the Western Cape despite ANC propaganda.

One of the comments that I regarded at the time as being far-fetched and unfair was when Robert said that the ANC did not want a well-educated and mature electorate; they were content that the education system was failing the vast majority of black people. He argued that in this way many blacks would believe the propaganda of the ANC: that the DA was racist and would reintroduce apartheid if they won ... that Nelson Mandela's spirit would haunt them if they did not vote ANC, and so on. Yet in May 2014 when I examined the voting patterns, one inverse conclusion was clear: the two provinces with the poorest matriculation (exam) results had the highest ANC support and the two worst results for the ANC were in the two best educated provinces of Western Cape and Gauteng. (See Table 3.5, page 100.)

And this is the problem the DA faces. The black community might not like Zuma's ANC, but they are not ready to commit 'heresy' and endorse the DA. In my conversation with numerous black people, it was clear that their ANC loyalty was solid. When I mentioned Jacob Zuma, none challenged my corruption accusation and could only invoke the mantra of Nelson Mandela.

Apartheid

The Afrikaans word 'apartheid' means separate development, and describes the segregation that took place between the races in South Africa. Numerous laws such as the Group Areas Act and the Pass laws were passed to divide the people and land on racial grounds.

The apartheid years 1948–94

It is important to have an understanding of the vast inequalities between the races created during the apartheid years – its legacy still exists today in South Africa.

The apartheid system was set up by the white group known as Afrikaners whose ancestors came mostly from the Netherlands. In 1948, they gained control of the country from the English-speaking whites and set up a government that denied all non-whites their political, social and economic rights. South Africa was to be white only, with just 13 per cent of the land area being given to the 70 per cent of the population who were black and given self-governing tribal homelands to live in. For example, the largest tribe, the Zulu, were to live in the homeland of KwaZulu-Natal and run their own affairs there. The black population were treated as foreigners, had to have permission to live outside their homelands and were expected to live in segregated areas called townships, the most famous being Soweto on the outskirts of Johannesburg.

The escalation of black unrest and international action against the white government of South Africa persuaded President F.W. de Klerk, leader of the National Party, that he must negotiate with Nelson Mandela, the imprisoned leader of the ANC. In 1990, Nelson Mandela was set free from prison, and the ANC declared legal. Prolonged negotiations took place and finally, in 1994, a new constitution was agreed and elections held (see analysis of results, right). For the first time the black population could vote; Nelson Mandela and the ANC won and formed the new government. All the political parties agreed to the setting up of a Truth and Reconciliation Commission (TRC) to investigate illegal actions that had taken place during the apartheid years (see below).

Truth and Reconciliation Commission

The TRC, chaired by retired Archbishop Desmond Tutu, was set up to establish as complete a picture as possible of the 'causes, nature and extent of the gross violations of human rights committed between 1960 and 1994'. The Commission had the power to grant an amnesty to anybody whose crime had a political purpose as long as they admitted their wrongdoing. Victims of apartheid had the opportunity to share their grief with the nation and to discover what had happened to their loved ones. The hearings, aired on television, shocked and horrified the nation. The revelations damaged the National Party and led to the resignation of de Klerk. In total 6000 people applied for amnesty and 22,000 victims testified to the Commission

(In 2011, Desmond Tutu, still the nation's moral conscience, denounced the infighting and corruption within the ANC. In his speech he called the ANC 'worse than the apartheid government'. However, he also asked whites to pay a wealth tax as an act of atonement for their privileged positions.)

1994 election analysis

- It was a triumph for democracy with the election remaining free from intimidation, fraud and violence.
- As expected, the ANC dominated the election, winning over 12 million votes but just failing to receive two-thirds of the votes (which would have enabled it to create a new constitution without consulting the other political parties).

At the provincial level the ANC won seven of the nine provinces with narrow defeats in the Western Cape and KwaZulu-Natal.

- The New National Party, by winning the support of white, coloured and Asian South Africans, gained an impressive 20.4 per cent of the vote and thus the post of deputy president. Its best performance was in the Western Cape where it won the Provincial election. The Democratic Party, a white party that had always opposed apartheid, did badly.
- The Inkatha Freedom Party (IFP) gained a narrow victory over the ANC in KwaZulu-Natal and won control of the province. The results reinforced the status of the IFP (and the New National Party) as regional rather than national players. While the IFP gained 1.8 million votes in KwaZulu-Natal, its combined vote in the eight other provinces was only 214,000.

Nelson Mandela

Nelson Mandela was born on 18 July 1918, the son of a tribal chief of the Xhosa nation. He graduated from the University College of Fort Hare and later set up a legal practice with Oliver Tambo in Johannesburg. Both men were leaders of the ANC Youth League which supported boycotts, strikes and acts of civil disobedience.

Figure 3.5 Nelson Mandela

The introduction of apartheid in 1948 and the brutal use of force by the white regime made him question the ANC's policy of non-violence. In 1961, Mandela went underground to organise the military wing of the ANC. On 2 August 1962 he was sentenced to life imprisonment for attempting to overthrow the government by violent revolution. It was not until 11 February 1990 that he gained his freedom, when he was released from prison by President de Klerk. He was reunited with his wife, Winnie, but their marriage ended and they were divorced in 1996. Nelson Mandela was elected president of the new democratic South Africa in 1994 and retained this post until 1999, when he retired from politics. Mandela preached reconciliation between the races and worked hard to create a new 'rainbow nation'.

An ailing Nelson Mandela died on 5 December 2013 and the 'rainbow nation' mourned. President Zuma stated 'our nation has lost its greatest son'.

Show your understanding

1. Outline the benefits to South Africa of holding the 2010 World Cup.
2. Describe the main racial groups in South Africa and discuss what conclusions can be reached about population change.
3. Create a brief profile of the nine provinces.
4. Describe the inequalities that non-whites experienced during the apartheid years.
5. What impact did the Truth and Reconciliation Commission have on the South African people?
6. Outline the main political parties that participated in the 1994 election and their performance.

Archbishop Desmond Tutu, 1994

'Apartheid has left a ghastly legacy. There is a horrendous housing shortage and high unemployment; health care is inaccessible and not easily affordable by the majority; Bantu education has left us with a massive educational crisis; there is gross maldistribution of wealth and an inequitable sharing of resources with which South Africa is so richly endowed. Some 20 per cent of the population owns 87 per cent of the land. Then there is the hurt and anguish of those who have been victims of this vicious system, those who were forcibly removed from their homes, nearly 4 million people. Those

Figure 3.6 Desmond Tutu, a former Archbishop and a South African Nobel Peace Prize winner

whose loved ones were detained without trial or banned, or who died mysteriously in detention, such as Steve Biko, or at the hands of death squads.'

Social and economic issues

Legacy of apartheid

The provision of the vote to all citizens ensured that the black South African people would run their own country. The *political* legacy of apartheid was removed by this action. Much more difficult for the new ANC Government would be the removal of the social and economic inequalities between the races. In its 1994 election manifesto, the ANC promised 'a job, a decent home and a chicken in every pot'. Over twenty years on, many Africans are still waiting for this to be achieved. The legacy of apartheid, which created vast inequalities between the races, is outlined in the statistical survey and comments that follow.

Education

The population growth within the black South African community is one of the challenges facing governments. Seventeen million of the 42 million black African population are under the age of 16. The paradox that South Africa faces is that, although it has an unemployment rate of

40 per cent, it is desperately short of skilled and educated black South Africans.

The culture of violence, with 'no education before liberation' being the slogan for a generation of young black South Africans, contributed to the decline of educational standards. This was reflected in the low matriculation results achieved by black South African students (see Figure 3.7). Overcrowded classrooms and few resources were also factors that help to explain poor educational performances and low African literacy rates.

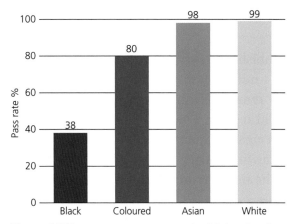

Figure 3.7 **Percentage pass rates for high school leaving exam by race, 1993**
Source: SA Department of Education, 1993

Health

Table 3.2 **Health inequalities, 1990**

	Infant mortality rate (per 1,000 births)	Life expectancy (at birth)
Black	65	60
Coloured	35	62
Asian	14	67
White	8	72

Source: SA Department of Health, 1990

During the era of apartheid, while the white South Africans enjoyed an excellent health service, the non-white population was condemned to a second-rate service that struggled to cope. In 1994, there was a white doctor for every 400 white people and an African doctor for every 44,000 Africans. The situation was worse in the rural areas of the homelands. Poverty, hunger and disease, combined with the lack of doctors and nurses, explained the high level of malnutrition and undernourishment among rural children.

The existence of a strong private health-care sector also created inequalities between the races. In 1994, 90 per cent of the white community relied on private medical care, while the vast majority of black people could not afford it.

Land

As Archbishop Desmond Tutu highlighted, almost 4 million non-white people were forcibly removed from their homes by the apartheid regime. The homeland and township systems created squatter camps, shanty towns and sprawling townships such as Soweto, where the majority of dwellings lacked basic amenities such as electricity and proper sanitation. In the rural areas many black South Africans were forcibly settled in arid lands that could not sustain them. The outcome was malnutrition, disease and abject poverty.

Cyril Ramaphosa, then ANC General Secretary, stated in 1993 that 'unless we settle the land question we tear South Africa to pieces'. As part of the 1994 peace agreement between de Klerk and Mandela, the white farmers were guaranteed that their land would not be taken from them through nationalisation or expropriation policies.

Show your understanding

1 Refer to the comments made by Archbishop Desmond Tutu in 1994. What evidence does he give to support his statement that 'apartheid has left a ghastly legacy'?
2 Outline the vast inequalities between the races that existed in 1994 in terms of: education, health and land.

Reducing social and economic inequalities

As indicated earlier, all ANC governments since 1994 have faced the apartheid legacy of vast social and economic inequalities and widespread poverty. President Mandela gave hope and raised expectations (1994–99), President Mbeki created disillusionment (1999–2007) and the current president, Jacob Zuma, again promises improvement.

RDP and GEAR

The Reconstruction and Development Programme (RDP) and Growth Employment and Redistribution (GEAR) have been central policies in bringing wealth to the African population and reducing poverty. The Government was prepared to upset the trade unions and the South African Communist Party by selling state-owned enterprises, such as electricity and gas, to the private sector. This policy of privatisation provided income to enable the Government to improve services. The downside was that private firms raised prices and consumers have had to pay higher charges for essential services. This has placed a heavy financial burden on the poorer sections of society.

GEAR encouraged growth and employment by providing economic stability which in turn encouraged foreign investment. GEAR also promoted a black enterprise culture. 'Wealthy, black and proud of it' is the slogan of the Government.

President Mbeki was aware of the need to transform South African society. The shift of power that took place in the political field must now cover all aspects of economic and social life. To try to narrow the huge gap between black and white, the Government embarked on a programme of Affirmative Action, which President Zuma has continued.

Affirmative Action

Mandela did not wish to antagonise the white population and did not pass legislation to compel employers or institutions to discriminate in favour of non-white people. His successor, Thabo Mbeki, used Affirmative Action legislation to speed up the 'transformation of South Africa's economic life'.

There are two major pieces of Affirmative Action legislation: the Employment Equity Act and the Black Economic Empowerment Act.

The Employment Equity Act

The Employment Equity Act, 1998, set up a directorate called 'Equal Opportunities' to ensure that organisations 'democratically represented' the black people of South Africa. The Act decreed that the correct balance of a workforce should be 75 per cent black, 52 per cent female, 5 per cent people with disabilities. The Act promoted reverse discrimination which meant that black South Africans were entitled to preferential treatment in hiring, promotion, university admission and the awarding of government contracts.

Any company that has more than 50 employees is covered by this Act and can be fined up to £100,000 if it does not meet its terms.

The Black Economic Empowerment (BEE) Act

The Department of Trade and Industry (DTI) states that 'Our BEE strategy is not affirmative action, although employment equity forms part of it. Nor does it aim to take wealth from white people and give it to blacks. It is essentially a growth strategy, targeting the South African economy's weakest point: inequality. The purpose of BEE is to stimulate economic growth and create employment.'

President Zuma has dismissed calls from the Afrikaner Freedom Front Party to end the discrimination towards young white people as they were not responsible for the inequalities created by apartheid. He stated that 'it was unthinkable for the ANC to abandon it'.

The controversial fabulous four

It is significant that former ANC leaders who fought against apartheid have crossed over from politics to the boardroom to become millionaires. The four who symbolise the new black elite are Cyril Ramaphosa, who re-entered politics to become deputy president in 2014, Tokyo Sexwale, former ANC provincial premier, Saki Macozoma, former political prisoner, and Patrice Motsepe, who is married to an ANC minister. They are aware of the growing criticism coming from fellow black South Africans, but they argue that their goal is to create a million black capitalists. In 2012, Ramaphosa bid 19.5 million rands for a prize buffalo – the average annual black wage is about 26,000 rands! However, Moletsi Mbeki, an economic analyst,

Figure 3.8 Cyril Ramaphosa, millionaire and now deputy president of South Africa, has been criticised for his involvement in the Marikana Massacre, see pages 109–10)

claims that BEE has struck 'a fatal blow against the emergence of black entrepreneurship by creating a small class of unproductive, but wealthy black crony capitalists'.

BEE: achievements and criticism

Table 3.3 **Achievements and criticisms of the BEE Act**

Achievements	Criticisms
The African middle class is now about 5 million and growing. Their new wealth has led to a consumer explosion. Their spending power is now far greater than that of their white counterparts. The number of black middle-class families living in the former white suburbs has increased from 20 per cent in 2004 to 55 per cent in 2013.	Many black-owned firms win government contracts despite submitting higher bids (the government rule is that bids from previously disadvantaged individuals, PDIs, can be up to 10 per cent higher than others). Having won the contracts they sub-contract the work to their losing competitors. In effect the PDI/10 per cent rule constitutes a special tax on all taxpayers with the proceeds going to the black businessmen who win the contract.
State-owned industries such as Eskom now have black majorities on their boards. Around 40 per cent of senior managers are black compared with about 4 per cent in 1996.	Several high-profile black empowerment businesses such as the African Bank and Community Bank have collapsed. Eskom, the state-owned power company, is regarded as inefficient and incompetent, and numerous power cuts took place in 2014.
To achieve government contracts, firms must now file a BEE scorecard to prove that they are promoting 'previously disadvantaged individuals' including black, coloured and Asian South Africans. The Government spends R12 billion a year on government contracts, much of which benefits black businesses and the black workforce.	Many BEE activities simply enrich a small number of individuals and do not offer any economic benefits to the black majority. White businessmen give directorships and shares to black business people to conform to BEE regulations (see Tenderpreneur, page 122).

The gap is closing

In a controversial speech in 2004 the then president Thabo Mbeki referred to South Africa as being a land of two nations – one white and rich, the other black and poor. While there are still significant inequalities between the races, progress has been made through the BEE project. There is now a rich African middle class, referred to as the 'Black Diamonds'.

The divide is now not so much based on race but on social class.

White poverty

It is true that rich, white South Africans have retained their wealth since apartheid ended, but many poorly educated white people have sunk into poverty and white beggars are a common sight in South African cities. In 2008, Jacob Zuma, then leader of the ANC, visited a poor white community in Bethlehem, Pretoria. Bethlehem has no electricity, running water or sewerage system and the people survive by selling vegetables they grow near the shacks. Solidarity, a union whose base is among white workers, claims that white poverty has increased from 3 per cent in 1994 to 13 per cent today and that their plight had been ignored by the Government. One Bethlehem resident stated 'When we tried to apply for food aid and social security payments, we were told by black social workers that you whites can suffer now. When we applied for jobs, we were turned away because of our colour. We are now the victims of the new apartheid.'

'Black Diamonds'

Evidence of the emergence of a black elite can be found in the number of black people now living in the wealthiest suburbs of South Africa's cities, once the exclusive domain of white citizens. Houghton, the grandest suburb in Johannesburg, has witnessed the growing number of black inhabitants. The new black elite now live in their walled estates and in luxury homes with a BMW in the driveway. Their children go to the middle-class mixed-race state schools or to the best private schools. These 'Black Diamonds' are categorised as educated, professional African workers who earn at least R7500 a month. They now number about 4 million and make up nearly a third of the country's buying power. Black Diamond women now represent 45 per cent of all female consumer spending power.

Figure 3.9 A 'Black Diamond', one of South Africa's new black elite

The coloured and Asian community

As stated previously, the coloured community is now the second largest racial group in South Africa (see Table 3.1). Eighty-five per cent of the 4.7 million coloured people live in the Western Cape, especially around Cape Town, and in the Northern Cape. The majority speak Afrikaans and many feel that they are being ignored by successive ANC governments and that their lives have not improved since 1994.

Many of the 1.3 million South African Indians have established themselves as successful business people, traders and professionals. Their economic and educational success over the last 40 years and their strong cultural beliefs have at times brought them into conflict with the African majority. In 2002, an African playwright wrote a song called 'Amandiya', which urged Africans to rise against the Indian community. The Indian and coloured communities feel that the policy of Affirmative Action discriminates against them: 'Under apartheid we were not white enough, now we are not black enough.'

What progress has been made with Transformation since 1994?

Distribution of income

Despite declining poverty levels and sustained economic growth, national income inequalities have not reduced. The GINI international index, which measures wealth inequalities (scale 0–1, where 0 means everyone is equal: see page 128), has increased from 0.63 in 1995 to 0.64 in 2013. The gap between the rich and poor in all race groups has grown since 1994. The richest 4 per cent of South Africans, a quarter of whom are black, now earn a hundred times more than the average person.

The growth in inequality is linked to the emergent black middle class and growing unemployment among the lower deciles of the black population.

A growing black middle class

- The emergent black middle class is the largest component in an increasingly multiracial national middle class.
- The public service has made substantial progress in achieving employment equity goals.
- Black representation in the public services increased from 76 per cent in 1995 to 90 per cent in 2012.
- In the private sector, white South Africans still hold 60 per cent of senior posts.
- Among the 295 companies listed on the Johannesburg Stock Exchange (JSE), black people comprise 45 per cent of directors.

Show your understanding

1 What is GEAR? Outline its achievements and criticisms.
2 What is Affirmative Action and why was it introduced?
3 Describe the main features of the Employment Equity Act.
4 Outline the achievements and criticisms of BEE.
5 What evidence suggests that social class rather than race is the main cause of wealth and poverty in South Africa?

Tackling poverty

The 2014 Presidency Report concluded that income poverty has declined in South Africa over the last 15 years and that there has been a significant decline in child poverty. The proportion of households living below the poverty line stands at 37 per cent compared with 53 per cent in 1996.

Social grants have played a critical role in this regard. In 1999, 2.5 million people benefited from grants. By 2013, this figure had risen to over 15 million. The social grants system is the largest form of government support for the poor. The two provinces with the highest number of social grant recipients are Eastern Cape (42.0%) and Limpopo (40.1%). The dependence on the ANC Government is astounding – almost 44 per cent of households rely on welfare payments to make ends meet.

South Africa is proportionally one of the world's biggest spenders on social grants and uses about 12 per cent of total government spending on social protection. President Zuma is considering increasing the eligible age for the child support grant to 18 years of age, subject to affordability.

Despite the decrease in the number of poor people, the report found a widening inequality gap in the country:

'While many poor South Africans were lifting themselves from abject poverty, the rich in South Africa, especially the new black middle classes, were getting richer.'

Education

Under Mbeki and Zuma much has been done to improve the horrendous legacy of African education from the time of apartheid. The Government is aware that education and training are crucial for the creation of economic prosperity. There is a shortage of skilled and highly educated black South African workers, yet an abundance of poorly educated, unskilled black South Africans who face a lifetime of formal unemployment.

In 2014, the Government invested 21 per cent of the entire budget in education. At over 6 per cent of the country's GDP, this is one of the highest rates in the world. Yet while much has been achieved, such as the introduction of the 'Mandela sandwich' (free school lunch), there are still major shortfalls. Fighting the culture of non-attendance and resistance to learning, the pressures caused by population growth, and the legacy of apartheid in terms of provision of resources between the races is a long uphill struggle, but one that is essential to enable South Africa to end poverty, unemployment and illiteracy among its people. Another major problem is the incompetence of many of the officials employed in provincial education departments. Appointment is not based on merit but on racial quotas (see pages 95–6). Again, corruption is a major issue.

South Africa's education system

South Africa has a single national Education Department and system. Provincial legislatures and local governments have substantial powers to run educational affairs (excluding universities and technikons – further education colleges) subject to a national policy framework.

Figure 3.10 **Inequality is still a problem in South Africa's school system**

The South African Schools Act, 1996, ensures that no state schools are racially segregated. While former white schools now take in pupils of all races, many former black South African and disadvantaged schools have no white pupils and have the highest number of matriculation failures. The Act also provided compulsory education for learners between the ages of 7 (Grade 1) and 15 (Grade 9). The first year of education, Grade R, and the last three years are not compulsory. From Grade 10 to Grade 12, students either attend school or engage in Further Education and Training (FET).

South Africa's education system accommodates more than 14 million learners and there is a sizeable and growing private sector. National norms and standards for school funding have

Table 3.4 **Percentage of population with no schooling, selected provinces, 1996 and 2013**

No schooling	Eastern Cape	Western Cape	Mpumalanga	Gauteng	Limpopo
1996	20.9	6.7	29.4	9.5	36.9
2013	10.2	2.0	12.8	2.7	14.2

Source: SA Department of Education

been set to address the inequalities between the races. Schools are divided into five categories based on needs: the poorest 20 per cent receive 35 per cent of the resources and the richest 20 per cent receive 5 per cent of the resources. Education is not free in South Africa for many pupils, and school fees are paid by parents. This explains why many pupils from the poorest communities – and those who are disadvantaged most in their quality of life – do not attend school. The Department of Education now exempts the poorest 60 per cent of schools (all black South Africans) from fees. However, provincial education departments do not always provide the poorest schools with the money to cover the non-payment of fees.

Matriculation results

The pattern of matriculation results (see Table 3.5), while highlighting significant progress since 2009, still reflects large inequalities in performance in spite of a more equitable allocation of resources across schools and provinces – clear evidence of massive regional inequalities that also cover wealth and health. The number presented for the exams in 2013 was

Table 3.5 **Percentage pass rate for Grade 12 Matriculation Senior Certificate**

Province	Pass rate	
	2009	2013
Western Cape	75.7	85.1
Eastern Cape	51.0	64.9
Gauteng	71.8	87.0
Limpopo	48.9	67.8

Source: SA Department of Education

654,723, the highest ever figure. However, many argue that standards have been lowered and so pass rates are now meaningless. Johnathan Jansen of the University of the Free State stated 'these pass rates are calculated at a base of 30 per cent in some subjects and 40 per cent in others'.

Modernisation of schools

Successive governments have made the upgrading of schools a priority and progress has been made in providing basic infrastructure within schools, such as electricity, water and sanitation (see Figure 3.11). However, as the situation in Eastern Cape indicates, much still needs to be done (see 'Crisis in Eastern Cape' box, page 101).

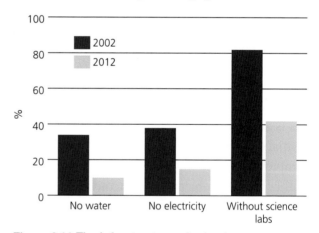

Figure 3.11 **The infrastructure of schools**
Source: National Education Management Infrastructure, 2013

Crisis in education

The Institute for Justice and Reconciliation (IJR) states that nearly 80 per cent of high schools are failing their children and that the overwhelming majority of children in the failing schools are black African. The IJR also states 'the best schools are those that were reserved exclusively for white children prior to 1994 and these schools today

Case study: Forte High, Soweto

Forte High School in the sprawling township of Soweto was once one of South Africa's ill-equipped and poorly performing schools. In 2007, it had no running water, no computers and no sports ground. Designed for 800 students, it had to cater for 1300. Only half of those who reached the final matriculation year gained the most basic certificate for finishing school. But thanks to new wealthy sponsors, a transformation has taken place. In 2012, the school achieved an 80 per cent pass rate and half of its matriculation students qualified for university.

An international charity, Art of Living Foundation, provided free food for the students as well as extra maths and science classes at weekends and during the holidays. One student who has flourished with this support is Albert Dove, a black student who lives with his unemployed and disabled father. He received six distinctions in his exams. He hopes to go to university to study science but is worried about the cost of fees. He stated 'I have enough food in my stomach so I will not go out and steal or go and gamble in the street … I will not smoke drugs to keep away the stress of having no food at home.'

should enrol the poorest children'. The standard of teaching is low. South Africa needs 25,000 teachers a year but only around 10,000 qualify. Maths and science teachers are especially in short supply. The IJR also argued that the 400 Dinaledi schools should be expanded as these schools were on the way to excellence. The Dinaledi project is a partnership between state schools and the business sector with the emphasis on maths and science.

Literacy and numeracy rates are low and these figures were confirmed in a 2013 report by the World Economic Forum. It ranked South Africa 146th out of 148 countries – and last in mathematics and science. National Planning Minister Trevor Manuel in his 2013 report indicated that the quality of schooling is sub-standard, especially in township schools. Violence (including rape of schoolgirls), pregnancy and poverty were factors in the high dropout rate in secondary schools. Teachers in black schools teach an average of 3.5 hours a day compared with 6.5 hours a day in former white schools.

Crisis in Eastern Cape

Examples reported in May 2013 included:

- Patumo Junior Secondary School, where there are 165 grade one learners in one classroom, with one educator and very few desks and chairs. In the whole school there are 14 toilets for 1175 learners.
- Ntapane Secondary School near Mthatha, where there is one tap for 835 learners, no sports field and no library, and where there are 100 learners per classroom.
- Nyangilizwe Secondary School in Mthatha, where 735 learners and 23 teachers share eight filthy pit toilets.
- Samson Senior Primary School in Libode district, where 235 learners are being taught in two mud huts and a nearby mud church, and where the nearest running water is 5 km away.
- Gwebityala High School in the Kotyana area, where there are 162 learners in one grade 10 class.

Despite ten years of struggle on the part of SADTU [the teachers' union], the problem of unpaid temporary teachers still prevails. The department remains under Administration, and while [the] Matric results improved in 2013, [Eastern Cape teachers] remain at the bottom of the pile with a 65% pass rate, compared to the national average of 78%.

Source: Zwelinzima Vavi, General Secretary, Congress of South African Trade Unions, speaking at the SADTU Eastern Cape Conference, East London, 8 July 2014

ICT task

See more on the crisis in Eastern Cape at:
www.cosatu.org.za/show.php?ID=9086

University and technikon students

Despite the shortcomings in attainment, a significant change has taken place in higher education. There is clear evidence of progress. Black South Africans now make up almost 70 per cent of university and technikon students. Under BEE legislation all higher education institutions must have equity targets to ensure that African students are not under-represented. White students argue that they are being discriminated against but can take no action as the Constitution supports 'Black Transformation'.

At the other end of the educational spectrum, the Government's Adult Basic Education and Training (ABET) programme has led to a steady increase in the literacy rate of adults, which now stands at 75 per cent. The Kha Ri Guide (Let us Learn) mass literacy campaign was launched in 2008. The Government pledged to spend R6 billion over five years to enable 4.7 million South Africans to achieve literacy by 2013. However, significant provincial inequalities remain. Provinces with the largest number of illiterates are KwaZulu-Natal, Limpopo and the Eastern Cape. The lowest numbers occur in the Western Cape and the Free State.

Show your understanding

1 Outline the impact of social grants.
2 Describe the South African education system and new exam reforms.
3 To what extent has progress been made in exam results, modernisation of schools and African entry to further and higher education?
4 What evidence suggests that South African education is in a poor state?

Health

Under successive governments significant progress has been made in improving primary health care (PHC) in both urban and rural areas. For those not covered by medical aid schemes, free health care is provided at public PHC facilities such as clinics and community health care centres. Some 40 per cent of all South Africans live in poverty and 75 per cent of these live in rural areas where health services are least developed. Regional inequalities reflect the urban–rural divide. Gauteng and Western Cape are highly urbanised and have the best health provision. Malnutrition is a major problem in rural areas alongside recent outbreaks of cholera in KwaZulu-Natal and tuberculosis in the Eastern Cape. Since 1996, 11 state-of-the-art hospitals have been built to tackle the poor hospital facilities available in provinces such as the Eastern Cape.

A key weapon against ill health and disease has been the availability of clean water. Over the last 15 years, 12 million South Africans have been provided with a clean water supply. As with other things, regional inequalities still exist in the percentage of households with no toilet facility. Child mortality rates double when there is no access to clean water.

There is a very strong private health service which inevitably reflects a racial imbalance in favour of white people and ensures that they have access to better health provision. The private sector spends R38 billion and serves 12 million people, while the public sector spends R38 billion and serves over 38 million people. At present hospital patients who do not have private health insurance pay for examinations and treatment on a sliding scale in accordance with their income and number of dependants. Those who meet the 'poverty criteria' have their fees paid by the provincial government.

State health provision faces severe problems. Under the previous president, Thabo Mbeki, state hospitals were under-funded despite the burgeoning AIDS epidemic (see pages 103–05). This was reflected in the low pay of state health care workers including doctors. Many health care workers have moved to the private sector or have gone abroad to countries such as the UK. This has led to staff shortages including 11,000 vacant doctors' posts and an estimated 50 per cent shortfall in nursing staff at the country's 386 hospitals. Health unions claim staff morale is low and that there is a shortage of vital medical equipment.

Table 3.6 **Doctors per 100,000 of the population, by province (selected), 2013**

Province	Doctors
Western Cape	38.0
Gauteng	36.0
Eastern Cape	13.4
Limpopo	11.2
North West	13.2

Source: SA Health Statistics, 2013

Primary health care

The primary health care programme offers a comprehensive range of services delivered by health professionals and associated organisations, such as school and nutritional services. Water and sanitation services, both of which have an obvious connection to health, are also included.

The strategy embraces health education, nutrition, family planning, immunisation, screening for common diseases, HIV/AIDS education and counselling, maternal and child health, oral health and the provision of essential drugs.

Projects such as the National Primary School Nutrition Project for needy primary school children have improved educational achievement as well as health standards. Every day about 6 million children in over 18,000 schools munch on a 'Mandela sandwich'. This has increased attendance at school and improved concentration and alertness levels.

Immunisation against tuberculosis, whooping cough, diphtheria, polio and measles is available free of charge to all children under the age of six. Such has been the success of this programme that South Africa has been declared polio-free by the Global Certification Commission.

Alongside the free health care programme for children under six and pregnant women, an impressive clinic building and upgrading programme has been implemented. Around 3500 primary health care clinics have been built and more than 700 mobile clinics set up, providing basic health care in the most remote and isolated areas.

HIV/AIDS

The one regret Nelson Mandela had of his period in office was his failure to tackle the outbreak of HIV/AIDS in South Africa (in 1994 2 per cent of those aged between 20 and 64 were HIV-positive). Unfortunately his successor, Thabo Mbeki, was very slow to react to the crisis. HIV/AIDS is the biggest health and social issue facing South Africa today and Mbeki was criticised, even by Nelson Mandela, for his failure to accept that AIDS is caused by HIV. For this reason Mbeki initially refused to give free anti-AIDS drugs to all HIV-positive pregnant women and their children.

In November 2001, a small group of AIDS activists, the Treatment Action Campaign (TAC), took the Government to the highest court of the land, the Constitutional Court, to force it to provide the anti-AIDS drug, Nevirapine, free to mother and child at birth. The Court ruled in favour of TAC and, in

October 2002, the Government announced that it would investigate ways of providing the anti-retroviral drugs that keep people alive – a dramatic reversal of policy.

TAC was especially critical of the then Minister of Health, Dr Manto Tshabalala-Msimang, who continually downplayed the AIDS epidemic and the use of anti-AIDS drugs. She argued that AIDS sufferers should use traditional remedies such as garlic and olives. In December 2009, Dr Tshabalala-Msimang died, and to the anger of many received an official state funeral. Dr Stephen Lewis, the United Nations' special envoy for HIV/AIDS in Africa until 2007, said that the policies of Tshabalala-Msimang and Mbeki were 'wrong, immoral and negligent, more worthy of a lunatic fringe than a concerned and compassionate state'. Independent studies from Harvard University claim that about 350,000 people died because of the delay in providing anti-retroviral drugs to AIDS patients.

Figure 3.12 Nkosi Johnson

'I want people to understand AIDS – to be careful and respect AIDS. You can't get AIDS if you touch, hug or hold hands with someone who is infected. Care for us, and accept us, we are all human beings, we are normal. We have needs just like everyone else. Don't be afraid of us. I just wish the Government would give anti-AIDS drugs to all HIV-positive pregnant women and their children.'

These are the words spoken by 11-year-old Nkosi Johnson at an International AIDS Conference held in Durban, South Africa, in July 2000. Nkosi had been born HIV-positive and abandoned by his mother. He was sent to a hospice to die. There he was adopted by a white woman, Gail Johnson, and he outlived both his parents (who died of AIDS). Within a year of speaking at the conference he was dead. Such was the impact he had made on the international community that his death was mourned around the world.

Fact file

AIDS pandemic: the present and the future?

- Life expectancy had dropped from 62 to 47 but has risen again to 59.
- Nearly 6 million South Africans suffer from AIDS.
- 35 per cent of deaths among pregnant women are caused by AIDS.
- Over 1 million children under the age of 18 have lost their mothers to AIDS.
- 600 South Africans die every day from AIDS.
- Almost 40 per cent of women aged between 25 and 29 are infected by HIV/AIDS.
- 500,000 people are infected each year.
- Racial divide – 13 per cent of black South Africans suffer AIDS, compared with 3 per cent of coloureds and Asians and 1 per cent of whites.

The National HIV Survey 2012 indicated that KwaZulu-Natal, Mpumalanga and the Free State have the highest HIV prevalence and that, among the races, Africans had the highest HIV prevalence (see fact file, left). According to government figures, 5.7 million South Africans suffer from HIV/AIDS and it is women in their mid- to late twenties who are the hardest hit.

The resignation of President Mbeki in December 2007 led to greater urgency in tackling the AIDS crisis through treatment and prevention. In December 2009, on World AIDS Day, President Zuma announced ambitious plans to expand the free treatment for HIV-positive babies and pregnant women by April 2010. Zuma had already appointed Dr Aaron Motsoaledi as his health minister, described by AIDS activists such as TAC as 'a man who trusts science and is willing to learn from past mistakes'. Zuma's Government had earlier set a target of getting 80 per cent of those who need AIDS drugs on them by 2011. Over 1.5 million South Africans now receive anti-retroviral drugs.

Table 3.7 **Life expectancy in South Africa (male and female), selected years, 1994–2013**

Year	Male	Female	All
1994	60.5	63.5	64.0
2002	50.0	55.2	52.7
2005	49.4	53.6	51.7
2013	57.7	61.4	59.6

Source: Statistics South Africa; General Household Survey, 2014

Show your understanding

1 Outline the progress that has been made in the provision of primary health care and other health improvements.
2 What evidence supports the view that health inequalities are a major problem? (Refer to regional inequalities and the role of the private sector.)
3 Why was President Mbeki criticised over his handling of the HIV/AIDS crisis and what action has President Zuma taken?
4 What evidence suggests that HIV/AIDS is the biggest health crisis in South Africa?

Land and housing

There is a distinct racial and urban–rural divide in terms of housing. The situation is not helped by an influx of people into the cities from the rural areas. Fifteen million people now live in RDP starter homes. The creation of an African middle class has led to a growth in the number of homes provided by the private sector. Between 2002 and 2012 the number of black property owners increased by just under 60 per cent, and over 50 per cent now own their own homes. Townships such as Soweto now have a middle-class area and a shopping mall. In the Diepkloof neighbourhood of Soweto new cars are parked next to elegant houses protected by security gates.

Spatial apartheid

In Cape Town there is a continuation of geographical or spatial apartheid. The majority of blacks and coloureds live in their own townships on the edge of the city or alongside dual carriageways, while most whites live in the wealthy suburbs. Government success in providing electricity, water and housing to the poor has had the unintended consequence of strengthening spatial apartheid by encouraging people to remain in their segregated communities.

In Johannesburg local officials are trying to break down this spatial apartheid by attempting to narrow the great distances between the black majority homes and the industrial centre. A stylish pedestrian bridge is being built that will link Alexandra township, where Nelson Mandela once lived, with Sandton, the city's wealthiest suburb, and also where massive shopping malls are located. The two areas are close to each other as the crow flies, but cut off from each other by a busy motorway. At least 10,000 people make their way between Alexandra and Sandton every day.

Progress has been made in providing basic amenities such as electricity and running water. The electrification programme has seen 3.6 million homes provided with electricity. The Community Water Supply Programme has brought clean water to over 10 million mainly rural homes. Unfortunately, a culture of non-payment of rents and amenities charges persists. The situation has not been helped by the privatisation of services, which led to an increase in charges.

A significant number of the new black middle class have moved into the former exclusively white areas. They live in mansions with spacious grounds or luxury apartments with controlled entry and security guards. In contrast, those black South Africans who live in informal settlements (squatter camps) have witnessed little progress since 1994. Their makeshift homes lack electricity and sanitation provision, crime is high and health is poor. Schooling is basic; many of the children do not complete secondary school and do not have the skills to contribute to or benefit from the BEE programmes. Gauteng and North West have the largest number of informal settlements. There has been a shift from rural to urban areas. Twenty per cent of people in the main urban areas are new migrants.

However, clear progress has been made since 2004. Then one household in eight had no toilet; now only 5 per cent are without a flushing toilet. The number of homes with electricity has increased from 77 per cent to 85 per cent. Two-thirds of homes now have their rubbish collected. Living standards have improved and this is reflected in 80 per cent of homes having a television, mobile phone and an electric stove.

Land reform

Land reform, especially in the countryside, is a major issue. A new Department of Land Affairs was created in 1994 with responsibility for developing and implementing a policy of land reform. The plan involves:

- compensating those who lost their land because of apartheid laws
- redistributing the productive land to those who were disadvantaged
- creating an independent Commission on Restitution of Land Rights as well as a Land Claims Court. Any claimant will have to prove that he or she was dispossessed after 1913 without financial compensation or alternative land being provided.
- setting up the Land Reform Pilot Programme to 'establish mechanisms for state-assisted entry into the land market for the most disadvantaged sectors of rural society'
- giving tenants the right to buy the land on which they farm and protection from eviction.

The original Reconstruction and Development Plan (RDP) promise of redistribution of 30 per cent of agricultural land within five years was totally unrealistic. The revised target date of 2014 was also not achieved. Black ownership of land increased from 13 per cent in 1994 to 20 per cent in 2014. Most people in urban areas prefer cash compensation to land redistribution. This, therefore, partly explains the limited increase in black land ownership. By 2014, all of the 80,000 land claims made by 1998 had been settled at a cost of R29 billion, including the transfer of 1.6 million acres benefiting 370,000 households. It was announced in May 2014 that there would be a reopening of land claims to run until 2019.

The 'willing buyer–willing seller' principle has been at the core of South Africa's land settlement, guaranteeing that land will be acquired by the state at fair prices and given to the landless black population. The Government has the power to force a compulsory sale if the white farmer rejects the original offer. This policy, despite its good intentions, has had an adverse effect on agricultural production. White farmers are reluctant to invest in improvements, while others have abandoned their farms. Agri SA, the white farmers' union, claims that about 700 of its members have responded to offers from neighbouring African states and are now farming in these countries.

Many white farmers are concerned about the brutal attacks on their farms and the lack of police action.

Crime

The fear and impact of crime is one issue that unites all races. While many white people and rich Africans seek safety in their walled estates, ordinary black and coloured South Africans protect their families as best they can. The availability of guns is a major problem. You can buy an AK47 rifle in any taxi queue for £30. On average, 47 murders take place every day. Of these, 26 are caused by guns.

Official government figures clearly indicate that South Africa is a less violent country than previously. The number of murders has declined by 30 per cent since 1994 – the 2014 figure was 17,068. The number of attempted murders has also declined from 30,076 in 2009 to 18,298 by 2014. However, this still represents 47 murders a day, making South Africa one of the most dangerous places to live. This figure equates to 37 murders per 100,000 South Africans. The Democratic Alliance argues that many crimes are not reported as the public have little faith in the culprits being caught. In a 2008 opinion poll, 57 per cent of the public believed that crime levels had increased. Crimes of rape and aggravated robbery at residential premises have increased and this explains the fear factor experienced by South African citizens.

Although the official figures show that the number of murders in South Africa has declined, it is nevertheless still a violent country (see page 108) and has the tenth highest murder rate in the

Case study: Why was there a crime explosion in South Africa after 1994?

- The dismantling of the rigid controls imposed by the security forces in the apartheid years has brought crime into the former white suburbs.
- The apartheid years created a culture of violence.
- The association of law enforcement and the rule of law with the apartheid regime have created a lack of respect for the police within the black community.
- The vast inequalities in terms of wealth in South Africa have created a 'war' between the 'haves' and the 'have nots'.
- Massive influxes of poor people from the countryside to the towns and the arrival of illegal immigrants (estimated at 4 million) from other African countries have created a group in society who ignore its laws.

South Africa's culture of violence and Oscar Pistorius

In September 2014, Oscar Pistorius was found guilty of the lesser charge of culpable homicide (manslaughter) for the death of his model girlfriend Reeva Steenkamp. He was given a five-year prison sentence. In February 2013, the world famous paralympic athlete had shot dead his girlfriend. He blamed South Africa's culture of violence for his actions. He said he was afraid that it was an intruder who might murder the couple.

Pistorius and Reeva Steenkamp were staying in a gated community in Cape Town, surrounded by an electric fence and high walls, yet he still

Figure 3.13 Oscar Pistorius

did not feel safe. The former wife of the last white president of South Africa, F.W. de Klerk, was shot dead in a similar well-protected gated community.

world. Many citizens do not trust the police and in fact the police officer initially in charge of investigations against Pistorius (see box above) is being investigated on a charge of murder (see 'Police brutality and corruption' box, page 109). For wealthier citizens, protection comes from private security firms and life in gated communities. For the majority of blacks, the threat of violence is constant and many vigilante groups dispense their own punishment to criminals, ranging from beatings to killings. In 2012, Andile Mtsholo was beaten, stabbed and 'necklaced' by Khayelitsha residents in a vigilante attack. No arrests have been made.

Police crime statistics, 2014

While the number of official murders had decreased by 9.2 per cent over the past ten years, 2013–14 figures displayed a substantial increase of 5 per cent. In absolute numbers, 17,068 people were murdered in South Africa between April 2013 and March 2014; this compares to 16,259 murders in the previous year and shows that 809 more people were murdered than in the previous year. South Africa's murder rate increased from an average of 45 murders per day to 47 murders per day.

Crimes relating to personal safety and business, such as house robbery, business robbery and carjacking increased overall by 10.8 per cent. Carjackings alone increased by 12.3 per cent, while truck hijackings recorded a 12.1 per cent increase, robbery showed a 13.7 per cent increase, while robbery in residential areas increased by 7.4 per cent. Property-related crimes increased by 1.7 per cent between 2009 and 2013 but slightly reduced by 0.2 per cent during the past financial year.

Source: adapted from the South African Institute for Security Studies Report, 22 September 2014

Police brutality and corruption

Reports of police brutality in South Africa have soared by 313 per cent in a decade, according to experts, yet only one in 100 cases against officers results in a conviction. There were 720 deaths in police custody or as a result of police action in 2011–12.

A series of high profile cases, including the shooting of striking mineworkers at Marikana and the killing of a Mozambican taxi driver dragged behind a police van, have left the reputation of the police service in tatters. Cases of police brutality leapt from 416 during 2001–02 to 1722 by 2011–12.

Gareth Newham of the ISS's Governance, Crime and Justice Division, said a total of 11,880 criminal cases were opened with the Independent Police Investigative Directorate (IPID) up to 2012. But this resulted in just 2576 prosecutions and 129 convictions, meaning that only 1 per cent of criminal cases opened against police officials end in a conviction.

'Police misconduct is met with impunity,' Newham said. 'The most likely outcome of a case against the police is no outcome.' This undermines the morale and public trust in the many honest police officers who do their work professionally and within the rules, he added.

The public is also paying the price through taxes. Police are facing civil claims valued at more than R840 million (£52m) in relation to assault, and R1.1 billion (£68m) in relation to shooting incidents. Total claims against the police have doubled in the past two years to R14.8 billion (£920m).

Newham highlighted figures showing that 1448 police employees have convictions for serious crimes, ranging from murder to rape. 'Why are convicted criminals allowed to continue to serve in the organisation responsible for law and order?' he asked.

The police budget increased 222 per cent to R66.7 billion (£4.15bn) over the ten years between 2003–04 and 2013–14, Newham said. The number of police personnel increased by more than 50 per cent, or 67,035 posts, during the period 2002–03 to 2011–12.

Low pay and morale, the daily risks involved in fighting violent crime and the recent 'militarisation' of the police, introducing army-style ranks and encouraging a 'shoot to kill' policy, have all been blamed for the country's culture of police brutality. The two previous police commissioners have been sacked for alleged corruption and the present police commissioner, Ms Phiyega, is an ANC appointee with no prior experience of policing.

Source: adapted from the South African Institute for Security Studies, 17 September 2014

Case study: The Marikana massacre

On 16 August 2012, the police shot dead 34 striking miners at Lonmin Mine, a platinum mine near Marikana in North West province. Archbishop Tutu, Nobel Peace Prize Laureate, summed up the shock of the nation when he said 'We thought we were having a nightmare … it was us in 2012 in our democracy.' Further disbelief grew after the National Prosecutor charged 259 miners with the murder of their colleagues, citing a 'Common purpose' law used by the white apartheid government. Under public pressure this charge was dropped, but it highlighted the political interference of President Zuma in the judicial process.

⇨

Case study (continued)

President Zuma commissioned an inquiry into the shooting to be headed by former Supreme Court of Appeals Judge Ian Gordon Farlam to 'investigate matters of public, national and international concern arising out of the tragic incidents at the Lonmin Mine in Marikana'.

What is clear is that the video and photographic evidence presented contradict the police version that they only opened fire after the striking miners had fired on police units.

Figure 3.14 Striking miners in Marikana

Photographs clearly show some of the dead miners on the ground without weapons at their sides; in the police photographs they are holding weapons.

The Marikana Support Campaign firmly places the responsibility for these murders on political interference and collusion between the state and Lonmin. It stated, 'The most central figure in this collusion is none other than the Deputy President of our country, and Lonmin shareholder and previous non-Executive board member, Cyril Ramaphosa.' The deputy president wrote in a string of emails:

'The terrible events that have unfolded cannot be described as a labour dispute. They are plainly dastardly criminal and must be characterized as such. In line with this characterization there needs to be concomitant action to address the situation.'

The inquiry completed its evidence in December 2014. The final report will be presented to the president in April 2015.

Added Value idea

The investigation into the deaths of miners in the Marikana massacre is hugely topical. This would be a good opportunity for your Added Value unit assignment. You will need to research and develop your own sources and present your findings in the form of report. Discuss this with your teacher.

Show your understanding

1 Describe the progress made in the provision of adequate housing and basic services in South Africa.
2 Outline the South African Government's policy on land reform.
3 Why has there been a crime explosion in South Africa?
4 What evidence suggests that serious crime is still a serious problem in South Africa?
5 What evidence suggests that the police in South Africa abuse their powers?

12-mark question

Evaluate the effectiveness of government policies to reduce social and economic inequalities.

The political system

The 1994 elections and the creation of a liberal, progressive Constitution transformed South Africa into a stable, multi-party democracy with all the features of a pluralist society including a free press and an independent judiciary. Five successive elections have been held and Nelson Mandela's dream of a rainbow nation has been achieved. The Truth and Reconciliation Commission (see page 91) has brought closure to the horrors of apartheid. Yet some fear that the dominance of the ANC and the corrupt activities of some of its members are turning the country into a one-party state where criticism of the government, especially when Mbeki was president, is seen as white racism or, if by blacks, as a betrayal of fellow Africans. Jacob Zuma's comment in 2008 that 'the ANC will rule South Africa until Jesus returns' horrified many South Africans for its arrogance.

While South Africa has on paper a federal system of government, the reality is that the central government totally dominates the provinces. Only in Western Cape is there an alternative to ANC rule; in 2009 the Democratic Alliance (DA) gained overall control of the province and retained control in the 2014 election. However, there is concern that the ANC will attempt to further reduce the powers of the provinces to weaken the power of the Western Cape provincial government.

The Constitution of South Africa

The Constitution includes a Bill of Rights which guarantees an extensive range of human rights. This includes equality before the law, the right to life including the abolition of the death penalty, and freedom of speech and religion.

The Constitution provides for an independent judiciary. The Constitutional Court is the highest court in the land. It deals with the interpretation, protection and enforcement of the Constitution and exclusively with constitutional matters. The Constitutional Court plays a crucial role in upholding the rights of the citizens of South Africa. There are 11 judges including the Chief Justice. One of its most recent decisions was to uphold the right of South African citizens living abroad to vote in national elections.

The Constitution makes clear reference to the need to address the inequalities created by apartheid. Article 9.2 states 'To promote achievement of equality, legislative and other measures designed to protect or advance persons or categories of persons disadvantaged by unfair treatment may be taken.'

Central government

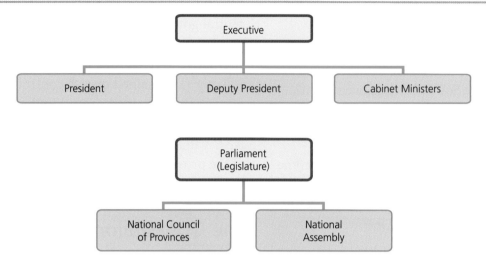

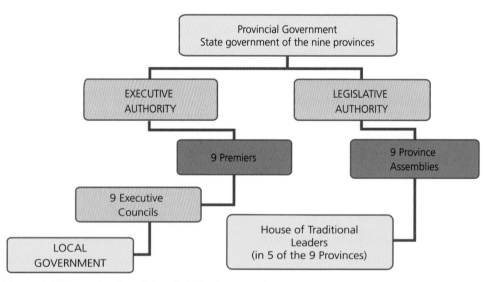

Figure 3.15 **Organisation of South Africa's central and provincial governments**

Parliament

South Africa has a bicameral (two-chamber) parliament consisting of a National Assembly (400 members) and the National Council of Provinces (NCOP). The council has two roles, both as an upper house and also as a body with special responsibilities to protect provincial interests. The NCOP consists of 90 delegates (ten from each province) and ten delegates representing local government. Elections for both houses are held every five years based on a system of proportional representation (PR).

Figure 3.16 **The South African Parliament in Pretoria**

The president and the Cabinet

The president is elected by the National Assembly from among its members. He or she is the executive head of state and leads the Cabinet. The president may not serve more than two five-year terms in office.

The present Cabinet consists of the president, the deputy president and 36 ministers (with 37 deputies). The significant increase in the Executive is part of Zuma's strategy to keep his supporters happy and loyal. The president appoints the deputy president and ministers, and may also dismiss them. Thabo Mbeki sacked Jacob Zuma as deputy president in 2005. However, Zuma's supporters forced Mbeki to resign in 2008.

Table 3.8 **Presidents of South Africa, 1994–2018**

President	Terms of office
Nelson Mandela	1994–99
Thabo Mbeki	2000–08 (forced to resign)
Kgaleme Motlanthe	2008–09
Jacob Zuma	2009–present

Law making

Legislation may be introduced in the National Assembly only by Cabinet members, deputy ministers or a member of a National Assembly committee. Bills amending the Constitution require

a two-thirds majority vote in favour in the National Assembly as well as a supporting vote of six of the nine provinces represented in the NCOP. Any bill amending Section 1 of the Constitution, which sets out the state's founding values, requires a 75 per cent majority vote in the National Assembly.

Provincial government

All nine provinces have their own legislature and government led by a premier. In 2014, eight of the nine premiers were appointed by Jacob Zuma. This ensures that the ANC leadership controls the provincial parties and weakens the powers of the provincial governments. Provincial constitutions and laws must correspond with the National Constitution as confirmed by the Constitutional Court. Provinces have legislative powers over agriculture, cultural affairs, education (except higher education), environment, health services, housing, local government, police, welfare services, and urban and rural development.

Local government

There are 283 local councils, which are referred to as municipalities, and large cities such as Cape Town and Johannesburg have their own

The South African Constitution:

Maintains unitary government. The Constitution of South Africa shall provide for the establishment of one sovereign state, a common South African citizenship and a democratic system of government committed to achieving equality between men and women and people of all races.

Supports cultural identity. The diversity of language and culture shall be acknowledged and protected, and conditions for their promotion shall be encouraged.

Offers limited powers to the provinces. The powers granted to the provinces are to be used to improve the well-being of their inhabitants in accordance with the policies and priorities of the national government.

metropolitan municipalities. The Zuma Government is at present reviewing the role of local government as many municipalities are failing to deliver basic services.

Participation opportunities

Apart from voting and being a member of a political party, South Africans can join pressure groups including trade unions and community groups. One pressure group, Section 27, is taking the Government to court for failing to deliver school textbooks.

Unfortunately, many local groups have lost confidence in their politicians and resort to illegal protests that in many cases become violent. Virtually every day in South Africa a violent protest occurs, especially in the townships denied the amenities promised by the Government. For example, in August 2013 residents in the informal settlement of Randfontein in Gauteng barricaded roads with burning tyres in protest at the lack of running water, electricity and sanitation, forcing the police to move in. In February 2014, the Dangerous Weapons Act came into effect, which prohibits the carrying of firearms, and other weapons such as spears and axes.

Many South Africans do not trust the police, and events such as the Marikana massacre of 2012 reinforce the view that official trade unions are there to serve the ANC and not the people. Workers are becoming disillusioned with the ANC-dominated unions. The leaders of the National Union of Mineworkers (NUM) receive a salary from mining companies. It was the breakaway union AMCU that organised the mining strikes across South Africa, including Marikana. It is ironic that the former leader of the NUM, Cyril Ramaphosa, is now a millionaire and deputy president (see page 96).

Political parties

African National Congress (ANC)

The ANC dominates South African politics and is the party of Nelson Mandela and black liberation. It has won all five of the national elections and in 2014, despite the cloud of corruption hanging over President Zuma, it won over 60 per cent of votes and 249 seats. Africans, especially the poor and poorly educated, remain loyal to the ANC.

Democratic Alliance (DA)

With the dissolution of the discredited Nationalist Party after the 2009 election, the DA leads the opposition to the ANC. It is the second largest party, with 89 seats, and in the 2014 election it

retained control of the Western Cape. The DA has increased its support in every general election. Its main supporters are whites, people of mixed race and Asians. It now has the support of a growing number of middle-class African voters.

Economic Freedom Fighters (EFF)

Julius Malema, the former ANC Youth leader, formed EFF in October 2013 and gained an impressive 6.4 per cent of the votes in the

2014 election. EFF won the support of the far left and young disillusioned and poor Africans. It advocates nationalisation of the mining sector, the doubling of public expenditure and land redistribution without compensations.

Inkatha Freedom Party (IFP)

The IFP, led by Chief Buthelezi, draws its support largely from Zulu-speaking South Africans and wants greater powers to be given to the provinces. It is a party in decline and it lost heavily to the ANC in the 2009 elections in Kwazulu-Natal. In the 2014 national election the party won only ten seats.

National Freedom Party (NFP)

Zanele KaMagwaza-Msibi and other former IFP members set up the NFP in 2011. This weakened

the IFP further. The NFP won six seats in the 2014 national election and in the provincial elections in KwaZulu-Natal it gained six seats.

United Democratic Movement (UDM)

The UDM was formed in 1997 and has witnessed a steady decline since the 1999 elections. Its leader is a former member of the ANC, Bantu Holomisa. Its power base is the Eastern Cape where it came third in the 2014 provincial elections. It retained its four seats in the national elections.

Congress of the People (COPE)

This was a new political party formed in 2008 by former Xhosa members of the ANC who had supported Thabo Mbeki. It came third in the 2009 elections but failed to win enough black support to challenge the ANC. It is now a divided party and in decline with only three MPs after the 2014 elections.

Elections

National elections are held every five years under the National List proportional representation system which closely matches votes to seats won by a political party. It encourages the formation of new parties: four new political parties contested the 2014 elections for the first time – NFP, EFF, Agang SA and African Independent Congress. However, this weakens the formation of a strong opposition as new parties divide and weaken the opposition to the ANC. The use of a party list means that the loyalty of ANC MPs is to the party and not to the people as there are no constituency links to the electorate. Many Africans do not choose to vote for the ANC based on their policies or their record, but base their support on their loyalty to the party of liberation and now to the memory of Nelson Mandela.

Voting turnout of those who were registered to vote in 2014 was a healthy 73.4 per cent, down from the 77.3 per cent of the 2009 national elections. But this figure excludes the millions who failed to register. And just under a third of those aged 18–19 – the 'born-free' generation – voted.

The 2009 national election

The 2009 election was a personal triumph for the ANC leader, Jacob Zuma. Despite being acquitted of rape and facing numerous accusations of corruption, he and his party won almost 66 per cent of the votes. The best result was in Kwazulu-Natal where Zuma used his Zulu heritage against the Inkatha Freedom Party. The IFP could no longer cast itself as the guardian of Zulu culture and the ANC as a group of Xhosas (previous ANC leaders Mandela and Mbeki were from the Xhosa tribe) out to destroy Zulu culture. In 1994, the IFP received 1.8 million votes in KwaZulu-Natal; in 2009 it received only 780,000. The ANC had lost votes in all of the other eight provinces, but KwaZulu-Natal was the exception: Zuma's '100 per cent Zulu Boy' campaign had sunk the IFP.

Figure 3.17 **Helen Zille, leader of the Democratic Alliance**

The Democratic Alliance (DA) further increased its support to 17 per cent of the national vote and achieved an outstanding victory in the Western Cape. Its leader, Helen Zille, continually reminded voters of past allegations of corruption and racketeering against Zuma and denounced the ANC as presiding over a 'failed state'. The DA had widened its racial support from white South Africans to embrace the coloured and Indian communities of the Western Cape. The Indian community switched its support from the (Asian) Minority Front to the DA. Helen Zille declared that 'The Western Cape is leading South Africa towards democracy. The voters here have shown the nation that democracy is not just about the right for everybody to vote, but about the regular change of government through the ballot box.' She further declared that 'the DA is the most non-racial party in South Africa'. Prior to the 2014 elections, the DA had hoped to nominate the former black activist Mamphela Ramphele as its presidential candidate. However, the deal quickly collapsed due to disagreements over the fate of Ramphele's party, Agang SA, in a merger with the DA.

The new party Congress of the People (COPE) gained 30 seats in the National Assembly and came second in four of the nine provinces, with its best result in the Eastern Cape where it gained 13 per cent of the vote. However, the party that had been created as a result of dissent within the ANC quickly descended into internal leadership squabbles. COPE also suffered from its links to former president Thabo Mbeki and his free-market policies.

The 2014 national election

As expected, the ANC won the 2014 national election with a clear majority – 62 per cent of the votes. Although it was the smallest majority the party had achieved in the five elections held since 1994, the victory was still impressive and displayed the affection still held for Mandela's party by the African population. Despite widespread ANC corruption, an economy with slow growth and massive unemployment, most Africans voted with their hearts and not their heads. About 44 per cent of households depend on welfare payments to make ends meet and the ANC has been criticised for using political rallies to give out state-funded food parcels to those who turn up. Turnout from the 'born frees' – those between the ages of 18 and 19, who had never experienced apartheid – was disappointing: just under 30 per cent voted.

The DA, with 22 per cent of the votes, achieved its best ever result and, more importantly, it retained control of the Western Cape and significantly increased its support in Gauteng – gaining 30 per cent of the vote. In total the DA won over 4 million votes compared to its previous high of just under 3 million in 2009. It is clear that the DA is widening its support to include educated and middle-class black Africans. The DA's control of the Western Cape

since 2010 has made it the least corrupt and most effective province. Its leader, Helen Zille, told Western Cape voters 'We have the lowest unemployment rate in the country, and the highest access to water and sanitation in South Africa and 78 per cent of our budget is redistributed among poor communities. This allows about 500,000 children to be provided with a meal every day and ensures that every child has a textbook for every subject.' In May 2015, Zille stepped down as leader of the DA.

The newly formed EFF became the third largest party with 25 MPs in the national parliament. Significantly, it came second in two of the poorer provinces, Limpopo and North West. With one million votes, EFF hope to win the further support of the unemployed and poverty-stricken citizens.

Julius Malema

The young leader of the EFF is a charismatic figure who preaches hatred towards white people and scorn towards the ANC's Black Diamonds. He was the leader of the ANC Youth League but was sacked by Zuma for his outspoken criticism of the ANC leadership. He taps into the anger and frustration of black youths who are experiencing an unemployment rate of over 50 per cent and who are trapped in a cycle of poverty and crime (they are ineligible for state welfare). His singing of 'kill the Boers' (Afrikaners) has been condemned as a hate crime by the courts and his demands that land should be taken from white people has encouraged further brutal attacks on white

farmers (see page 120). Helen Zille described him as a 'dictator in waiting'.

Figure 3.18 Julius Malema, leader of the EFF

Table 3.9 **National Assembly election results for the African National Congress (ANC) and Democratic Alliance (DA), 2004–14**

Party	Seats			Votes		
	2004	2009	2014	2004 (per cent)	2009 (per cent)	2014 (per cent)
African National Congress	279	264	249	69.9	65.9	62.1
Democratic Alliance	50	67	89	12.6	16.7	22.2

Table 3.10 **Election results for the province of Western Cape, selected parties, 2009–14**

Party	2009		2014	
	Votes	Seats	Votes	Seats
African National Congress	620,918	14	697,664	14
Democratic Alliance	1,012,568	22	1,259,645	26
Congress of the People	152,356	3	12,000	–
Economic Freedom Fighters	–	–	44,762	1
African Christian Democratic Party	28,995	1	21,696	1

Table 3.11 **Election results of parties elected to National Assembly, 2014**

Party	Votes	Per cent	+/–	Seats	+/–
African National Congress	11,436,921	62.15	−3.75	249	−15
Democratic Alliance	4,091,584	22.23	+4.65	89	+18
Economic Freedom Fighters	1,169,259	6.35	New	25	New
Inkatha Freedom Party	441,854	2.40	−2.15	10	−8
National Freedom Party	288,742	1.57	New	6	New
United Democratic Movement	184,636	1.00	+0.16	4	–
Freedom Front Plus	165,715	0.90	+0.07	4	–
Congress of the People	123,235	0.67	−6.75	3	−27
African Christian Democratic Party	104,039	0.57	−0.24	3	–
African Independent Congress	97,642	0.53	New	3	New
Agang SA	52,350	0.28	New	2	New
Pan Africanist Congress	37,784	0.21	−0.07	1	–
African People's Convention	30,676	0.17	−0.04	1	–

Show your understanding

1 Describe the main features of the South African Constitution. Refer to the Bill of Rights, an independent judiciary, a unitary government, limited power to the provinces and Article 9.2.
2 Describe the political structure set up by the 1996 Constitution. Refer to parliament, the president, the Cabinet and provincial governments.
3 Assess the impact of the 2014 elections on the four major parties.

The dominance of the ANC

In 2013, the ANC celebrated its centenary and 2014 marked 20 years of ANC rule. The ANC dominates South African politics and the South African people display intense loyalty to the party. The 'Triple Alliance' between the ANC, SACP (South African Communist Party) and COSATU (Congress of South African Trade Unions) remains solid despite criticisms of Mbeki and Zuma's free-market economic policies. The Triple Alliance supported Zuma in his power struggle against former president Mbeki. The latter was forced to resign as president in 2008, despite clear evidence of Zuma's corruption (see page 122).

However, there is tension between the ANC and COSATU. The Secretary General of COSATU Zwelinzima Vavi, who has been a vocal critic of ANC corruption, was suspended after stating that under Jacob Zuma's Government 'We are heading rapidly in the direction of a full-blown predator state in which a powerful, corrupt and demagogic elite of political hyenas increasingly controls the state as a vehicle for the accumulation of wealth.' Vavi quickly became the victim of a smear campaign that claimed he was part of a plot to overthrow the Government. The National Union of Metal Workers of South Africa (NUMSA) withdrew its support for the ANC in the 2014 elections. In retaliation, COSATU expelled NUMSA from its membership in November 2014. In March 2015 Vavi was expelled from COSATU.

As the former head of intelligence in the ANC, Zuma has placed his loyal supporters in control of the State Security Agency (SSA) in order to install a culture of fear in the ANC and to use the SSA to punish those who challenge his authority.

Jacob Zuma, 'The People's Man'

The president of South Africa is a controversial figure. For some he represents the unacceptable face of democracy, a man accused of massive corruption and of a lavish lifestyle, supporting his six wives and his 20 children. On the other hand, his humble rural background and his lack of formal education make him highly popular among the majority of black South Africans who are poor. He is a '100 per cent Zulu Boy' who offered hope to those who live in poverty. However, while Nelson Mandela brought out the best in the ANC, Jacob Zuma has brought out the worst.

Figure 3.19 Jacob Zuma

Opposition to the ANC

As discussed in the section on Elections, the National List proportional representation system encourages the formation of political parties, which can weaken the opposition. Aware of this fragmentation, opposition parties had discussed forming a multi-party group with a new name to contest the 2014 general elections. The parties involved were the Democratic Alliance (DA), the Independent Democrats (ID), the Congress of the People (COPE) and the United Democratic Movement (UDM). As expected the talks broke down. The ANC has tried to undermine the DA by calling Helen Zille a white racist. In return, opponents of the ANC might argue that ANC now stands for African/Nepotism/Corruption.

The Afrikaner community

There is deep anger and frustration among the Afrikaner community over the erosion of its culture, especially the Afrikaans language. Only one per cent of all schools in South Africa are now single-medium Afrikaans schools. Stellenbosch University and other Afrikaans universities have lost their status as Afrikaans-medium institutions. Dan Roodt, an Afrikaner journalist, stated, 'What nation-building really means in South Africa is the complete destruction of Afrikaans culture and the Afrikaner identity.' This frustration and anger led to the re-emergence of white, right-wing terrorist attacks. In 2012, five Afrikaners were each sentenced to 35 years in prison for setting off bombs and plotting to kill Nelson Mandela.

BEE legislation discriminates against poorly educated white people who cannot get jobs and about 10 per cent of white people live below the poverty line. White beggars are common sights in South Africa's towns and white squatter camps dot the cities. President Zuma has made conciliatory gestures to the Afrikaner community. He has acknowledged the existence of white poverty and has referred to the Afrikaner people as being the real white South Africans. He also appointed Pieter Mulder, the leader of Freedom Front Plus, to his Cabinet in 2009. In the Western Cape, Afrikaans is the language of the large coloured population as well as the Afrikaans-speaking white community.

However, President Zuma sang 'Shoot the Boer' at the ANC Centenary Celebration event in January 2012. He claimed that its use at the ANC Centenary was not intended as a hate speech, but rather to commemorate the struggle against apartheid.

Despite President Zuma's proclaimed intent, his singing of the song may be contributing to an increasingly hostile environment that threatens the safety of white South Africans. The number of murders of Boer farmers increased each month in 2012. Over 3000 white farmers have been murdered since 1994. The South African police have not made investigation and prosecution of these farm murders a priority, dismissing them as crimes by common criminals. The Government has disbanded the commando units of white farmers that once protected their farms, and has passed laws to confiscate the farmers' weapons.

In April 2010, Eugene Terreblanche, the leader of the paramilitary extreme Afrikaner group the AWB (Afrikaner-Weerstandsbewegig), was savagely murdered on his farm by two black farm workers. Terreblanche had consistently demanded the creation of an Afrikaner Volkstaat (homeland). After his murder, Pieter Steyn, one of the AWB leaders, stated 'All we want is a piece of land in South Africa where we can settle ourselves and call it our own and govern ourselves with our religion and laws.'

A recent outbreak of violent farm invasions has led to casualties among white South Africans. The farm invasions are also direct results of calls by EFF leader Julius Malema and his deputy, Ronald Lamola, for whites to give up their land without compensation, or face violence by angry black youths 'flooding their farms'.

Towards a one-party state or a successful democracy?

Chief Buthelezi once stated 'I am very worried … if we are not careful we are going to become a one-party state.' This worry is shared by many. One of the two provinces that offered an alternative to the ANC and a protection of minority rights, KwaZulu-Natal, is now under the complete control of the ANC after the 2009 and 2014 elections. Only in the Western Cape Province is there an alternative to the ANC.

To what extent is South Africa a successful democracy?

Table 3.12 **Arguments for and against democracy in South Africa**

Arguments for	Arguments against
1. South Africa is a stable model of democracy for Africa. There have been five peaceful elections based on PR. Over 35 political parties participated in the 2014 elections with 13 parties sitting in the National Assembly. The PR system encourages the formation of new political parties.	1. There is a fear that South Africa is becoming a one-party state. The ANC controls eight of the nine provinces. Only in Western Cape is it in opposition. The NNP merged with the ANC in 2004. The ANC has 249 of the assembly seats. In contrast, the official opposition, the DA, has 89 seats.
2. A peaceful transition from Mandela to Mbeki occurred. The power struggle between Mbeki and Zuma was resolved peacefully with the resignation of Mbeki as president in September 2008.	2. There is an issue of corruption with leading ANC members such as Tony Yengeni being sent to jail. Zuma was under investigation for eight years over charges of corruption. The charges were dropped in April 2009 in controversial circumstances.
3. South Africa has a federal system of government with powers divided between central and provincial governments. Local government structures provide local services. The Western Cape is controlled by the Democratic Alliance and this has prevented the ANC from totally dominating politics. Helen Zille, leader of the DA, called her victory 'a triumph for democracy'.	3. The federal system exists only on paper. Minority rights, such as Afrikaner and Zulu culture, are under threat. Zuma appoints all eight premiers of the provinces under ANC rule and there is a lack of democracy within them. The people do not directly choose the president or premiers of the provinces.
4. South Africa has a liberal Constitution guaranteeing freedom to its citizens. It provides for an independent judiciary. The Constitutional Court ordered Mbeki to provide drugs to combat AIDS. There is a free press and civil society able to criticise and monitor the actions of the Government. The success of the Truth and Reconciliation Commission highlights the openness of South African society.	4. Mbeki was intolerant of criticism. He accused critics of being racists and even attacked Archbishop Tutu. The policy of Transformation Politics could threaten the independence of judges and the rights of non-black South Africans. The South African Broadcasting Corporation (SABC) is regarded as being the mouthpiece of the ANC. Zuma could threaten the independence of the judiciary through new appointments to the Constitutional Court.

Corruption

Every country has its corrupt politicians and the dominance of the ANC in every walk of life inevitably provides opportunities for politicians and officials to enrich themselves. Standards of public auditing are abysmal and every year huge sums of public money are stolen. A recent report from South Africa's anti-corruption body, the Special Investigating Unit (SIU), said it had identified 400,000 civil servants who were getting welfare payments to which they were not entitled. Kgalema Motlanthe, a former deputy president, has stated that 'corruption was far worse than anyone imagines at all levels of government and too many ANC comrades regard election to public office as simply a chance to get rich'. President Zuma has promised to root out corruption but he himself had been accused of taking bribes from foreign firms when he was deputy president. His financial adviser, Schabir Shaik, was found guilty, but controversially Shaik was pardoned by the president in January 2010.

Under President Zuma, corruption has intensified. In 2010, South Africa was ranked 54 out of 183 countries on Transparency International's Corruption Perception Index (1 is the cleanest and 183 the most corrupt). In the 2013 rankings, South Africa had fallen to 72.

Millions for Malema, naught for the victims

This is an extract from the editorial of the South African *Sunday Times* which exposes the everyday actions of tenderpreneurs (see 'ANC corruption' box, page 123). Malema, who is no longer an ally of Zuma, is now under police investigation – a common fate for those who become Zuma's enemies.

Malema is accused of defrauding the Limpopo Department of Roads and Transport of millions of rands through their company, On-Point Engineering and the Ratanang Family Trust.

'It provides a rare window into the world of tenderpreneur corruption, which eats at this society's moral fabric and undermines its ability to deliver needed services and infrastructure to its citizens.

'It details how a shelf company was purchased one month before a tender for "goods and

services" was advertised, and falsely converted into On-Point Engineering, which claimed to be a "nine year-old company". According to the Madonsela Report "The reality was at the time of the submission of the bid On-Point had existed for one month, no employees, no assets or annual turnover."

How the scam worked?

The money the department paid On-Point was then moved to the Ratanang Family Trust, the sole trustees of which were Malema, his son and, later, his 84-year-old grandmother. The trust then paid money towards the purchase of a farm and the construction of houses.

The victims are the people who were supposed to receive "goods and services" and the honest bidders who were shafted by the corrupt.'

Source: adapted from the Sunday Times *(South Africa), 14 October 2012*

Tenderpreneur

This term is applied to those ANC members and supporters who get rich from government contracts or from accepting payments for awarding contracts. The Auditor General states that about 40 per cent of all government contracts have been awarded to companies owned by officials or

their families. An investigation in Eastern Cape in 2013 discovered that 80 per cent of government contracts had been allocated to officials or their families. Those who were investigated for suspected corruption include two ministers, the head of the police and the now leader of EFF, Julius Malema (see above and page 117).

ANC corruption

- A popular saying in South Africa is that there are two types of ANC politicians: those who were in jail and those who should be in jail.
- Many leading ANC leaders have been found guilty of corruption including Tony Yengeni, Chief Whip of the ANC, and Winnie Madikizela-Mandela.
- In January 2010, the wife of the Minister of State Security, Siyabonga Cwele, was arrested and charged with drug trafficking.
- In August 2010, the former chief of police and a senior ANC figure, Jackie Selebi, was jailed for 15 years for accepting bribes.
- Despite attempts to ban it, the media disclosed that President Zuma's state-of-the-art ranch mansion was costing the taxpayer R328 million (see 'Zuma's private home in Nkandla' below).
- Julius Malema owed the South African Revenue Services (SARS) more than R16 million by the time he was expelled from the ANC. By the age of 30, Malema, who has never worked, had become a very wealthy individual. (See *Sunday Times* extract on previous page.)
- Tshwane ANC regional secretary Paul Mojapelo's consulting company has received R75 million in contracts from the municipality between 2012 and 2014.
- President Zuma's daughter Thuthukile, at the age of 25, is the youngest head of a minister's office on a salary of almost a million rand a year. She was appointed in May 2014 without the post being advertised and her previous position was as a lowly public liaison officer.

Zuma's private home in Nkandla

In an official report leaked to the *Mail and Guardian* in December 2013, the full cost of Zuma's new private home was exposed. In total R328 million (about £20 million) of public money was used to build a house which includes a swimming pool, amphitheatre and cattle enclosure. In 2012, Zuma had told parliament that his family had paid for all of the building work except for the security features. In November 2012, a government edict forbade the publication of details of the Nkandla compound. Newspapers responded with defiance and splashed the house on their front page.

The judiciary and the media

Critics of those who argue that South Africa is now moving towards a one-party state highlight not only the democratic electoral system and the numerous political parties, but also the existence of an independent judiciary, a free press and active pressure groups such as TAC (see pages 103–104) and COSATU. They rightly claim that South Africa is not Zimbabwe.

Administration of justice

As highlighted on page 111, the Constitution grants judicial authority to its courts, which are independent and subject only to the Constitution and the law. The Public Protector, a body created by the Constitution, published a report in March 2014 that criticised Zuma's extravagance (see above). A court has ordered that Zwelinzima Vavi should be reinstated as leader of COSATU (see page 119). The

Constitutional Court has already played an important part in monitoring the activities of the Government (see availability of anti-AIDS drugs, page 103.

An issue of concern to many commentators is the future independence of the judiciary. The dominance of white judges in the higher levels of the judiciary, especially the Constitutional Court, has led to demands from the ANC that the judiciary must reflect 'the racial and gender composition of South Africa'. This campaign of white judge-bashing was witnessed in the trial of Schabir Shaik and during the investigations into corruption charges against Jacob Zuma when the judges were called 'white racists' by members of the Communist Party, which is affiliated to the ANC.

The decision in 2009 to drop all charges against Jacob Zuma again raised concern over the future independence of the judiciary. Helen Zille, leader of the DA, accused the Zuma Government of using the transformation of the judiciary (60 per cent are now black) as a smokescreen to control the judges. She stated 'It [the Zuma Government] wants a bench that is subservient to the racial ideology, policies and political control of the party-state.' Further concern was raised when Zuma stated, in a pre-election address, that judges were not gods, and he was accused of trying to undermine the independence of the judiciary. Desmond Tutu also criticised the appointment of a discredited Zuma loyalist, Menzi Simelane, to the post of National Director of Public Prosecution. In contrast, the respected advocate Jeremy Gauntlett was not appointed to be a High Court Judge in 2014. The reason given was that 'he lacked humility and judicial temperament': code words for being white and being independent of the ANC!

The media

South Africa has a thriving free and independent press with liberal newspapers such as *The Mail and Guardian* keeping a close and critical watch on the actions of the Government. (The newspaper was a fierce critic of the apartheid government in the 1980s.) The ANC has passed through parliament the Protection of State Information Act which will place restrictions on access to government information backed up by severe punishment of up to 25 years in jail. An ANC spokesperson stated that 'the media can be a serious obstacle to advancement'. In a democracy dominated by one party a free press is essential to highlight abuse of power by the Government. The former president of South Africa, F.W. de Klerk, stated in 2014 that the bill 'undermined the constitutional requirement that government is accountable, responsive and open'. Amnesty International referred to the so-called secrecy bill as being 'a dark day for freedom of expression'.

Television plays an important role in maintaining the culture and languages of South Africa. The impartiality and independence of the South African Broadcasting Corporation (SABC) is an issue of major debate in South Africa. Tony Leon, a prominent South African politician, has accused the SABC of 'becoming a virtual propaganda arm' of the ANC. COPE also complained that the SABC failed to provide live coverage of its final rally before the 2009 elections, and refused to accept that it had been a technical fault. Again in the 2014 general election, the television political broadcast by the DA was pulled off the air. The SABC claimed it violated the electoral code.

Show your understanding

1 Why is Jacob Zuma a controversial politician?
2 Describe the division within the ANC between 2005 and 2009 and outline the outcome.
3 What is the Triple Alliance and why is there tension within it?
4 Explain why the Afrikaner community feels threatened by the ANC.
5 Why is the future of the IFP bleak? (Refer to pages 92, 115 and 118.)
6 With reference to Table 3.12, outline the arguments for and against South Africa being a successful democracy.
7 What evidence suggests that South Africa has a corruption problem?
8 Outline the role of the judiciary in South Africa.
9 To what extent is there a 'free' media in South Africa without government interference?

20-mark question

To what extent does the South African political system provide an effective check on its government?

International relations

Under the apartheid era (1948–94) South Africa experienced international isolation. It was suspended from the United Nations and from the Commonwealth. International sanctions were also applied by the world community. The international stature of Nelson Mandela ensured that the new South Africa that emerged in 1994 would play a leading role among the countries of the developing world and in international organisations such as the United Nations and African Union. South Africa is the dominant regional power in Southern Africa and is the only country in sub-Saharan Africa to be a member of the G20 group of countries, which includes the European Union. Further evidence of South Africa's global influence is its membership of the BRICS bloc (see page 127).

South Africa – the regional superpower?

A regional superpower is a country that completely dominates its neighbours in terms of population, military and economic strength and international influence. With one-third of the GDP of sub-Saharan Africa and two-thirds of that of the Southern African Development Community (SADC), the South African economy is the powerhouse of African development in this region.

The Southern African Development Community (SADC)

South Africa is the dominant nation within the SADC, which consists of 14 African countries (see Figure 3.20). The SADC is working towards regional integration in order to accelerate economic growth, reduce poverty and establish peace and security in a region with a population of over 250 million. The SADC's headquarters are in Gaborone, Botswana.

ICT task

Read more about the SADC at:

www.southafrica.info/africa/sadc.htm

Figure 3.20 **Map of the countries within the SADC**

Table 3.13 **Selected countries within the SADC**

Country	Population (m)	GDP per capita ($)	Literacy rate (%)
Angola	17.9	5,783	40
Democratic Republic of the Congo	75.2	315	75
Malawi	14.3	404	72
Mozambique	20.5	532	47
Namibia	2.1	4,315	87
South Africa	50.5	8,910	88
Zimbabwe	2.7	789	97

Source: www.southafrica.info

However, Nigeria is now challenging South Africa's economic dominance of sub-Saharan Africa. In April 2014, under revised GDP (Gross Domestic Product) estimates, Nigeria surged past South Africa to become the biggest economy in Africa, although based on population size South Africa's per capita is way above Nigeria's (see Table 3.14). Nigeria's internal problems and political instability, illustrated by the activities of the Islamist militant group Boko Haram, have exposed the weakness of the Nigerian Government and division in society. In August 2014, the South African economy was classified as being in recession.

Table 3.14 **Nigeria and South Africa: GDP growth and GDP per capita**

	Nigeria	**South Africa**
GDP growth	6.00%	2.50–3.00%
GDP per capita	$2,800	$8,910

South Africa, with its stable democracy and progressive Constitution and Bill of Rights, is rightly regarded as a beacon of democracy for its fellow African neighbours. The world image of many African states is one of corrupt government, tribal conflict and denial of human rights to its citizens. The recent tragic civil war in the world's newest state, South Sudan (see page 156), unfortunately reinforces this perception. South Africa's reputation as a successful democracy with a sophisticated economy attracts millions of immigrants from neighbouring states such as Zimbabwe.

South Africa is an active member of the African Union (AU). The AU consists of 54 African states and its role is to provide 'African solutions to African problems, to support economic growth and to achieve conflict resolutions between states'. Ms Dlamini-Zuma, a leading member of the ANC, was elected chairwomen of the AU Commission, highlighting South Africa's influence in the organisation.

South Africa has played a central role in seeking to end various African conflicts in Burundi, Democratic Republic of the Congo (DRC), Comoros and, more controversially, in Zimbabwe. Here, South Africa has been criticised for its failure to force President Mugabe to end his brutal persecution of political opponents. President Zuma's support for Colonel Gaddafi and his belated attempts to resolve the Libyan crisis was an embarrassing flop. South Africa's peace-keeping activities in the Central African Republic were also a disaster with the death of 14 South African soldiers.

South Africa is also increasingly playing a role in post-conflict reconstruction and development and humanitarian affairs in the African continent and beyond. DRC, Sierra Leone, South Sudan, Somalia, Zimbabwe and Haiti have all benefited from technical expertise and financial support from the country.

The BRICS

The BRICS, which South Africa joined in 2010, consists of Brazil, Russia, India, China and South Africa, and plays an important role in the shifting and distribution of power internationally. The BRICS bloc represents 43 per cent of the world's population, approximately one-fifth of global gross domestic product (GDP). South Africa also sees its role in BRICS to promote the African Agenda. As a government minister stated 'Our belief is that the membership of South Africa to BRICS represents the 1 billion people on the continent of Africa.'

Obviously South Africa is hardly in the same league as its fellow members – it has a smaller economy and population (see below). But its inclusion brings to the group representation from all the developing-world continents (Latin America, Asia and Africa). The African branch of the planned BRICS development bank will be based in South Africa.

However, South Africa's strong ties with China have been criticised within South Africa (see page 128).

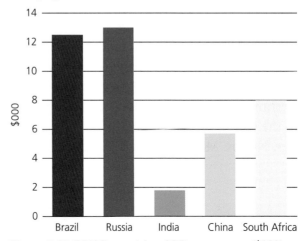

Figure 3.21 **BRICS countries GDP per person ($000)**

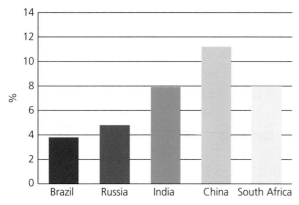

Figure 3.22 **GDP average annual growth (%), 2002–12**

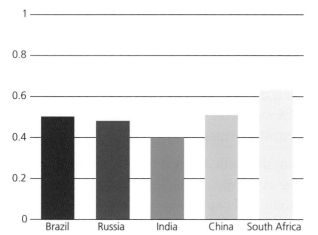

Figure 3.23 **GINI coefficient (Wealth inequality: 0 = everyone equal), 2012**

Source: IMF Euromonitor International, 2014

United Nations

South Africa was one of the original members of the United Nations when it was set up after the Second World War with its headquarters in New York. However, as stated earlier, it was forced to leave the UN because of the apartheid policies of the white South African Government. South Africa rejoined the UN after the end of apartheid and its new leader, Nelson Mandela, had significant international influence. Today, South Africa is an active member of the United Nations and was elected in 2006 and again in 2010 by the UN General Assembly to serve on the Security Council as a non-permanent member. However, South Africa has been criticised by the West for placing its loyalties to the countries of the developing world ahead of human rights issues. In particular, a 'no' security vote on a resolution criticising the Burmese Government, and South Africa's original intentions to vote against economic sanctions to be imposed on Iran, attracted widespread criticism.

However, South Africa argues that the USA and Europe have too much influence in the Security Council of the UN. President Zuma argues that 'the Security Council should be opened up. In other words, regions of the world should be represented in the same way. You have one region that dominates, the European Union.'

South Africa's close ties with China have been criticised by many South Africans. In October 2014, Archbishop Desmond Tutu attacked the Government for refusing a visa to the Tibetan spiritual leader, the Dalai Lama. In a statement, Tutu said that he was 'ashamed to call this lickspittle bunch my government'. The event was the 14th World Summit of Nobel Peace Laureates, which was to be held in Cape Town to celebrate the memory of Nelson Mandela, a former Nobel Peace Laureate. The meeting was cancelled as the other Nobel Peace Laureates refused to attend in protest and the summit was moved elsewhere. Economic interest and the desire not to upset the Chinese came before support for human rights and respect for Nelson Mandela.

Below is an extract from a South African Government website that highlights the international influence of South Africa.

South Africa's expanding global influence

In the space of just two decades, South Africa has gone from being an international pariah, shunned because of its apartheid policies, to being an influential player in world affairs and a powerful advocate for global political and economic reform.

This is according to the Government's 20 Year Review, a report reflecting on South Africa's progress in reconstruction and development since 1994, and on the challenges facing the country as it enters its third decade of democracy.

The report, released by President Jacob Zuma in Pretoria on Tuesday, notes that South Africa has sought to improve north–south relations while pushing for reform of the global economy and global governance, better market access for developing countries, more favourable terms for debt relief, and new forms of partnership for development.

Pushing for peace, global reform

The country has served on the United Nations Security Council for a two-year non-permanent term, become a member of influential emerging economy blocs BRICS and IBSA (the India, Brazil, South Africa Dialogue Forum), and is still the only African country on the G20.

To promote the interests of developing countries, South Africa has pushed for a rules-bound international political and economic order, and sought to transform north–south relations through dialogue while consolidating south–south collaboration by participation in groupings like the Non-Aligned Movement (NAM) and the UN Conference on Trade and Development (UNCTAD).

South Africa also works with other African states and multilateral organisations like the UN, African

Union (AU) and Southern African Development Community (SADC) to promote international respect for human rights, democracy and good governance.

It has helped Madagascar, Zimbabwe and South Sudan resolve their problems and assisted with peacekeeping in Ethiopia/Eritrea, the Democratic Republic of the Congo (DRC) and Burundi, among others.

The country has also hosted numerous major international conferences and events since 1994, including the Non-Aligned Movement Summit (1998), Commonwealth Heads of Government Meeting (1999), UN Aids Conference (2000), UN World Conference Against Racism (2001), World Summit on Sustainable Development (2002), and the UN Climate Change Conference (COP17) which delivered the landmark Durban Platform that rescued the Kyoto Protocol in November/December 2011.

The democratic South Africa has prioritised the development of political and economic relations with African countries. Since 1994, it has signed 624 agreements and established 40 bilateral mechanisms with countries on the continent.

Expanding, shifting trade relations

South Africa's export markets have changed considerably over the past 20 years, with new markets emerging at the same time as the country's share of exports to some traditional markets, such as the United Kingdom, Japan and Europe, have declined.

China has emerged as South Africa's most important export trading partner since 2009, with its share of non-gold merchandise exports measuring 12.9 per cent in 2012 compared with 0.8 per cent in 1994.

India is now South Africa's fifth-largest export destination, having overtaken both the United Kingdom and Switzerland, and African countries have also become increasingly important export markets, especially for manufactured goods. ⇨

'Exports to the entire African continent increased from 10 per cent in 1994 to 17.6 per cent in 2012,' the review states. 'SADC countries claimed most of these exports, accounting for 12.9 per cent of overall exports in 2012, up from 8.3 per cent in 1994. Africa accounts for around a third of South Africa's exports of more advanced manufactures.'

South Africa has also benefited substantially from the United States' African Growth and Opportunity Act of 2000 (AGOA). Bilateral trade between South Africa and the US grew from R15.9 billion in 1994 to more than R129 billion in 2013, with the trade balance in South Africa's favour.

Looking to the future

Looking forward, the report says South Africa's foreign policy should continue to be shaped by the interplay between prevailing diplomatic, political, security, environmental, economic and regional factors.

'It should remain cognisant of global power shifts, the stratification of regional groupings, threats to human and state security, internal and external sovereignty and natural resources, and the need to promote South Africa's national interests.'

The report notes that regional and continental integration are important both for Africa's socio-economic development and political unity and for South Africa's prosperity and security.

'The country will strengthen its support for regional and continental institutions that work towards achieving peace and resolving security crises, and it will take further steps to strengthen regional integration, promote intra-African trade and champion sustainable development on the continent.'

The review states that co-operation between state institutions that deal with international relations policy and cross-border issues should also be strengthened.

'Closer collaboration and partnerships between government, business, civil society and labour must be pursued to ensure that the country operates holistically in the competitive and unpredictable international arena.'

Source: SAnews.gov.za

ICT task

Read more about South Africa's expanding global influence at:

www.southafrica.info/news/international/20years-review1.htm

Show your understanding

1 To what extent is South Africa the regional superpower in Southern Africa?
2 Describe South Africa's involvement in the United Nations and in the BRICS bloc.

12-mark question

Analyse the international influence of a world power you have studied.

4 Development issues in Africa

Understanding 'development'

Throughout this chapter you will learn about the causes and consequences of a lack of development in Africa. Firstly, it is important to understand how we identify countries that are developed and less developed. It's not a simple process; a complex set of factors are analysed to determine a country's development status. There is no universal, agreed-upon criterion for what makes a country developed versus developing. There are general reference points such as a nation's gross domestic product (GDP) per capita compared to that of other nations. For the World Bank, a 'developed' country is one with a high gross national income (GNI) per capita. It then classifies countries according to their income level. But this doesn't tell the whole story – it doesn't give the distribution of wealth across a population like the GINI index attempts to do. The GINI index, or coefficient, is a number between 0 and 1, where 0 corresponds to perfect equality and 1 corresponds to perfect inequality (where one person has all the income and everyone else has zero income; the GINI index therefore measures the gap between the rich and the poor). The human development index (HDI), reported on in the United Nations' annual Human Development Report, attempts to draw on a wider vision of development, including measures of education, health and standard of living in countries across the globe. From our point of view as Modern Studies experts, the HDI is a better way to learn about a country's social, economic and political issues.

Overview

Africa is a continent of over 1 billion people. The population has grown rapidly from 220 million in 1950. In many African countries, particularly those south of the Sahara, more than 40 per cent of the population are under 15 years of age. Africa is made up of 54 independent countries; among these are 34 of the least developed nations in the world. Seventy per cent of Africa's population subsist on less than $2 a day, yet Africa is full of natural resources such as minerals, oil, land and sea ports. How can this be?

There is no simple answer. A complex combination of social, economic and political factors interact to impede development. Some of these factors operate outside Africa while others operate within. No one factor explains the situation. Natural disasters hit the headlines and

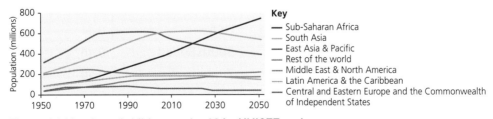

Figure 4.1 **Number of children under 18 by UNICEF region**
Source: UNICEF, 2012. Generation 2025 and Beyond

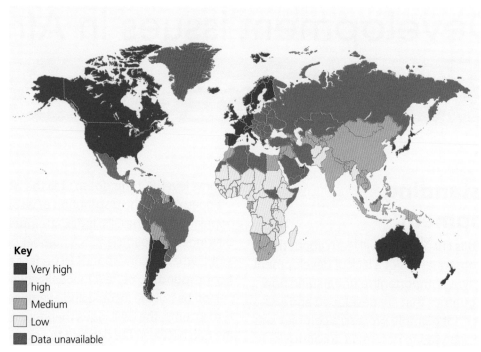

Key
- Very high
- high
- Medium
- Low
- Data unavailable

Figure 4.2 **Level of human development according to the UN Human Development Index by country, 2014**
Source: United Nations

lead us to believe that nature alone is the cause of the bleak situation facing many African people. Undoubtedly drought, flooding, crop failures and climate change play a major part in creating wide-scale food shortages, but unfortunately there are a plethora of other factors that blight the continent. A lack of democracy, widespread political corruption, a lack of basic infrastructure, and a history of colonisation all combine to cause the desperate situation in many African countries today. The inability of social, economic and political structures within a country to respond to the variety of problems is the key issue.

A comparison between the profiles of the African country Chad and the United Kingdom reveals stark contrasts and provides a vivid insight into the gulf that separates the industrialised developed world from the developing world (see page 135).

From Table 4.1 you can see that Chad, a developing country, has around the same level of inequality as the UK. This does not mean Chad is as wealthy as the UK, it means the gap between the richest and poorest in society is roughly the same. Relatively speaking, the difference between the poor in the UK and the poor in Chad is quite simply the ability to afford food and shelter and access readily available health and education provision.

Table 4.1 **GINI coefficient by country, 2014**

Country	GINI coefficient
Denmark	0.25
Norway	0.26
Germany	0.28
United Kingdom	0.37
Chad	0.39
USA	0.41
South Sudan	0.46
Zimbabwe	0.50
South Africa	0.63
Namibia	0.64

ICT task

Visit www.hdr.undp.org/en to access and investigate the latest UN Human Development Report.

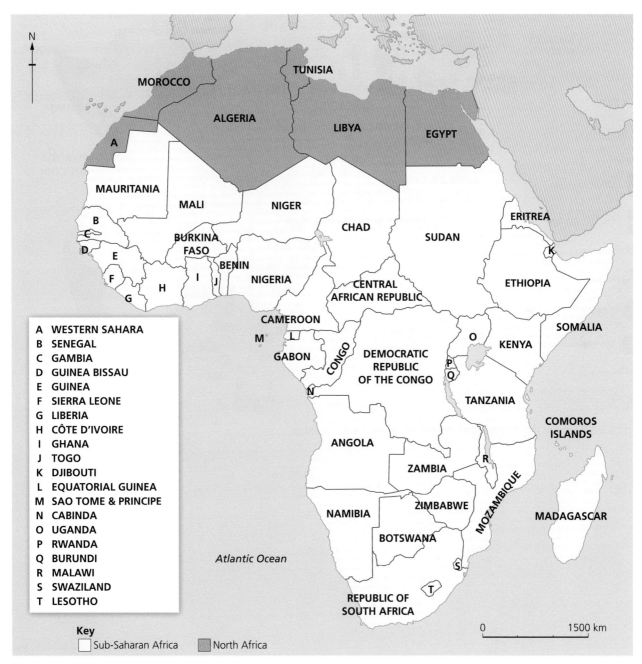

A WESTERN SAHARA
B SENEGAL
C GAMBIA
D GUINEA BISSAU
E GUINEA
F SIERRA LEONE
G LIBERIA
H CÔTE D'IVOIRE
I GHANA
J TOGO
K DJIBOUTI
L EQUATORIAL GUINEA
M SAO TOME & PRINCIPE
N CABINDA
O UGANDA
P RWANDA
Q BURUNDI
R MALAWI
S SWAZILAND
T LESOTHO

Key
Sub-Saharan Africa North Africa

Figure 4.3 **Africa**

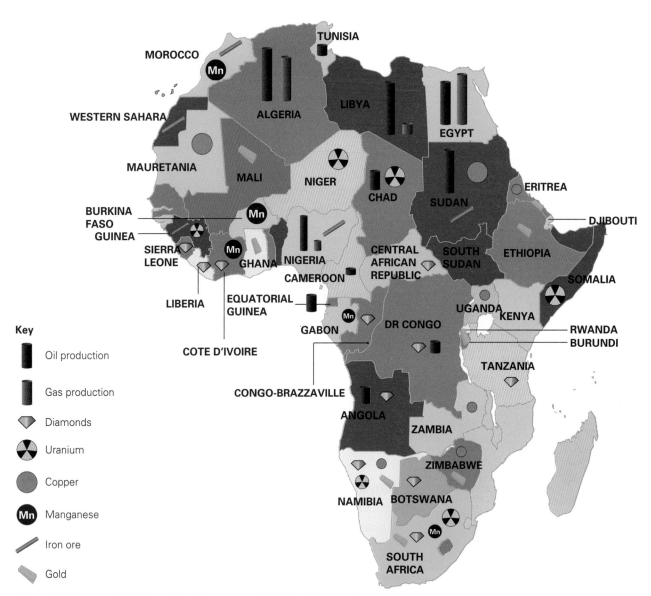

Key

Oil production

Gas production

Diamonds

Uranium

Copper

Mn Manganese

Iron ore

Gold

Figure 4.4 **Some of the key natural resources in Africa by country**

Profile of Chad

Population
12 million

Health
Life expectancy: 49 years
People with HIV/AIDS: 4.8%
Immunisation levels:

- TB 68% ● Polio 56% ● Measles 64%

Percentage of GDP* spent on health: 4.3%
Access to a clean water source: 50.7%

Education
Male literacy: 52%
Female literacy: 34%
Primary school enrolment: 52%
Secondary school enrolment: 16%
Percentage of GDP spent on education: 2.3%

Economy
**GDP per capita: $1035
Unemployment rate: 34%
Percentage below poverty line: 80%

Women
Risk of death in childbirth: 540 in 100,000
Infant mortality rate: 77 in 1000
Child labour rate: 48%

Profile of United Kingdom (UK)

Population
63 million

Health
Life expectancy: 79 years
People with HIV/AIDS: 0.2%
Immunisation levels:

- TB 100% ● Polio 91% ● Measles 81%

Percentage of GDP spent on health: 9.3%
Access to a clean water source: 100%

Education
Male literacy: 100%
Female literacy: 100%
Primary school enrolment: 99%
Secondary school enrolment: 98%
Percentage of GDP spent on education: 6.2%

Economy
GDP per capita: $36,500
Unemployment rate: 7.2%
Percentage below poverty line: 16.2%

Women
Risk of death in childbirth: 12 in 100,000
Infant mortality rate: 5 in 1000
Child labour rate: 0%

*GDP is the total monetary value of all final goods and services produced in a country in a year.
**GDP per capita is an approximate total value of goods and services produced per person in the country, dividing the gross domestic product (GDP) by the country's population.
Source: United Nations 2014

Show your understanding

1. What are the various ways we can determine a country's development status?
2. Describe the demographics of Africa.
3. Study the comparison between Chad and the UK. Outline some of the key differences.

Social, economic and political factors affecting development

In this section you will learn about the causes and consequences of a lack of development in Africa. Such causes, and indeed the consequences, are many and it is therefore better to understand them under social, economic and political sub-sections.

Social factors affecting development

Health issues

The causes of health-related issues in Africa range from debt and poor governance to a lack of education and infrastructure. No country in Africa has universal health care, never mind having health care that would rival the standard of our National Health Service. The UK spent £110 billion (roughly 10 per cent of GDP) on health care in 2014, with African countries such as Ethiopia, Kenya and Nigeria each spending between 4 per cent and 6 per cent of GDP. Health care in Africa differs widely, depending on the country and also the region – those living in urban areas are more likely to receive better health care services than those in rural or remote regions. Many communities lack clean water and proper sanitation facilities, particularly in rural areas. This means that illnesses caused by poor hygiene, such as cholera and diarrhoea, are common in some countries and can be life threatening without decent health care.

HIV/AIDS

There is an HIV/AIDS epidemic in Africa; HIV/AIDS is one of the three major killers in Africa. An estimated 25 million adults and children were living with HIV in sub-Saharan Africa at the beginning of 2015. During 2014, an estimated 1.5 million Africans died from AIDS. The epidemic has left behind approximately 11.6 million orphaned African children. HIV/AIDS is one of the biggest challenges confronting many African countries but some progress has been made. In the period 2002–12 life expectancy increased by 5.5 years due mainly to the dramatic scaling up of anti-retroviral treatment. However, life expectancy in many countries remains very low. Swaziland, which has the highest HIV prevalence in the world, has a life expectancy of just 50 years. Lesotho's situation is worse still at 48.7 years.

Table 4.2 shows current life expectancy of people in the countries in sub-Saharan Africa worst affected by the HIV/AIDS epidemic.

Table 4.2 HIV prevalence and life expectancy, 2014

Country	HIV prevalence (per cent)	Life expectancy (years)
Botswana	23	50
Lesotho	23.1	48.7
Malawi	10.8	54.8
Mozambique	11.1	50.7
Namibia	13.3	62.6
South Africa	17.9	53.4
Swaziland	26.5	50
Zambia	12.7	49.4
Zimbabwe	14.7	52.7

Fact file

HIV/AIDS in Africa

- At the height of the HIV epidemic in sub-Saharan Africa between 1990 and 2000, average life expectancy stagnated at 49.5 years.
- AIDS could slash the wealth of some African countries by as much as 20 per cent.
- 75 per cent of all people in the world infected by AIDS live in Africa.
- Half of all people with HIV become infected before they are aged 25.
- In some African countries, AIDS is the major cause of children being orphaned.
- Food is often the main need of poor families living with HIV/AIDS. Malnutrition increases as HIV progresses.
- Without good food, the anti-retroviral drugs used to treat the condition are not as effective as they could be.
- By 2020 it is estimated that HIV/AIDS will kill 20 per cent of southern Africa's farm workers.
- Education is the most cost-effective means of preventing HIV transmission.

Case study: Swaziland

In Swaziland, one in four adults are living with HIV. AIDS has spread through Swaziland at an alarmingly fast rate in the last 30 years and in 2014 Swaziland had the highest HIV prevalence in the world. As elsewhere in sub-Saharan Africa, the impact of so many AIDS-related deaths in Swaziland exacerbates existing poverty for families, and has resulted in a very youthful population. More than a third of the population are under 14 years old and only 5.2 per cent are over 65.

However, the problem is being tackled head on. Swaziland is one of just five sub-Saharan African countries to achieve the target of getting more than 80 per cent of eligible people on anti-retroviral treatment. Among pregnant women, treatment access is also high at 83 per cent. Consequently, the number of AIDS-related deaths in Swaziland is declining. More people are also coming forward to be tested for HIV, showing that people are less fearful of the stigma attached to the disease. The stigma of HIV has been a major issue in tackling the epidemic across the whole of Africa in the last few decades.

The consequences of HIV/AIDS

HIV/AIDS places huge burdens on societies in Africa. The vast majority of Africans living with HIV/AIDS are between the ages of 15 and 49, which is the prime of their working lives. The effects on the labour supply and the economy are dramatic, with employers, schools, factories and hospitals having to constantly find and train staff to replace those who have become too ill to work. For example, in some countries more teachers die of HIV/AIDS-related illnesses than are being trained. The HIV epidemic has had a severe and wide-ranging impact upon households in sub-Saharan Africa. Many families have lost their chief income earners, who have died or are too sick to work. This puts a heavy financial burden on families who have to pay ever-increasing medical costs, forcing many into poverty. In many cases, households simply dissolve because parents die and children are sent to relatives for care and upbringing.

Furthermore, the already limited medical services in African countries struggle to cope with demand as around 50 per cent of hospital beds in some countries have been given over to AIDS sufferers. Overall, the true impact and cost of HIV/AIDS on the economies of sub-Saharan Africa is difficult to measure. A country needs a healthy population to fuel the economy with their labour and HIV/AIDS certainly hinders this. However, clearly the social problems caused by the disease are immense.

Anti-retroviral treatment is not a cure for HIV, but it can stop people from becoming ill for many years. The treatment consists of drugs that have to be taken every day for the rest of someone's life.

Malaria

The World Health Organization's World Malaria Report in 2013 highlighted that one child died almost every minute from malaria in 2012. This amounted to around an estimated 483,000 children under five years of age. That is 1300 children every single day.

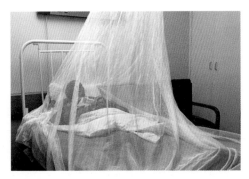

Figure 4.5 **An insecticide-treated malaria net will help to save lives**

Figure 4.6 **Children in an African classroom**

Malaria is an entirely preventable and treatable mosquito-borne illness. In 2013, 97 countries had on-going malaria transmission. Malaria thrives in hot temperatures that enable the parasite that causes the disease to mature more quickly in the bodies of the mosquitoes that carry it. Malaria is Africa's biggest killer and the consequences of malaria for African development are similar to those of HIV/AIDS. It is estimated that malaria accounts for economic losses totalling £10 billion per year among African countries.

However, malaria is preventable. When insecticide-treated malaria nets are used properly, malaria transmission is cut by 50 per cent, child deaths are cut by 20 per cent and the mosquito population drops by as much as 90 per cent. It is estimated, however, that fewer than 5 per cent of children in sub-Saharan Africa currently sleep under any type of insecticide-treated net. International targets for reducing malaria cases and deaths will not be attained unless considerable progress is made in the 18 most affected countries, which account for an estimated 80 per cent of malaria cases. About 40 per cent of malaria deaths occur in just two countries: Nigeria and the Democratic Republic of the Congo.

Education

Education transforms lives. Whether in Scotland or in Malawi, education is a route out of poverty and in to prosperity. In the same way, education

is vital to a thriving society. A society without education will become a breeding ground for violence and intolerance. An educated society will promote tolerance and peace, justice and understanding, innovation and advancement, and positive, self-fulfilment. Mass literacy across a population allows people not only to take part in society but to actively contribute to it. A fully educated population leads to development in other areas as well, such as improved health, economic growth, political participation and greater equality.

Unfortunately, the provision of education in many African countries is lacking. In a similar way to health care, education is a privilege. Public spending by African nations on education averages around 5 per cent of GDP but there is a lack of finance targeted at providing universal access to primary school for every child. This has resulted in 35 million children in the sub-Saharan region missing out on school completely.

From 1999 to 2009, Burundi brought the number of out-of-school children down from 723,000 to 10,000. Over the same period, Burundi increased its investment in education from 3.2 per cent of GDP to 8.3 per cent. But what made the real difference was the decision to dedicate a much larger proportion of the budget to primary education, effectively moving public money away from secondary schools and universities.

Nevertheless, it must be remembered that tight budgets and poor financial management have not been helped by a population boom that continues today. The children who do manage to make it through primary and secondary school will experience sub-standard facilities and resources. Schools find it difficult to employ qualified professional teachers, especially in rural areas. Class sizes are often upwards of 50 pupils and resources such as teaching aids and textbooks are limited.

Brain drain

Those who attain a high level of education in Africa often choose to emigrate to more prosperous countries such as Britain. This is often referred to as a 'brain drain' of the country concerned. Brain drains cause countries to lose valuable professionals such as doctors, scientists and engineers. When these people leave, their country is harmed in two ways. First, expertise is lost with each emigrant, diminishing the supply of that profession. Second, the country's economy is harmed. Professionals often earn larger salaries, so their departure removes significant consumer spending from the country.

Women's rights

As with other regions around the world, gender inequality is a problematic and thorny issue in Africa. Traditional gender roles are more entrenched than in the UK. For example, in Sudan there are clearly defined gender roles. Men make the decisions but also bear the responsibility of providing financially for their mothers, sisters and aunts. Women take care of children, the sick and elderly, as well as running the household. Women frequently have a high amount of work, such as gathering firewood and water or tending family fields.

Girls are less likely to attend school and more likely to drop out than boys. In sub-Saharan Africa, 81 per cent of boys were enrolled at primary school during 2010–14, compared with only 77 per cent of girls. The tradition of early marriages in some cultures is also hindering social development. The practice of forced marriages highlights a backward nature to human rights: UNICEF estimates that two-fifths of all African girls are married before the age of 18. In some countries the proportion is much higher. For example, in Chad and Niger, a third of young women (aged 20–24) said they were married by the age of 15.

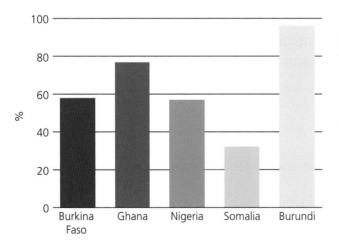

Figure 4.7 **Primary school enrolment in selected African countries**

Figure 4.8 **Collecting water is a role allocated to women in some African countries**

Farming, food, famine and malnutrition

Famine is caused by the shortage of food or the inability of people to obtain food. This might be caused by low food production resulting from drought or other factors such as armed conflict or bad governance. Poor farming practices such as deforestation, overcropping and overgrazing are exhausting the land in many African countries. Increasingly, fertile farmland is under threat from erosion, salination or desertification. Added to these problems is poor irrigation and water management. These combined factors result in limited agricultural yields, which can cause mass food shortages.

Around one-third of all people who live in sub-Saharan Africa are undernourished and there are an estimated 275 million people in Africa who, each day, go hungry. Children are the most visible victims of malnutrition. Children who are poorly nourished suffer up to 160 days of illness each year. Poor nutrition plays a role in around half of all child deaths in Africa. Malnutrition magnifies the effect of every disease, including measles and malaria.

> 'Every morning our newspapers could read, "More than 20,000 people perished yesterday of starvation."' (Professor Jeffrey Sachs, leading expert on development)

Economic factors affecting development

Debt

The causes of Africa's debt crisis are neither single nor simple; they are the result of the complex interaction of many factors. When many African countries gained their independence from colonisation in the 1950s and 1960s they had the task of self-governance and social and economic development. This led to developing nations accepting loans that they struggled to pay back (unfortunately much of this money was misspent or embezzled – see page 144). In turn, further loans have followed from institutions such as the World Bank and the International Monetary Fund (IMF).

Today, Africa has a $300 billion debt burden which creates a major obstacle to the continent's development. African countries spend almost $14 billion annually on repaying debt, resulting in vital resources being diverted away from essential social programmes.

The money African governments have borrowed from the IMF or World Bank comes with high interest rates and strict conditions. Such conditions when lending money can lead to extreme hardship for the countries involved. For example, the IMF can insist that education

Show your understanding

1 Why do many Africans lack access to health care?
2 a) Outline the HIV/AIDS situation in Africa with reference to Table 4.2 (page 136), the fact file and the case study on Swaziland.
   b) What are the consequences of the HIV/AIDS epidemic?
3 What are the problems surrounding malaria in Africa?
4 a) What are the benefits of an educated population to a country?
   b) To what extent is educational provision experienced by African people?
5 Describe some of the issues surrounding women's rights in Africa.
6 What are the consequences of poor farming and famine?

programmes and health programmes are cut to reduce government spending. If such conditions are not followed, then finance can be stopped.

The inability of African governments to invest in social services and promote economic development is the enduring consequence of the debt burden. This can be understood by looking at Angola, which is a nation rich in natural resources. It is Africa's second largest oil producer and also has a wealth of diamonds, iron ore and coffee. These natural resources should mean that Angola is economically rich, yet this is not the case due to its troubled history of civil war and huge accumulation of foreign debts that have resulted from this. During the civil war that lasted from 1975 to 2002, the Angolan Government borrowed money from rich nations to fund its military. Angola's current debt stands at $18.1 billion. This means that Angola spends 6.8 per cent of its GDP on loan repayments and only 1.5 per cent on health care.

In 2005, some African countries had some of their debt cancelled. The resulting benefits have been considerable. After receiving partial debt cancellation, Zambia introduced free health care for people living in rural areas, scrapping fees that for years had made health care inaccessible for millions. In Ghana, debt cancellation has been used with success to fund free early education, and in Mali funds were invested in improving the water supply and roads. These examples indicate the progress that could be possible if debts owed by African countries were cancelled completely. However, the 2005 debt cancellation saw only around 60 per cent of Africa's debt cancelled and many countries are still indebted to the IMF, the World Bank or the developed world.

Trade

Being rich in natural resources, Africa should be a prosperous continent with many products available to trade and sell to the rest of the world. If Africa could earn more through trade, African countries would be able to rely less on foreign aid and loans. In 1980, Africa had a 6 per cent share of world trade. By 2013, this had

Case study: BRICS Bank – a new lender in global development

The leaders of the BRICS (Brazil, Russia, India, China and South Africa) emerging market countries have launched a $100 billion (£58.3 billion) development bank and an emergency reserve fund in their first major step towards reshaping the Western-dominated international financial system. The long-awaited bank is the first major achievement of the BRICS countries since they joined forces in 2009 to press for a bigger say in the global financial order created by Western powers after the Second World War, which centres on the IMF and the World Bank.

The bank will begin with a subscribed capital of $50 billion divided equally between its five founders, with an initial total of $10 billion in cash put in over seven years and $40 billion in guarantees. It is scheduled to start lending in 2016 and will be open to membership by other countries, but the capital share of the BRICS cannot drop below 55 per cent.

The NGO [non-governmental organisation] ActionAid International said that while it was pleased that plans for the new development bank were gathering pace, more needed to be done to ensure it was inclusive. 'There are still no clear indications of how other stakeholders, including civil society, can have input into the bank's policies,' said its advocacy co-ordinator, Sameer Dossani. This is crucial to avoid the mistakes of the World Bank and others in the past, such as placing detrimental conditions on loans.

Source: adapted from Reuters.com, 16 July 2014

dropped to just 3 per cent. If Africa could regain just an additional 1 per cent share of global trade it would earn $70 billion more in exports each year – several times more than the amount the region currently receives in foreign aid.

Cash crops and terms of trade

Trade varies greatly from country to country. Sudan and Nigeria are blessed with large oil reserves and can export millions of barrels per day, whereas countries like Malawi and Ethiopia depend heavily on growing and exporting cash crops such as fruit, tea and coffee, cocoa and cotton. These crops are called 'cash crops' as they are grown for money rather than as food. Around 60 per cent of workers employed in Africa work in agriculture, with 40 per cent of farmers working in the cash crop industry. Cash crops are highly controversial in many ways.

Buyers from developed nations can force down the price of cash crops and therefore reduce the finance flowing into developing countries. As the price of coffee has increased in the coffee shops of Scotland, the likelihood is that the price of the coffee beans acquired from Africa has decreased. Companies prioritise profits often at the expense of the African farmer. Moreover, the desire of

African farmers to grow cash crops and export produce to large companies means that food is not grown for the purpose of the African population. Indeed, the situation remains that Africa sends food all over the globe while thousands of Africans die every day of starvation.

Another consequence of cash crops is the increasing proportion of African land being leased to foreign companies (e.g. Monsanto) to grow their own cash crops. For example, Mozambique has leased 20 per cent of its agricultural land, while Ethiopia has leased 8 per cent. If this continues, communities will be left without access to resources and unable to make a living to feed themselves and their families. With 60 per cent of Africa's farmers being subsistence farmers, this is a serious ongoing issue. Many development experts have called this increase in agribusiness the 'new scramble for Africa'.

Lack of infrastructure is also a huge problem for many African nations, and the transportation of goods is not always easy. This severely hinders trade between African countries but also provides hope for future trade – if infrastructure can be improved, profit can be made through the consequential trade increase.

Case study: The controversial role of multinational corporations in Africa

Part of the reason why African countries are not wealthy, despite their plentiful natural resources, lies in the role and conduct of multinational companies in Africa. Post-colonial Africa was encouraged to be a free market economy, similar to that of European countries where private businesses are free to provide services to citizens in return for profit. As African nations required financial support from the IMF or the World Bank, the loans they received often contained conditions that they must sell off their natural resources to big companies; this is called privatisation. This is not necessarily a bad thing; many UK enterprises have been privatised

Figure 4.9 Iron ore mining in Africa

Case study (continued)

over the years. However, problems have occurred in Africa because many sub-Saharan countries have suffered civil war, corruption and dictatorships among other economic and political troubles. Multinationals have been accused of 'exploiting' such countries and 'plundering' their natural resources. Large oil companies such as Shell and Elf have been implicated in corruption and bribery scandals, with companies somehow managing to operate in countries that lack democratic governance and transparency.

Furthermore, multinationals are accused of failing to pay their correct share of tax from the profits received through extracting African resources. This is due to two reasons. Firstly, multinationals are not properly taxed because African authorities lack the capacity to put in place tax systems and secondly, multinationals have advanced and complex ways of avoiding tax. Tax avoidance and siphoning off profit is called 'capital flight' and costs Africa at least $160 billion per year, according to Christian Aid.

Susan Hawley, of Corruption Watch UK, states that 'Multinational corporations' corrupt practices affect Africa in many ways. They undermine development and exacerbate inequality and poverty. They disadvantage smaller domestic firms and transfer money that could be put towards poverty eradication into the hands of the rich.'

ICT task

An interesting insight into the role of multinationals in Africa is discussed in the documentary *Stealing Africa – Why Poverty?* Access this and other relevant documentaries at www.whypoverty.net/video/stealing-africa.

Show your understanding

1 a) What is the extent of debt faced by African countries?
  b) What problems does debt cause for African countries?
2 What is BRICS Bank and why might it be beneficial to poorer countries?
3 Why is trade important to African countries?
4 What are the various controversies surrounding cash crops?
5 Outline the controversial role of multinational corporations in Africa.

Political factors affecting development

Poor governance, corruption and kleptocracy

Bad (or poor) governance means the government cannot be trusted to deliver key services, taxes are not efficiently collected, there is corruption, the police are dishonest, human rights are abused and the legal system is not independent. Bad governance also means that there are no democratic elections and there is a lack of transparency that allows those in power to rule unchallenged.

Kleptocracy can go hand in hand with bad governance. Kleptocracy describes a situation where an elite group, and/or a dictator, exercises power to the benefit of themselves at the expense of the population at large. Funds or aid are diverted to equip the military which will ensure the government remains in power.

Corruption has also been a huge problem in African politics. It has been stated that the day corruption ends in Africa is the very day we shall see the development of the continent. The lack of democracy has allowed many dictators to remain in power for decades enjoying lavish lifestyles while the population starves. Money and aid that should flow to the population and be spent on health centres or primary schools is siphoned off into the bank accounts of government officials. Former DR Congo dictator Mobutu Sese Seko amassed a personal fortune estimated by various sources (including Transparency International) at somewhere between $1 billion and $5 billion. Experts believe virtually all of it was illicitly acquired from the nation's funds and stashed away in Swiss banks. He owned a range of Mercedes cars and divided his time between plush palatial residences in Paris and Lausanne, Switzerland. He also developed a special taste for pink champagne and flew in fresh cakes from Paris for his consumption. All this while the population of DR Congo barely survived on $1 a day.

It is estimated that corruption today costs the continent around $150 billion a year with Somalia perceived to be the most corrupt nation on earth in 2014 (according to Transparency International). World Bank President Jim Yong Kim recently stated 'in the developing world, corruption is public enemy number one'.

Case study: Political corruption in Zimbabwe

Zimbabwe was once the economic leader in Africa and a successful exporter of food but, as a consequence of government mismanagement, the country has experienced a series of economic disasters. The current president, Robert Mugabe, came to power in 1980 and continues to rule today. Zimbabwe has regular general elections every five years. However, as with every previous election, the 2013 election was marred by allegations of corruption and intimidation. The Zimbabwe Election Support Network stated that the election was also tainted

Figure 4.10 Robert Mugabe

by media bias and tampering with the electoral roll. It was estimated that in an area where the main opposition party had many supporters, over 300,000 people were turned away from polling stations and 207,000 were 'assisted' with filling out their ballot papers. Unsurprisingly, the dictatorship of Mugabe has hindered economic and social development, with human development indicators suggesting living standards are grim for Zimbabweans. Poverty is rife, infant mortality is high and life expectancy is only 52 years. Human rights in Zimbabwe do not conform to the UN charter as Mugabe suppresses any political protest and he is a strong supporter of anti-gay legislation in the continent.

The economic and social decline of Zimbabwe

- The country has no set currency as hyperinflation has devalued the Zimbabwean dollar.
- US dollars and the South African rand are being used as currency in the country.
- Per capita income was lower in 2014 than in 1980.
- Life expectancy is 52 years – there has been no improvement during Mugabe's reign.
- Around 70 per cent of the population lives below the poverty line.
- There is no freedom of speech or right of assembly.
- Zimbabwe has the fastest rise in rates of infant mortality in the world.
- The rate of HIV infection is one of the highest in the world with 14 per cent of the population being infected. Every week 3500 people die from a combination of HIV/AIDS, poverty and malnutrition.
- Foreign investment and tourism have collapsed.
- There is an extreme shortage of medicines and medical equipment
- Out of a population of 12 million, over 4 million have emigrated abroad, many of whom are the skilled and educated – a brain drain (see page 139).

Civil war and armed conflict

'I dream of an Africa which is in peace with itself.'
(Nelson Mandela)

Figure 4.11 **Soldier/rebel with rifle**

Since the end of colonialism in Africa, there has been constant conflict, with the region being dubbed 'the Kalashnikov continent'. At any one point over the last 50 years, numerous countries have suffered from civil wars which have plagued social, economic and political development. Civil war is both a cause and a consequence of poverty and underdevelopment. But further causes of conflict in Africa include ethnic, religious and tribal differences that are complex in nature and trace back thousands of years. Current examples of tribal conflict include the world's newest country, South Sudan, where various tribes are fighting over power and land. This conflict has caused 1.5 million people to be displaced from their homes, and charities are warning that the conflict could cause critical food shortages due to farmers being forced off their land. Along with HIV/AIDS and malaria, armed conflicts are now a leading cause of world hunger. Armed conflict leads to food shortages on a large scale and for long periods of time, destroying any prospect of economic and social development. In 2014, the Democratic Republic of the Congo, Somalia, Sudan and Chad were all involved in armed conflicts. The effects of armed conflict are catastrophic for the countries involved and it can take decades to reconstruct after the conflict has ceased.

Oxfam reports the enormous impact of armed conflicts in many African countries. Civil wars cost Africa on average $18 billion per year. The charity has demonstrated that the cost to the continent's development over a 15-year period was nearly $300 billion. In addition, African countries involved in conflict have, on average, '50 per cent more infant deaths, 15 per cent more undernourished people, life expectancy reduced by 5 years, 20 per cent more adult illiteracy and 12.4 per cent less food per person'. Additionally, in non-conflict African countries, there are approximately 2-3 more doctors per patient compared with those involved in conflict. The report goes on to say that the cost of conflict was equal to the amount of money received in aid during the same period.

'Scorched earth policy' is a common military strategy used in Africa during civil wars that involves destroying anything that might be useful to the enemy while advancing through or withdrawing from an area. This includes burning down homes and villages, burning food stocks, bombing fields and destroying transport and communication facilities.

'Peace is the greatest weapon for development that any people can have.' *(Nelson Mandela)*

Case study: The economic consequences of armed conflict

In 2011, when fighting in Côte d'Ivoire made access to the key Ivorian seaport of Abidjan virtually impossible, foreign trade was disrupted in Mali, Burkina Faso and Niger. Mali's cattle exports halted almost completely and Burkina Faso's total exports of cattle and animal products fell by 65 per cent. The economic disturbances caused by the Ivorian conflict weakened the financial position of the affected countries. Burkina Faso and Mali each lost nearly $30 million in government revenues in the first three months of the war in taxes, customs duties and other sources of revenue.

Tourism is also important to Africa. It is an essential source of foreign exchange to many countries, and for Kenya the largest source. However, armed violence deters millions of potential visitors. Oxfam's research of international opinion showed that more than half of people from the world's top tourism spenders (France, Germany, Japan, UK and the USA) said they would be less likely to go on holiday to a country with a reputation for armed violence or gun crime than to a country without such a reputation.

Case study: Conflict – the rise of terrorism in Africa

In the last decade the threat of terrorism has traditionally come from Afghanistan and Pakistan. More recently there has been a shift towards increased terrorist activity in North Africa. Groups linked to al-Qaeda have grown in countries such as Somalia and Nigeria where they are able to take advantage of the lack of infrastructure and policing. They are able to recruit and train in the desert and move freely without restrictions from the law or the army. In Somalia, militant group al-Shabaab has wreaked havoc over the last few years taking control of towns and villages across the country. They have carried out suicide attacks in neighbouring countries that

Figure 4.12 Terrorist training in North Africa

have attempted to assist the Somali Government in fighting the group. The biggest attack was on Nairobi's Westgate shopping centre in 2013 when at least 68 people died.

The results of armed conflicts

- Children suffer seriously from armed conflict. Children often become orphans or can be dragged into conflict to fight.
- Millions of people can be uprooted from their homes and land, destroying any prospect of being self-sufficient.
- Vast numbers of refugees are created who are without food, water, shelter and medical support.
- Emergency aid can be severely disrupted or temporarily stopped because of the dangers caused by shooting, fighting, attacks and highjacking of aid trucks.
- Food becomes a weapon, with soldiers destroying food and livestock, adopting a scorched earth policy. Wells are often contaminated or mined, which forces farmers off the land.
- Food production is seriously affected by armed conflict with areas affected suffering annual losses of more than 12 per cent of production. In the extreme case of Angola, food production was reduced by 44 per cent.

Show your understanding

1 What is kleptocracy?
2 To what extent is corruption an issue in some African countries?
3 Read the case study on corruption in Zimbabwe. What evidence is there that corruption is rife?
4 Describe the extensive consequences of civil war and armed conflict. Make reference to the case study on Côte d'Ivoire and the fact file.
5 Outline the issue of terrorism in North Africa.

12-mark question

Analyse the causes of a world issue you have studied.

20-mark question

To what extent has a world issue you have studied had an impact in different countries?

Responses to development issues in Africa

The starvation of children, the widespread contagion of disease, widespread corruption and the plague of conflict means the general state of Africa is an international issue of huge significance to the global community. International organisations, non-governmental organisations (NGOs), individual countries and groupings of countries all have a part to play in addressing the issues faced by many African countries. There is no single silver bullet that can solve the complicated problems facing African people. Aid and support can come in many forms and what might be appropriate in one situation may not be suitable in another. At times, immediate short-term emergency aid is essential, while at other times a prolonged programme of long-term support and aid is required. There is even debate as to whether aid is an appropriate way to help Africa – does it support or does it create reliance (see page 163–4)?

Types of aid

Bilateral aid

Figure 4.13 **The UK Government gives aid to the government of Ethiopia**

Bilateral is government-to-government assistance, where one country gives aid directly to another. The aid is usually long term and part of a programme of development. It can take the form of emergency assistance at times when disaster strikes. Increasingly, aid comes without strings attached, though much assistance still comes in the form of tied aid.

Multilateral aid

Figure 4.14 **The flags of the EU and the UN**

This is aid provided by multinational organisations such as the United Nations (UN), the European Union or the African Union. There is the advantage that aid is not usually tied and these organisations can operate on a large scale because of their economic power.

Non-governmental organisation (NGO) aid

This is provided by voluntary organisations such as Save the Children, ActionAid, Oxfam, Mary's Meals and SCIAF (Scottish Catholic International Aid Fund). Often NGOs will target particular groups, such as children, or will provide specialist services. They are motivated by humanitarian concern and have no political ties.

Tied aid

Tied aid refers to aid given to a country but with conditions attached. Aid is conditional on the recipient country purchasing goods and services from the donor country. Tied aid has been a target of fierce criticism. It is estimated that tying aid can increase the prices of the goods and services by up to 25 per cent.

Criticisms of tied aid

- It favours companies in the donor country rather than the recipient country.
- Spending on goods and services takes place in the donor country, not in the recipient country.
- It can increase the costs of aid programmes because the best price is ignored in favour of buying from the donor country.
- It excludes and discourages companies and businesses in the recipient country from participating so local people do not benefit.
- It results in an over-reliance on knowledge, technology and spare parts from the donor country. Self-reliance is discouraged, leading to aid dependency.

Ten years ago, many aid donors pledged to end tied aid. The UK formally untied all development assistance in 2001, with the justification that 'tied aid reduces value for money' and tends to lead to inappropriate and expensive projects that do little to tackle the needs of the poorest. However, the UN has identified that a large majority of its members continue to tie aid. Much of this aid money is referred to as 'boomerang aid' – funds that flow to developing countries return immediately to donor countries. The USA makes sure that 80 cents in every dollar is returned home (see case study on page 149).

The benefits of non-tied aid

- Competitive tendering would be encouraged, attracting bids from local companies.
- It would assist the development of the private sector in recipient countries, thereby creating more jobs.
- Local ownership would be encouraged.
- The value of aid would be worth more to the recipient.
- Dependency on outside support would be reduced, so self-sufficiency would be more likely.

Case study: Tied aid – US food aid

The USA is the largest donor of international humanitarian aid, contributing roughly $8 billion in emergency food aid since 2010. But a significant portion of that food aid is 'tied', which means the food must be sourced from US suppliers and transported on US ships, even if cheaper alternatives exist. The benefits of tying go to companies in the US at the expense of aid recipients. For example, the Cargo Preference Act of 1954 dictates that 75 per cent of all US food aid must be shipped on private US commercial vessels, on which 75 per cent of the crew are US citizens. These policies translate into big gains for US shipping interests. The US might report a food aid shipment of $5 million to Ethiopia but $3.5 million of this is actually consumed by freight and logistics costs – in other words, profit for US companies.

What makes aid 'good aid'?

Good aid is targeted at the people most in need and is not tied. It involves local people who are consulted about possible solutions. It is monitored to ensure that it is delivering what was intended and goes hand in hand with improving good governance in the recipient country. Ultimately, good aid should address the issues that hamper development so that, in the future, the recipient country becomes self-sufficient and capable of dealing with the social and economic hurdles that get in the way of development.

UK aid to African countries

Figure 4.15 **The office for the Department for International Development**

The Department for International Development (DFID) is the part of the UK Government that is responsible for Britain's aid to developing countries. The focus of the department is to promote development in the developing world, particularly in countries where people are suffering from extreme poverty. The department is led by a Cabinet Minister. DFID works with charities, businesses and international organisations such as the World Bank and the UN in working towards achieving the Sustainable Development Goals (SDGs; see page 155).

An example of the work of DFID is in combating one of Africa's biggest killers, malaria. In 2005, only two-thirds of Ethiopians had access to health services. Rural areas in particular suffered from a lack of medical facilities and health workers. Since 2010, the Health Extension Programme, the flagship programme of the Ethiopian Ministry of Health, has aimed to extend health care with a primary focus on reducing malaria cases. DFID funding is currently supporting more than 3900 health extension workers to deliver health services to around 9 million people in Ethiopia. Additionally, the DFID is supporting the Health Extension Programme through a financial contribution to the government of Ethiopia, which pays for the delivery of services.

Fact file

Department for International Development aid statistics

- The UK Government has made a commitment to invest 0.7 per cent of gross national income (GNI) on official development assistance. The GNI target of 0.7 per cent is recommended and encouraged by the United Nations.
- In 2013 Bilateral spend for DFID was £4.5 billion, which makes up around 60 per cent of DFID aid, while multilateral spend was £3 billion.
- In 2013, DFID spent £8.8 billion on aid to poorer countries.
- In 2013, DFID provided bilateral assistance to 68 countries, of which 31 countries received direct financial aid.
- In 2013 Africa received £2.2 billion.
- The top three recipients of UK net bilateral aid in 2014 were India (£292 million), Afghanistan (£274 million) and Ethiopia (£266 million).
- DFID's bilateral humanitarian assistance in 2014 totalled £354 million.
- In 2014, the largest recipient of bilateral humanitarian assistance was Somalia (£79 million).
- In 2014, the European Commission's development programme received the largest amount of DFID multilateral assistance (£1.2 billion), followed by the World Bank (£1 billion) and the United Nations (£377 million).
- Much of the finance donated by DFID comes with political conditions. The receiving country must be committed to tackling poverty, upholding human rights and must manage public money wisely.

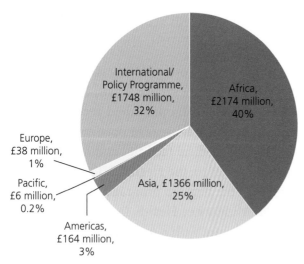

Figure 4.16 **Regional breakdown of UK bilateral aid spending, 2014**

How successful is DFID?

The UN recommends, and its members have agreed, that 0.7 per cent of GNI should be allocated to overseas aid. However, some countries contribute more, for example, Denmark, Sweden, Finland and Luxembourg give more than Britain. While being among the richest countries in the world, Britain is around the middle in terms of the contributions it gives in aid, leading some to say Britain should give more. Concerns have been expressed that former British colonies are given preference when it comes to deciding which countries in Africa should receive aid. In addition, it is claimed that aid is used to control the internal affairs of African countries through political conditions. Necessarily, any government has to be selective when deciding which countries will receive aid, meaning that, however good the intentions are, many countries will not be helped.

The DFID came under criticism in 2014 for providing agricultural aid that benefited private companies. Companies were invited to the

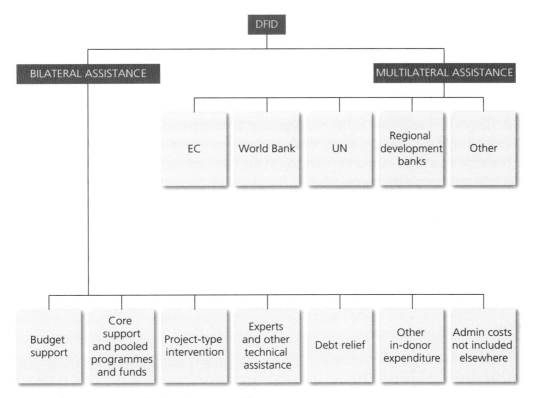

Figure 4.17 **The flow of UK development aid**

table through the G8 New Alliance for Food Security and Nutrition initiative that pledges to accelerate agricultural production and lift 50 million people out of poverty by 2022. But small farmers, who are supposed to be the main beneficiaries of the programme, were shut out of the negotiations.

ICT task

Visit the DFID's aid tracker to find out how the UK invests in developing countries at http://devtracker.dfid.gov.uk.

Scottish aid to African countries

The Scottish Government's International Development Policy seeks to build upon both the historical and contemporary relationships that exist between Scotland and the developing world, even although Scotland's financial contribution is included as part of UK aid. The Scottish Government's £9 million fund focuses on seven countries around the world. The Scottish Government has a partnership agreement with the government of Malawi and around half of funding goes to projects in that country. Support also goes to projects in three other countries in sub-Saharan Africa. The Small Grants Funding Round exists to provide funding to smaller NGOs for projects in the seven priority countries. In addition, the Scottish Government provides emergency humanitarian funding in response to crises. In 2014, £500,000 was donated to help people affected by the war in Gaza (Palestine). The Scottish Government is also funding projects in sub-Saharan Africa through the Climate Justice Fund.

Case study: Scottish Government multilateral aid

Organisation: Tearfund (a charity)

Project title: Water and Climate Justice in Malawi (£499,694)

This project seeks to support the better management of water resources and helps empower communities to hold duty bearers accountable for those resources. In terms of impact, the project leads to the improved socio-economic standing of the targeted households by reducing the number of people suffering from waterborne diseases. The project achieves three main aims:

1 Increased availability of clean and safe water
2 Increased water resource governance at district and community level
3 Households in targeted communities will employ strategies to adapt to climate change to improve water resource management.

Source: adapted from Scotland.gov.uk

Show your understanding

1 Explain the various types of aid.
2 Why is tied aid controversial? Make reference to the case study of US food aid.
3 Outline the work of DFID – make use of the fact file.
4 Has the UK been successful in providing aid to those in need?
5 Describe the provision of aid by the Scottish Government.

Multilateral responses to development issues

The European Union

The European Development Fund (EDF) is the main instrument for European Union (EU) aid to Africa. It is managed by the European Commission (EC) but is not part of the EC Budget. The majority of the UK's multilateral aid goes towards the EDF. The EDF sets a budget over a multi-annual period with the current budget covering 2014–20. The budget is around £24 billion. In 2000, the Cotonou Agreement was signed, which is a 20-year programme for delivering aid to African countries. During the first five years, the EU supported African governments to create a balanced economy, expand the private sector and improve social services in the countries covered by the agreement. Another continued objective is to integrate African states into the global economy.

The EC funds most African aid programmes in four stages. Indicative programmes identify overall priorities before money is allocated via commitments to specific projects. Then contracts with third parties to deliver projects are agreed through individual commitments. Payments are then made to the contractors for the delivery of projects. In delivering aid, the EC faces many challenges. This includes dealing with the world's very poorest countries, many of which have weak government structures and shaky economic policies. The EC must make best use of European taxpayers' money by ensuring that anti-poverty programmes are tailor-made to meet local needs and that they deliver concrete, lasting results.

Case study: EU aid and the Democratic Republic of the Congo (DRC)

The Democratic Republic of the Congo is a vast country with immense economic resources. From 1998 until 2003 it was at the centre of what some observers called 'Africa's world war'. This five-year conflict pitted government forces, supported by Angola, Namibia and Zimbabwe, against rebels backed by Uganda and Rwanda. This has left DRC in the grip of a humanitarian crisis that still goes on today. The EU's approach is to help rebuild the country politically (governance) and physically (transport infrastructure and health care). The EU also supports regional initiatives and measures to protect the environment. The multi-annual indicative programme in the DRC for the current spending round has budgeted £450 million for these priorities.

Figure 4.18 The location of the DRC

The EU's activities in the DRC also involve cross-cutting issues such as democracy, good governance, human rights, the rights of children and indigenous peoples, gender equality, long-term environmental protection and the fight against HIV/AIDS.

The African Union

Figure 4.19 **The logo of the African Union**

In 2002, the African Union (AU) was established. The AU seeks to create a strong and united Africa, with particular attention paid to the needs of women and young people. Peace and security are viewed as essential elements in creating development and a united Africa. Its official vision is to create 'an integrated, prosperous and peaceful Africa, driven by its own citizens and representing a dynamic force in the global arena'. However, many have challenged its success in realising this vision.

Aims of the AU

- To eliminate the remaining problems left by colonialism.
- To seek to unite African states in a common cause, creating solidarity among African countries.

- To accelerate economic development by co-ordinating and intensifying co-operation.
- To protect individual African states and their right to run their own affairs.
- To promote and encourage international co-operation, especially within the United Nations.
- To promote and defend African concerns on a variety of issues relevant to African people.

Has the AU been effective in resolving development issues?

The AU has had some successes over the last decade. In dealing with political corruption and dishonesty, AU observer missions are now sent as a matter of routine to cover elections in all member states, in accordance with the African Charter on Democracy, Elections and Governance (2007). Furthermore, there has been a significant fall in conflicts and coups, and an increased number of successful elections in the region in the past decade, suggesting the AU has added value to Africa's 'political performance'.

Perhaps the most significant development has been the creation of the Peace and Security

Council, designed to address regional conflicts in Africa that are the cause of so much poverty and suffering. Africa is therefore aiming to take responsibility for addressing its own security problems rather than relying on outside intervention, which has often been inadequate or unsuccessful. In 2013, terrorist groups seized control of territory in northern Mali, and the AU intervened with a military response to fight the terrorist threat.

The AU faces huge challenges in Africa. It is a comparatively new organisation and is still finding its way. It has struggled to boost the African economy in any great way, with poor internal trade still a major barrier to development. Despite numerous protocols to facilitate the free movement of goods and people across borders, the AU's record in stimulating the removal of trade barriers between countries in the union is less than impressive and the value of intra-African trade is still abysmally low as a percentage of total trade. Proposals for an African central bank and an African monetary union (like the euro) are still on the drawing board, as vested interest and concerns about sovereignty hold back the necessary political will to drive the process. There is no doubt the AU has been beneficial but it could still do better.

The United Nations

The United Nations (UN) plays a significant role in attempting to deal with development issues in Africa. One of the main aims of the UN is to co-operate in order to promote economic and social progress throughout the world and it is this aim that guides the work of the specialised agencies through which aid and assistance is channelled. The UN Declaration of Human Rights describes the rights that the citizens of all members should enjoy.

Millennium Development Goals (MDGs)

In September 2000 at the United Nations Millennium Summit, nearly 190 countries signed up to a range of goals and targets designed to reduce world poverty and hunger and improve life for people in developing countries. The goals were practical in nature and designed to encourage the international community to stop talking about making a difference and join together to start taking action. Eight precise targets were drawn up that the countries involved had to aim to meet in a specified time – before 2015. The idea of setting a time limit to achieve the goals meant that those involved and those benefiting from assistance had a clear goal to reach. However, when we look at the MGDs in more detail, it can be understood why some criticised them for being too modest and unambitious. For example, the targets to address extreme poverty and hunger stated that by 2015 the number of people living on less than $1 a day and the proportion of people suffering from hunger would be halved. Without doubt this meant progress, but not to the extent required. Other MDG targets were more ambitious, such as ensuring that by 2015 all children would be able to complete a full course in primary education.

Fact file

The eight MDGs

- Eradicate extreme poverty and hunger.
- Achieve universal primary education.
- Promote gender equality and empower women.
- Reduce child mortality.
- Improve maternal health.
- Combat HIV and AIDS, malaria and other diseases.
- Ensure environmental sustainability.
- Develop a global partnership for development.

Have the MDGs been reached?

Over the 15-year term some excellent progress was made in attempting to realise the eight MDGs. However, ultimately, most of the goals have not been reached. This has led to severe criticism and questions being asked about the worthiness of the goals. The successful MDGs include the halting and reversing of the spread of HIV/AIDS, halving the number of people in extreme poverty and halving the proportion of people without access to basic sanitation. This sounds impressive but in reality 22 per cent of people still live in extreme poverty and over 30 per cent of people cannot access basic sanitation. The other goals have not been reached, which has led to the drafting of a new set of goals that run from 2015 until 2030. The goals rework, build upon and add to the original MDGs and are called the Sustainable Development Goals (SDGs). The targets include fully eradicating extreme poverty and, regarding hunger, call for doubling agricultural productivity and the incomes of small-scale farmers. The health targets include ending preventable deaths of newborns and children under five years old. The SDGs are more extensive and less 'headline' focused, which may mean they are more achievable over the next 15 years. Only time will tell.

Added Value idea

The MDGs were highly controversial. Research the arguments for and against the notion that they were a success. Looking at their progress in a specific African country would be a good way to focus your work.

Show your understanding

1 Outline the role of the EU in providing aid.
2 What are the aims of the African Union?
3 Has the AU been effective in resolving development issues and meeting its aims?
4 To what extent have the MDGs been successful?
5 What are the Sustainable Development Goals?

The work of the United Nations agencies and NGOs

The work of specialised UN agencies

The UN plays a significant role in attempting to deal with development issues in Africa. When the UN was established in 1945 one of its main aims was to encourage countries to work together and co-operate to improve the lives of human beings all around the world. Nowhere is

A selection of the 17 SDGs

1 End poverty in all its forms everywhere.
2 End hunger, achieve food security and improve nutrition.
3 Ensure healthy lives and promote well-being for all at all ages.
4 Ensure inclusive and equitable quality education and promote life-long learning opportunities.
5 Achieve gender equality and empower all women and girls.

6 Ensure availability and sustainable management of water and sanitation for all.
7 Build infrastructure, promote inclusive and sustainable industrialisation and foster innovation.
8 Reduce inequality within and among countries.
9 Make cities and human settlements inclusive, safe, resilient and sustainable.
10 Take urgent action to combat climate change and its impacts.

this required more than in many African countries. The UN operates a series of specialised agencies that work to deliver multilateral aid and assistance. Each agency has a particular focus and remit when it comes to meeting the needs of developing nations.

It is through the variety of agencies as well as in working with member states and other organisations that the UN attempts to meet the targets set in the Sustainable Development Goals. We will analyse the work of several UN agencies and look at how they attempt to resolve development issues in Africa.

The United Nations Children's Fund (UNICEF)

Figure 4.20 **The logo of UNICEF**

UNICEF is a huge agency that focuses on the needs of children and their mothers. UNICEF deals with providing emergency aid when disasters strike and will provide specialist assistance with a particular focus on helping children and women. In addition, UNICEF takes on long-term projects such as supporting governments to build and equip health systems,

train health workers and provide food and clean water, so every child can be as healthy as possible.

Furthermore, UNICEF is the world's largest distributor of vaccines to the developing world. It supplies vaccines for 36 per cent of the world's children in over 190 countries. In 2014, UNICEF procured over 2.5 billion doses of traditional and new vaccines worth half a billion pounds. UNICEF also works to support families and communities to care for children and protect them against exploitation and abuse. The UN Convention on the Rights of the Child sets out the basic rights every child around the world is entitled to – UNICEF works to make sure these rights are fulfilled.

The World Health Organization (WHO)

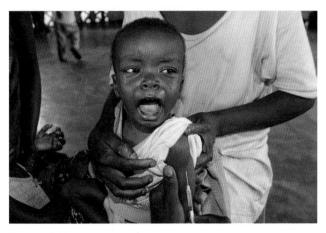

Figure 4.21 **WHO immunisation programme in Liberia**

Case study: The work of UNICEF – emergency assistance to South Sudan

In 2014, the children of South Sudan were facing an emergency of grave proportions. Critical shortages of food and water had left the country on the verge of famine. Conflict has blighted South Sudan since its independence in 2011. As the fighting continued, children were threatened by disease and malnutrition, and by forced recruitment into armed groups as child soldiers.

In 2014, a quarter of a million children under the age of five were at risk of severe malnutrition and 50,000 were in danger of dying if they did not receive life-saving food. This led to emergency intervention from UNICEF which provided essential food and clean water, as well as education and protection from abuse and exploitation. UNICEF also helped treat tens of thousands of children for severe malnutrition and vaccinated more than 300,000 children against measles.

Case study: UNICEF project work – improving access to water and sanitation in rural schools in Tanzania

Schools with inadequate water and sanitation facilities usually have the poorest attendance records and highest dropout rates. In Tanzania, 89 per cent of schools do not have adequate water or sanitation facilities. A study in Tanzania showed a 12 per cent increase in school attendance when water was available within 15 minutes compared to more than half an hour away. Girls often have to walk long distances to fetch water and firewood in the early morning. After such an arduous chore, they may arrive late and tired at school. Being 'needed at home' is a major reason why children, especially girls from poor families, drop out of school. Providing water closer to homes increases girls' free time and boosts their school attendance. When girls get older they are often forced to skip classes or drop out of school because there are no separate toilets for them that guarantee a minimum of privacy. Providing water, sanitation and hygiene facilities in schools is a cost-effective intervention that can significantly reduce hygiene-related diseases, increase student attendance and learning achievements, and contribute to dignity and gender equality.

UNICEF provided 25 rural schools with safe drinking water points, separate toilets for boys and girls and hand-washing facilities to benefit at least 25,000 school children. Hygiene education also encourages children to act as agents of change and promote improved hygiene practices at home and in their wider community.

Some of the work done by WHO is visible and familiar: the response teams sent to contain outbreaks, the emergency assistance to people affected by disasters, or the mass immunisation campaigns that protect the world's children from killer diseases. Other work is visible because the diseases being addressed – HIV/AIDS, tuberculosis or malaria – have such a high profile for global health. However, some work undertaken by WHO is largely invisible, such as setting standards to help maintain the quality of medicines and vaccines. WHO specifically aims to reach the most disadvantaged and vulnerable groups. These groups are often hidden, living in remote rural areas in countries such as Mali or Burkina Faso. From 2000 to 2015, WHO was tasked with meeting three of the Millennium Development Goals and will continue to strive to reduce child mortality, maternal death in childbirth and the spread of HIV/AIDS. With particular regard to Africa, the fight against HIV/AIDS has been WHO's priority focus for the past three decades, with HIV rates finally beginning to fall throughout the continent.

Case study: WHO and the Ebola virus epidemic of 2014

Ebola is a viral illness and the initial symptoms can include a sudden fever, intense weakness, muscle pain and a sore throat. Subsequent stages are vomiting, diarrhoea and – in some cases – both internal and external bleeding. The disease infects humans through close contact with infected animals. It then spreads between humans by direct contact with infected blood, bodily fluids or organs, or indirectly through contact with contaminated environments. Ebola has a high fatality rate of around 60 per cent and there is currently no licensed treatment or vaccine. In 2014, the virus broke out in Western Africa with WHO declaring in September 2014 that the Ebola virus was an 'international health emergency'.

Case study (continued)

In Liberia, Sierra Leone and Guinea, three of the world's poorest countries, Ebola caused the already threadbare health-care systems to almost collapse. Hospitals were in disarray as supplies ran out and as staff abandoned posts after watching their colleagues succumb to the virus. WHO deployed teams of experts to West African countries, including epidemiologists to work with countries in surveillance and monitoring of the outbreak and medical experts to support mobile field labs for early confirmation of Ebola cases. WHO also deployed clinical management experts to help health-care facilities to treat affected patients. Lastly, WHO set up logistics to dispatch needed equipment and materials and gave national and international advice to citizens on how to avoid contracting the disease.

The World Food Programme (WFP)

Figure 4.22 **A bag of Pakistani rice, donated by Germany, for Laos in south-east Asia, as part of the World Food Programme**

Acute hunger and starvation is often highlighted on our TV screens. We see adverts from charities asking us to donate money to finance food aid to famine-struck countries. WFP is the world's largest humanitarian agency, fighting hunger worldwide. Each year, on average, WFP feeds more than 90 million people in more than 70 countries. In recent years, the number of hungry people in the world has grown to almost 1 billion, which means that one person in seven does not get enough food to be healthy and lead an active life. Of those hungry people, 265 million live in sub-Saharan Africa. WFP is on the front line, using food assistance to help break the cycle of hunger at its roots.

Fact file

The extent of hunger and starvation in Africa

- 24.8 per cent of the population in sub-Saharan Africa are hungry.
- 38.8 per cent of Burundi's population are hungry.
- Almost one in three of the world's hungry live in sub-Saharan Africa.
- 23 million school-age children attend classes hungry every day.
- In every minute of every day, six children die of hunger in Africa.
- Hunger kills more people in Africa than AIDS, malaria and TB combined.
- Undernourished children lose their curiosity and motivation and millions do not carry on with their education as a consequence.
- For the cost of 6p a child can be fed in school for a day in Africa.
- Women are much more affected by hunger than men. Seven out of ten of the world's hungry are women and girls.

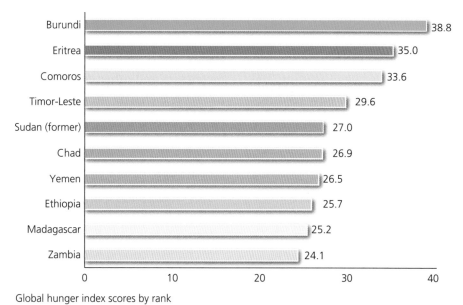

Global hunger index scores by rank

Figure 4.23 **Eight of the ten countries with the highest hunger levels are in Africa**
Source: Global hunger index

Show your understanding

1 What is the remit of UNICEF?
2 Describe the work of UNICEF in Africa. Give examples using the case studies.
3 What is the remit of WHO?
4 How did WHO assist with the Ebola outbreak of 2014?
5 Using the fact file, describe the work of the WFP and explain why it is so important.

The work of non-governmental organisations (NGOs)

NGOs raise money from voluntary and private sources to fund projects in developing countries. They are free from government interference and can determine for themselves what their aims and policies are. They provide emergency relief at times of crisis and are most obviously in the public eye at these times when they are involved in high-profile fundraising, for example, during the famine in South Sudan.

NGOs work in partnership with other bodies providing short-term and long-term aid. There are literally hundreds of NGOs. Some provide specifically targeted aid to groups, such as Save the Children, while others act on a broader scale, such as Oxfam. By focusing on the work of two NGOs, a fuller picture of the role and work of NGOs will generally unfold.

Mary's Meals

Figure 4.24 **The logo for Mary's Meals**

Mary's Meals is a Scottish charity that provides international aid to several countries around the globe. The charity sets up school feeding programmes in some of the world's poorest communities, where hunger and poverty prevent children from gaining an education. Mary's Meals provides one meal per day in a place of learning to attract chronically hungry children into a classroom where they receive an education that can, in the future, be their ladder out of poverty. Mary's Meals began feeding 200 children in Malawi in 2002 and is now feeding around 1 million children across 12 countries. In addition to this, many of the schools where Mary's Meals provide food have a school garden which encourages the children to learn about agriculture. The produce of the garden (e.g. cabbage, peppers, avocado, pineapples) goes to supplementing the children's lunches. The children are also taught the importance of hand washing before eating, and Mary's Meals supplies soap to each school.

Mary's Meals is mainly financed through fundraising by supporters of the charity. Money is also received in donations from churches, businesses and other contributors. Mary's Meals has several charity shops across Scotland which help to fund the school feeding programmes.

ICT task

Visit www.child31film.com and watch *Child 31*, a documentary that explores the work of Mary's Meals and gives an insight into the lives of children coping with the realities of extreme poverty.

Case study: Mary's Meals in Liberia

Mary's Meals started working in Liberia delivering shipments of emergency aid during the devastating civil war that ended in 2003. The school feeding programme began in 2006 and has steadily grown to reach more than 128,000 children, making it Mary's Meals' second biggest project. After the civil war, schools re-opened and pupils started to catch up on years of missed education. Most of the schools receiving Mary's Meals in Liberia are in small villages in rural areas. Children are often too hungry to attend school, or are helping to find wild food (fruit and fish), and even if they do attend, they are too hungry to concentrate and learn.

Mary's Meals helps to relieve the burden for families and other community members, tackling child malnutrition and crucially encouraging children back to the classroom. The schools, communities and volunteers are key partners in the feeding programme. The schools and communities provide storage and management of supplies, daily record keeping, organisation of volunteers and daily meal preparation. Mary's Meals provides project management, financial oversight, purchase and delivery of food, equipment and training with support visits from field monitors twice a week.

Mary's Meals has a long-term commitment to feeding the children of Liberia and is planning to reach a further 40,000 children over the coming years.

Response to Ebola outbreak in Liberia and Western Africa

During the Ebola outbreak in 2014, Liberia was in a state of emergency with all schools closed to minimise the spread of the virus. This brought a halt to the standard delivery methods for the feeding programme Mary's Meals operates on a daily basis. However, Mary's Meals launched an emergency response to Ebola by distributing meals to children's homes and to embattled health-care workers, as well as those being treated in Ebola holding and treatment centres.

Source: adapted from marysmeals.com

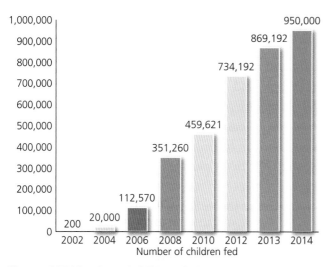

Figure 4.25 **Number of children fed a daily meal by Mary's Meals worldwide**

Oxfam

Figure 4.26 **The logo for Oxfam**

Oxfam has a general aim of fighting poverty all over the world. Oxfam focuses its work on vital issues to tackle the root causes of poverty, from life's basics – food, water, health and education – to complex questions around aid, climate change and human rights. With this extensive field of activity, Oxfam is one of the world's oldest and largest NGOs. Like other NGOs, Oxfam relies on private and voluntary donations; however, Oxfam also has a nationwide chain of charity shops in the UK that help with funding. Oxfam is also a pressure group with thousands of members in the UK. As a pressure group, Oxfam works to improve the lives of many people around the globe, especially in developing countries in Africa. Political campaigning by NGOs is another way to help achieve development in Africa as well as more traditional aid-based methods.

Case study: Oxfam – Inequality and Poverty Campaign

Across the world, the gap between the rich and the rest is growing faster than ever. And this increasingly extreme inequality is destabilising economies, damaging societies and pushing more people into poverty. Oxfam is determined to change that world by mobilising the power of people against poverty. Oxfam is spearheading an online activist movement to bring about awareness among the general population that extreme inequality is not inevitable – it is the result of years of deliberate policies and rules that have been rigged in favour of the few. Oxfam also organised a letter-writing campaign aimed at getting its members and followers to send a letter or email to their MP to pressure elected representatives to challenge inequality.

Source: adapted from Oxfam.org.uk

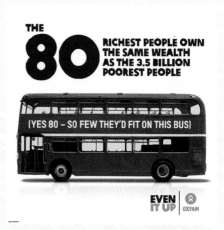

Figure 4.27 An online viral campaign by Oxfam to raise awareness about wealth inequality across the world

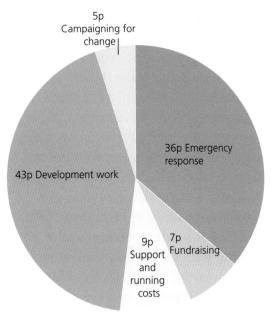

5p
Campaigning for change

36p Emergency response

43p Development work

9p
Support and running costs

7p
Fundraising

Figure 4.28 **For every £1 donated to Oxfam in 2014 …**

Show your understanding

1 How are NGOs financed?
2 Outline the different varieties of NGOs operating in Africa.
3 Describe the aims and work done by Mary's Meals. Make reference to the case study on Liberia.
4 Why are political campaigns a useful method for bringing about development in Africa? Refer to the Oxfam case study.

12-mark question

Analyse the actions taken by international organisations to resolve a world issue you have studied.

20-mark question

International organisations have been successful in resolving a significant world issue.

Discuss with reference to a world issue you have studied.

How successful are NGOs?

The issues affecting Africa's development are immense and dwarf the resources of all NGOs, let alone one particular NGO. However, at their best NGOs can make a striking and important contribution to improving the lives and futures of many African people. The examples in the preceding case studies show how lives have been changed for the better. For example, without Mary's Meals a million more children in the world would go hungry every day.

Needless to say, NGOs have their shortcomings. One growing concern is the so-called 'compassion fatigue' felt by the public as they are asked to donate to yet another important cause. Some NGOs are accused of spending too much on administration, which can put people off donating. Other NGOs are well meaning, but lack expertise and fall short of the standards expected of an aid organisation. In comparison to the UN and international governments, individual NGOs operate on a small scale and consequently their impact is inevitably limited.

There are numerous examples of superb work being done by various organisations, but their impact in addressing the multiple causes that impede development is on a small scale. In addition, many NGOs target particular groups so their success can only be measured within the narrow framework in which they work. NGOs are one part of the jigsaw that is the possible solution to addressing the issues surrounding Africa's development.

Criticisms and controversies of NGOs

Some NGOs, like Oxfam, genuinely contribute to development. However, others are sometimes ideologically biased or religiously committed and promote their particular views. Many NGOs promote Western values such as women's liberation, human rights, civil rights, the protection of minorities, freedom and equality. Not everyone finds these liberal values acceptable and they may clash with traditional views.

NGOs are self-appointed and answer only to themselves. They are unelected and cannot be voted out. They frequently attempt to tell those who are elected democratically, and those who voted them into office, how to organise their countries.

NGOs in places like Sudan, Somalia and Zimbabwe have become the preferred agencies for delivering Western aid. According to the Red Cross, more money goes through NGOs than through the World Bank. Their power over food, medicines and funds creates the power of an alternative government and sometimes corruption takes place.

Is aid the way forward to assist Africa's development?

The great aid debate

Over the past 50 years there has been a general school of thought that those in developing countries should be entitled to aid from richer countries. Indeed, the developed world has seen it as a moral obligation to donate aid to those countries, mainly in Africa, that require support and assistance. However, more recently some academics have questioned the merits of development aid and cited that aid is actually detrimental to developing counties.

The following opinions are from two experts with opposing views on development aid:

Aid is counter-productive

Richard Dowden, Director of the Royal African Society

Dowden argues a radical view claiming that aid is not the answer to Africa's problems. He concedes that humanitarian relief will always be needed when a disaster hits a country; however, he questions the view that aid can transform societies. At best, he argues, aid can only accelerate a process that is already under way. He explains that nearly a trillion dollars has been spent on aid to Africa since the 1960s but the situation now for African people is not much better. Much aid was spent without consultation with local people and what are left are abandoned and useless projects.

Africa is a continent in which countries were created artificially by colonial powers and have not produced effective governments.

This means that aid providers have had to work alongside bad governance, making it impossible to deliver the development needed. Dowden highlights the fact that South Africa and Botswana have better-run governments and do not need aid. On the other hand, where governments have collapsed, such as in Somalia, it is impossible to put development aid into action effectively. The countries in the middle, such as Mozambique, have become aid dependent and have had their self-reliance undermined. Dowden argues that good governance is the essential component to facilitate development. Only by African governments raising appropriate taxes and spending them wisely can development take place. Short-term aid to assist countries moving in this direction may be appropriate, but otherwise aid will be wasted. The people themselves must undertake development.

Aid works

Bill Gates, Gates Foundation

Broadly speaking, aid is a fantastic investment, and we should be doing more. It saves and improves lives very effectively, laying the groundwork for economic progress (which in turn helps countries stop depending on aid). Also remember that healthy children do more than merely survive. They go to school and eventually work, and over time they make their countries more self-sufficient. This is why I say aid is such a bargain. The US Government spends more than twice as much on farm subsidies as on health aid. It spends more than 60 times as much on the military.

Another argument from critics is that aid holds back normal economic development, keeping countries dependent on generosity from outsiders. This argument makes several mistakes. First, it lumps different kinds of aid together. Second, the 'aid breeds dependency' argument misses all the countries that have graduated from being aid recipients, and focuses only on the most difficult remaining cases. Even in sub-Saharan Africa, the share of the economy that comes from

aid is a third lower now than it was 20 years ago, while the total amount of aid to the region has doubled. There are a few countries like Ethiopia that depend on aid, and while we all – especially Ethiopians themselves – want to get to a point where that is no longer true, I don't know of any compelling argument that says Ethiopia would be better off with a lot less aid today.

Critics are right to say there is no definitive proof that aid drives economic growth. But you could say the same thing about almost any other factor in the economy. It is very hard to know exactly which investments will spark economic growth, especially in the short term. However, we do know that aid drives improvements in health, agriculture and infrastructure that correlate strongly with growth in the long run. Health aid saves lives and allows children to develop mentally and physically, which will pay off within a generation. Studies show that these children become healthier adults who work more productively. If you're arguing against that kind of aid, you've got to argue that saving lives doesn't matter to economic growth, or that saving lives simply doesn't matter at all.

Source: adapted from the 2014 Gates Foundation annual letter

Case study: The controversy surrounding Band Aid 30

In late 2014, the famous charity single 'Do they know it's Christmas?' was released for the third time in an effort to raise money to help tackle the Ebola outbreak. The re-release was met with considerable controversy, with notable musicians such as Adele and Lily Allen refusing to take part. This led to public debate about the view of Africa that the song (and its music video) portrays. The lyrics of the song have been criticised by many for being outdated and guilty of perpetuating negative stereotypes of African countries. Sir Malcolm Bruce MP, chairman of the International Development Select Committee, stated, 'Africa is a continent with many different countries with many different challenges. There's a danger that this kind of appeal (Band Aid) is slightly patronising and gives the impression that Africa doesn't have the capacity to do things for itself.' Conversely, Band Aid 30 reached number one in the UK charts and raised over £1 million.

Figure 4.29 Bob Geldof promoting Band Aid 30

Development summarised for the twenty-first century

No one agency, charity or government can solve the problems confronting many African countries. The social, economic and political factors that explain Africa's development issues are complicated and cannot be addressed satisfactorily by short-term solutions.

Huge levels of international debt, corrupt or inefficient governments, trade that favours developed nations, not to mention the power of international corporations, the devastation caused by HIV/AIDS and desperate poverty, must all be tackled. This will require an effort of will and commitment by governments unparalleled in scope. Currently, admirable work is being undertaken by a variety of providers, but each has its limits and shortcomings. The Sustainable Development Goals which will run until 2030 may take us a long way to creating a fully developed world – but progress will need to be better than the development goals we initiated at the millennium.

Show your understanding

1 What are the limitations and criticisms of NGOs?
2 a) Provide arguments for and against the view that aid is the best way to assist African countries to develop.
   b) Overall, which view do you support? Give detailed reasons to support your view.

Added Value idea

There is considerable controversy surrounding development aid. You could centre your research on the merits and drawbacks of aid, coming to a conclusion about whether the UK should increase or cut back aid to developing nations.

Assessment

Welcome to the new Curriculum for Excellence (CfE) Higher Modern Studies!

The Higher award is made up of internally and externally graded assessments. To achieve the award you need to pass the internal assessment for each of the following units:

- Democracy in Scotland and the United Kingdom
- Social Issues in the United Kingdom
- International Issues.

The Added Value unit for CfE Higher Modern Studies is an externally assessed course assessment. This consists of two components:

- question paper
- assignment.

To gain the course award, all units and overall course assessment must be passed. The marks awarded for the question paper and the assignment are added together and an overall mark indicates pass or fail. The course award is graded A to D.

The question paper

The question paper is worth a total of 60 marks, with 20 marks for each unit of the course. Essay questions are allocated 44 marks in total and source-based questions 16 marks in total. The duration of the exam is 2 hours and 15 minutes.

Essay questions/extended response

Essay questions are allocated either 12 or 20 marks. Examples of the style of question are given below.

Evaluate the effectiveness of parliamentary representatives in holding the Government to account. (**12 marks**)

Analyse the different lifestyle choices that may result in poor health. (**12 marks**)

To what extent does a world power you have studied have influence in international relations? (**20 marks**)

International organisations have been successful in resolving a significant world issue. **Discuss** with reference to a world issue you have studied. (**20 marks**)

Source-based questions

These questions are allocated 8 marks and appear in any two of the three sections of the exam. There will be no choice of source-based questions – for example, if there is a source-based question in the International Issues section it will be either a World Power or a World Issues question.

There are two types of source-based questions:

- one that asks '**to what extent**' something is accurate or true, and
- one that asks you to '**draw conclusions**' about a topic.

Both of these questions require you to draw on data that is provided in the form of sources, extracting information that is relevant to the question being asked, and to justify your answer using evidence from these sources.

For an example of some source-based questions, have a look at SQA's Specimen Question Paper on the (CfE) Higher Modern Studies page of their website: www.sqa.org.uk/sqa/47924.html.

Unit assessment

You will be expected to answer a skills-based question/activity and a knowledge and understanding question/activity. For the internal assessment of the International Issues unit the skills and knowledge that will be assessed are as outlined in outcome 1 and outcome 2 below.

Outcome 1

Use between two and four sources of information to draw and support conclusions about international issues, focusing on either a major world power or a significant world issue.

Outcome 2

Draw on factual and theoretical knowledge and understanding of international issues, focusing on either a major world power or a significant world issue.

Assessment evidence

Evidence for successful completion of both outcomes can be based on a range of activities:

- written responses
- slides in support of an oral presentation
- video/audio recording
- candidate's notes used to support an oral presentation.

The assignment

The assignment is worth 30 marks out of a total of 90 marks for the course, and contributes 33 per cent of the total marks for the course. The assignment task is to research a Modern Studies issue with alternative views. You will use your two one-sided A4 sheets (Modern Studies research evidence) to support you in presenting the findings of your research. The duration of the write-up is 1 hour and 30 minutes.

The assignment applies research and decision-making skills in the context of a Modern Studies issue. You can choose a political, social or international issue. The information collected should display knowledge and understanding of the topic or issue chosen. SQA recommends that you should devote about 8 hours for the research stage, including preparation time for the production of evidence.

The results of the research will be written up under controlled assessment conditions and must be completed within 1 hour and 30 minutes. Your Modern Studies research evidence recorded on up to two single-sided sheets of A4 will consist of materials collected during the research stage of the assignment. The allocation of marks is based on the following success criteria.

1 Identifying and demonstrating knowledge and understanding of the issue about which a decision is to be made, including alternative courses of action

You should choose a decision about which there are alternative views, for example:

To recommend or reject the continuation of the death penalty in the USA

or

To recommend or reject the continuation of positive discrimination in favour of black South Africans

You should agree an issue to research with your teacher. It has to relate to one or more of the issues that you have studied in your course:

- Democracy in Scotland and the United Kingdom
- Social Issues in the United Kingdom
- International Issues.

2 Analysing and synthesising information from a range of sources including use of specified resources

You will research a wide range of sources to widen your knowledge and understanding of the issue and to provide contrasting views on your chosen issue. By linking information from a variety of sources and viewpoints, you will be able to enrich and synthesise the arguments that are developed in your report. Remember it is important to provide balance in your report and to consider the arguments against your final decision/recommendation.

3 Evaluating the usefulness and reliability of a range of sources of information

You will comment on the background and nature of the source. Does it provide only one point of view, are its findings up to date and are its comments still relevant today?

4 Communicating information using the convention of a report

Remember you are *not* writing an essay. Your report style should include:

- a title
- a formal style that refers to evidence rather than personal opinion
- section headings breaking up the information to present evidence and contrasting arguments in a clear and logical structure
- references to the evidence you have used, especially the research evidence referred to in your A4 sheets

- a statement of the decision you have reached based on the evidence provided.

5 Reaching a decision, supported by evidence, about the issue

Your decision should be based on your research evidence and your own background knowledge of the issue.

Possible International Issues titles for your assignment

- Should the death penalty be abolished in the USA?
- Should positive discrimination legislation in favour of black South Africans be abolished in South Africa?
- Should the European Union continue to enlarge?
- Should NATO forces be based in the Ukraine?
- Should China end its one child policy?

Research methods

In Modern Studies we look at a range of political, social and international issues that affect everyone's lives. Many of these issues are based on evidence gathered by research carried out by a whole series of people and organisations – from the government to charities.

How do I carry out a piece of research?

When researching a topic in Modern Studies, it is important to consider where you will get your information from. In the twenty-first century, you have access to huge amounts of information at your fingertips on the internet. However, you need to be conscious of its accuracy and the likelihood of it containing bias and exaggeration.

Figure 5.2 **Gathering evidence by research**

Where do I gather information from?

The information gathered from research can be broken down into two parts – primary information and secondary information – and both provide qualitative and quantitative information.

Primary information

Primary information is evidence that you have gathered by yourself and is unique to your personal research. The ways in which you gather primary evidence can vary greatly. Here are some examples:

- surveys/questionnaires
- interviews
- emails
- letters
- focus groups
- field studies.

Secondary information

Secondary information is evidence that you have gathered from research carried out by others. You should use it to help support your personal (primary) research. There are vast amounts of secondary information available. Here are some examples:

- newspapers, magazines and books
- official statistics
- internet search engines and websites
- television and radio programmes
- mobile phone apps
- social media such as Twitter
- library research.

Qualitative and quantitative research

Qualitative research is more focused on how people feel, what their thoughts are and why they make certain choices or decisions. Focus group meetings or one-to-one interviews are typical forms of qualitative research .On the other hand, quantitative research largely uses methods such as questionnaires and surveys with set questions and tick-box answers. It can collate a large amount of data that can be analysed easily and conclusions formulated. Table 5.1 compares both types of research.

Table 5.1 **Qualitative and quantitative research**

	Qualitative research	**Quantitative research**
Objective	To gain an understanding of underlying reasons and motivations To cover prevalent trends in thought and opinion To provide insights into the setting of a problem, generating ideas and/or a hypothesis for later quantitative research	To quantify data and generalise results to the population of interest To measure the incidence of various views and opinions in a chosen sample Sometimes followed by qualitative research which is used to explore some findings further
Sample	Usually a small number of non-representative cases. Respondents selected to fulfil a given quota	Usually a large number of cases representing the population of interest. Randomly selected respondents.
Data collection	Unstructured or semi-structured techniques, e.g. individual depth interviews or group discussions	Structured techniques such as online questionnaires, on-street or telephone interviews
Data analysis	Non-statistical	Statistical data is usually in the form of tabulations (tabs). Findings are conclusive and usually descriptive in nature
Outcome	Exploratory and/or investigative. Findings are not conclusive and cannot be used to make generalisations about the population of interest. Develop a sound base for further decision-making	Used to recommend a final course of action

Source: www.snapsurveys.com/qualitative-quantitative-research